ANTHONY JONES

9, ADELA ROAD,

RUNCORN

WA7 4TU

The Nebraska Indian Wars Reader, 1865–1877

Edited by R. Eli Paul

University of Nebraska Press
Lincoln and London

Acknowledgments for the use of previously published material appear on pages
ix–xii, which constitutes an extension of the copyright page.
© 1998 by the University of Nebraska Press
All rights reserved
Manufactured in the United States of America

♾ The paper in this book meets the minimum requirements of American
National Standard for Information Sciences—Permanence of Paper for Printed
Library Materials, ANSI z39.48-1984.

Library of Congress Cataloging-in-Publication Data

The Nebraska Indians Wars Reader, 1865–1877 / edited by R. Eli Paul.
    p.   cm.
Includes bibliographical references and index.
ISBN 0-8032-8749-6
1. Indians of North America—Nebraska.   2. Indians of North
America—Wars—1866–1895.   I. Paul, R. Eli, 1954–
E78.N3N44   1998
978.2′00497—dc21   97-32942
                                                                  CIP

Contents

Illustrations

Maps

Figures

Preface

No comprehensive history of the Indian wars in western Nebraska exists, which is somewhat surprising. The subject is a fascinating one, as vast as the state's open plains and as rich as its soil. Luckily the dearth in this particular area of historical writing does not mirror a similar paucity of surviving documentation. To the contrary, many participants left accounts of the events, places, and personalities of the Plains Indian wars, over which countless students and scholars have pored and pondered, subsequently putting their own thoughts on paper.

One goal with this anthology, *The Nebraska Indian Wars Reader, 1865–1877,* is to display the contributions of both the eyewitnesses and the later scholars. Another is to do some historical chinking. Until some ambitious historian tackles the entire topic in a book-length study, this collection of articles goes far to fill this gap in the literature.

Nebraska History, the medium in which all but one of these essays originally appeared, has been the quarterly journal of the Nebraska State Historical Society since 1918. Hundreds of historical articles have graced its pages, documenting the state's land and its people. Many of the articles comprise studies of Indian–white relations on the Great Plains, providing the editor of an anthology with an abundance of possibilities.

The easy editorial choice was narrowing the anthology's subject and scope. Here I drew upon historian James T. King's "Forgotten Pageant" (Introduction), which divides Nebraska's Indian wars history into four periods, spanning the years 1854–90. (Luckily, King's article also serves as an excellent introduction to *The Nebraska Indian Wars Reader,* a literary effort that I did not feel compelled to duplicate.) The dozens of pertinent articles in *Nebraska History* blanket all four of King's periods, and anthologies for each, equaling this one in size, could have been readily organized.

I have confined this collection to King's third period, the one covering western Nebraska for the years 1865–77, and the decade in which, wrote King, "the military frontier . . . reached its full development" (p.8). This was a time when the blue-clad frontier regular replaced his volunteer replacement during the Civil War years, and, in turn, raised the heat on their Indian foes. Recent Historical Society research projects have also focused on themes central to this period, specifically on publications about Crazy Horse's people (*The Crazy Horse Surrender Ledger,* Nebraska State Historical Society, 1994) and on Fort Robinson (a forthcoming two-volume history). This anthology sprang from those efforts.

Once the focus narrowed to the 1865–77 period, though, the compiler's decisions became more difficult, the most challenging being: *Why these selections?* I wanted to feature all the major personalities—"Buffalo Bill" Cody, Frank North, Red Cloud, and Crazy Horse—and the major adversaries—the Pawnee, Lakota, and Cheyenne tribes arrayed for or against the United States Army. Spotlighted as well are the major places and events—building and guarding the transcontinental railroad across Nebraska, the Republican River Expedition of 1869, the Battle of Massacre Canyon, the flagpole incident at Red Cloud Agency, Camp Robinson in the Great Sioux War of 1876–77, and the killing of Crazy Horse. These are all Nebraska stories, illustrating the integral role western Nebraska played in the Plains Indian wars.

The initial selection of articles—twice the number that survived—not only covered these topics, but fell neatly into four categories. The group headings, "Seizing Control of the Platte and Republican Rivers," "Pawnee Triumph, Pawnee Tragedy," "Red Cloud Agency in the Spotlight," and "Sioux War Saga," reflect the shifts in Nebraska's cultural and historical geography during this relatively brief period. Although the number of articles in each section was whittled away, the balance I sought remained.

Soon I saw that this anthology might evolve beyond a mere "best of" compilation. To make the final cut each candidate article had to possess strengths in two areas. First, it could *stand alone* on its historical and scholarly merits. Second, the articles *taken together* had to present a comprehensive story that discussed the important persons, places, and events while avoiding redundancy. To turn a stale phrase, the sum of the whole had to exceed the sum of its parts. This mathematical impossibility has, to some degree, been achieved by the gathering of articles that have never appeared together, thereby providing a fuller context for all, and the inclusion of a previously unpublished article as an epilogue.

Although the death of Crazy Horse, the dramatic denouement of the Great Sioux War, figures largely in Eleanor Hinman's "Oglala Sources on the Life of Crazy Horse" (Chapter 10), several loose ends remained. Most are drawn together by James E. Potter's "The Pageant Revisited" (Epilogue), a study appearing for the first time in this book. Potter's tracing of the record of Nebraska Medal of Honor recipients in the frontier army provides another overview to the Indian wars in western Nebraska, complementing King's introduction and the chapters to follow.

Looking at both sides of this epic struggle and striving to reach a balance in the storytelling required the inclusion of first-person, eyewit-

Preface

ness accounts by participants—Indian, white, and mixed-blood—in addition to the traditional, analytical studies by professional historians. This mix also reveals the predilections of *Nebraska History*: the magazine for decades has welcomed reminiscences and oral histories. These intimate accounts by persons who were there cannot be overlooked. They are also exceptional reading.

Articles appearing in *Nebraska History* based on personal experiences and oral traditions, though, inevitably succumbed (as did the storytellers) to studies published in the journal based on archival sources, scholarly research methods, and an expanding historiography. These too are vital to our understanding and appreciation of the era, and *Nebraska History* continues as a venue for both types of articles, the major change being the increased annotation of first-person accounts demanded by modern scholarship.

Current scholarship also required that I examine each article to smooth out inconsistent citations as well as terms and spelling. The style imitates the one developed and followed by *Nebraska History* for the past decade.

One last question remains: *What else needs to be written about the era covered by the anthology?* The lives of three historical figures immediately spring to mind—George Crook, Crazy Horse, and Eli S. Ricker. Historian King called for a "re-evaluation" of Crook in another article in *Nebraska History* ("Needed: A Re-evaluation of General George Crook," 45 [Sept. 1964]:223–35). Neither he nor any other historian has met the challenge of providing a sorely needed biography of this influential officer, although fascinating works on such military contemporaries as Philip H. Sheridan, Nelson A. Miles, Ranald S. MacKenzie, John G. Bourke, and Charles King have appeared recently. Those interested in Crazy Horse's life must return, by necessity, to Mari Sandoz's *Crazy Horse, Strange Man of the Oglalas*, an increasingly unsatisfying work that has been purchased, read, and cited for half a century. A new biography is desperately needed before Crazy Horse is forever lost to the world of myth. Lesser known, of course, is Judge Ricker, the Chadron, Nebraska, amateur historian, whose early twentieth century interviews of Indians, soldiers, and frontiersmen are universally recognized as premier source documents of the Indian wars. His interview of Billy Garnett (Chapter 8) is one of only a handful that have been published in *Nebraska History*. Editing the approximately 5,500 handwritten pages of interviews and the several boxes of Ricker's voluminous correspondence have thus far proven to be beyond our energies, although not beyond our dreams.

It may seem contradictory to look wistfully to future scholarship when drawing so heavily from the past in creating this book. From the great body of knowledge found in *Nebraska History*, and partially encapsulated in these essays and reminiscences, however, comes a wealth of facts and a source of encouragement. The tradition continues—to question, understand, and disseminate our discoveries about the past.

Inspiration also comes from colleagues in the field of western history. Paul L. Hedren, editor of *The Great Sioux War, 1876–77: The Best from Montana The Magazine of Western History*, and Charles E. Rankin, head of the Montana Historical Society Press, were exceedingly helpful in the development of this anthology, which is, of course, a shameless attempt to duplicate the success of their valuable collaboration. John D. McDermott and Jerome A. Greene, two esteemed frontier military historians, read and commented on the manuscript. The advice from this quartet was graciously given and warmly received.

The articles found in *The Nebraska Indian Wars Reader*, as in *The Great Sioux War*, have become increasingly difficult and expensive to obtain in their original form, the best example being the Hinman interviews on the life of Crazy Horse. The original 1976 issue of *Nebraska History* in which the interviews appeared sold out immediately. The Historical Society reprinted the article, and it too sold out quickly. It also appeared the same year as a costly, numbered, John Carroll edition. All sport hefty premiums on the western rare book market. I would encourage other state historical organizations, as Paul and Chuck encouraged me, to look at their journals as invaluable and underperforming assets offering important writings still relevant to students of history and a book-buying public.

My colleagues at the Nebraska State Historical Society were their usual dependable selves. Thomas R. Buecker, curator of the Fort Robinson Museum and contributor to this volume, helped in the selection of all articles but his own. James E. Potter, the editor of *Nebraska History* and also a contributor, reviewed the manuscript as did Patricia Gaster, his assistant. Debra Brownson of the Exhibits Department fashioned the design and layout of the book, and Dell Darling drew its maps. To them and to the authors whose writings are herewith presented again go my deepest thanks.

R. Eli Paul
Lincoln, Nebraska

Introduction

Forgotten Pageant: The Indian Wars in Western Nebraska

James T. King

The dramatic conflicts between the Indian and the white man on the successive frontiers of the United States form a colorful chapter in the nation's history. As each new wave of white population moved westward, the attempts of the Indian to preserve his birthright resulted in a new Indian war. Early in the decade of the 1850s, it was Nebraska's turn to feel the impact of a conflict that would continue intermittently for a quarter of a century.

Although many other states have placed greater emphasis upon their participation in the Indian wars, Nebraska may claim a similar era in her history—one which was often as vivid and stirring as that of any other state. Notable expeditions marched through Nebraska's river valleys and over her plains, battles were fought on her soil, and military posts protected her burgeoning population. Yet the sites of these events are often unmarked, and the names of the men who participated in them are often only dimly remembered. Followed by other such dramatic events as the coming of the cattleman and the farmer and the rise of urban centers, the pageant of Nebraska's military frontier has been largely forgotten.

Any undue neglect is to be regretted, for these were years that—for all the violence and tragedy of Indian war—were both exciting and of significance to the developing state of Nebraska. It is not the purpose of this paper to refight these wars bullet-for-arrow, but rather to attempt a survey of the military frontier of Nebraska, with special emphasis upon that period when the Indian-fighting army was most closely associated with the people of western Nebraska.

Nebraska's involvement in the Indian wars lasted just as long as the period of warfare in the entire Great Plains region—from 1854 to 1890. If the Indian wars may be called a "pageant," then Nebraska arrived at curtain time and stayed for the whole show. But it was during the late

1860s and the early 1870s that the military frontier was most directly a part of Nebraska's life. And of the entire state, it was the western and southwestern sections that were most directly involved.

The Indian wars in Nebraska may be conveniently divided into four periods: the first, beginning in 1854, when the primary concern was the protection of overland travel; the second, during the Civil War, when the purpose was to hold the line against Indian attempts to overrun weakened western defenses; the third, after the war, when the Indian-fighting army began offensive operations to wrest the central Great Plains from their Indian inhabitants and thus clear the way for the advance of white population; and the fourth, ending in 1890, when the last flickering embers of Indian resistance were snuffed out.

Before the 1850s, there seemed little reason to believe that the region later to become Nebraska might be disturbed by the violence of an Indian war. The region beyond the Missouri River, popularly assumed to be a "Great American Desert" unsuitable for use by the white man, had been set aside as a permanent Indian domain, and a line of eleven military posts—including Fort Atkinson, Nebraska—was established from the Great Lakes to the Gulf of Mexico to protect the frontier.[1]

But the Mexican War had given the United States a western coast; gold was discovered in California, Oregon was a region of potential wealth, and thousands of Americans undertook the hazardous journey to the Pacific. Now the Platte Valley had become one of the pathways to the West. With increasing travel over the Oregon Trail and the extension of military power to such new points as Fort Kearny, the first steps were taken towards the destruction of the "permanent" Indian frontier. The next step was the Treaty of Fort Laramie in 1851 by which representatives of such tribes as the Cheyenne, Lakota, and Arapaho were cajoled into permitting the construction of roads and forts in the Indian country. The end of the concept of a permanent Indian domain came with the Kansas–Nebraska Act of 1854, which provided for the organization of the Plains into white man's territories.[2]

Thus begins the first period of Nebraska's Indian wars. White population at this time was sparse and confined almost entirely to the Missouri River area. The territorial boundary was large, extending west to the Rocky Mountains and north to the British possessions. The military frontier in Nebraska was still primarily one of punitive and scouting expeditions, rather than of permanent establishments.

The incident that began the hostilities occurred far to the west in a part of Nebraska Territory that is now eastern Wyoming. A dispute over a cow belonging to Mormon travelers had brought death at the hands of the Sioux to Lt. John L. Grattan and his small detachment. The secretary of war, alarmed at the prospect of Indian hostilities, sent an expedition under Col. William S. Harney into the Platte River Valley.[3] Harney's victory over the Sioux at Ash Hollow, Nebraska, in September 1855 ended organized Indian opposition for a time, but conditions remained unsettled throughout the decade.

A second expedition penetrated into the Republican River Valley in 1858. Led by Col. Edwin V. Sumner—who earned his nickname, "The Old Bull of the Woods," by his habit of removing his false teeth to bellow orders above the noise of his dragoon column—the expedition scouted the country as far north as Fort Kearny before returning to Fort Leavenworth.[4] In 1860 Capt. Samuel Sturgis of the First United States Cavalry led yet another column into the Republican Valley, where he sparred with the Indians along Beaver Creek and the Republican River, and led a determined but inconclusive fifteen-mile running skirmish in the vicinity of present-day Cambridge, Nebraska.[5] There was not yet a general Indian war in Nebraska; however, the continued harassment of overland traffic and the Pony Express was enough to demonstrate the protest of the Plains Indian tribesmen.

The second phase of Nebraska's Indian conflicts came with the outbreak of the Civil War. Emboldened by the withdrawal of military forces to the East, the Plains tribes began to exert pressure on the line of white settlement. The military frontier now became a defensive one, relying on volunteers rather than on regulars, intended to restrain the Indians until the national war had ended. Nebraskans heard with horror of the bloody Sioux uprising in Minnesota in 1862, and the Second Nebraska Cavalry was mustered in to participate with other regiments in a campaign in Dakota Territory. Fearing that Confederate agents were urging a similar uprising on the central Plains, the Union government strengthened the garrison at Fort Kearny, and sent the Seventh Iowa Cavalry to establish Camp McKean, which later was renamed Fort McPherson.[6]

Nebraskans of today might be surprised at the thought of soldiers from the southern states fighting Indians in the Platte Valley. Yet former Confederates helped to defend Nebraska's frontier during two critical years of Indian war. By the third year of the Civil War it was clear that some sort of help was needed on the frontier, for the understrength federal volunteers were becoming increasingly inadequate for the task facing them. Late in the summer of 1864 the Cheyenne, Arapaho, and Sioux tribes had closed the overland trail for a month, broken telegraph communications, halted mail service, and driven the white population in terror to the east. Every stage station from Fort Kearny to Julesburg had been attacked in one massive raid. In October 1864 the desperate troops halted Indian raids for a few weeks by burning the prairie from Fort Kearny to Julesburg and south to the Republican River.[7]

Col. John M. Chivington's vicious attack upon peaceable Indians at Sand Creek, Colorado, only infuriated the hostile tribes more, and it appeared that 1865 might bring a general retreat of white population. Indeed, in January of that year the Legislative Assembly of Nebraska in a joint resolution sent to the secretary of war declared "the firm conviction of this body, founded on facts constantly within our observation, that without [increased military protection] everything must be given up to the control of hostile Indians."[8]

But in 1865 sagging frontier defenses were strengthened by six regiments of "Galvanized Yankees." Officially styled "United States Volunteers," these were units made up of captured Confederates who were willing to swear allegiance to the Union and fight in the West upon the assurance that they would not be asked to fight their own brethren in the South. In Nebraska the "Galvanized Yankees" were stationed at such points as Plum Creek (now Lexington), Fort Kearny, Fort McPherson, and Camp Mitchell. Although they skirmished and fought with the Indians from the Little Blue River to the border, their signal service in Nebraska was the protection of stage and railroad stations in the valley of the Platte River.[9]

In the decade after the Civil War the military frontier in Nebraska reached its full development. With the mustering-out of the last of the volunteers, the regular army resumed the task of protecting the frontier, and the professional soldier became an integral part of Nebraska frontier society. Many new military posts were constructed; to the few lonely outposts previously located in Nebraska were added such new installations as Camp Sargent at North Platte, Fort Sidney, Camp Ogallala at what was then Ogallala Station, Camp Red Willow just east of present-day McCook, Fort Hartsuff, and Camp Sheridan. The army's campaigns against the Indians increased in range and intensity until Indian power on the central Plains was broken. The third phase of Nebraska's military frontier had begun.

The importance of this martial activity is understood by the rapid economic and social growth of Nebraska as the territory reached statehood. The Union Pacific Railroad, publicized by the ebullient George F. Train and financed through the uncertain economic structure called the Credit Mobilier, was being rushed to completion. One traveler reported that "the *shibboleth* of Omahans in 1868 was 'Great is Omaha, George Francis Train, and the Credit Mobilier'" and, he added, "he who was not prepared to swear by this local trinity was jocularly advised to emigrate or make his will."[10] To the west, the railroad had superseded the Oregon Trail as the pathway to the mountains and the Pacific, and Nebraska itself was beginning to beckon to westward-moving pioneers. The image of the Plains as a great "desert" was receding before the enthusiastic boomerism of Nebraska's growing population. Early in the critical year 1869, the *Nebraska City News* cried a hearty "Come Hither" to "all ye who seek a new and healthy prosperous home in the strong and sturdy west."[11] But there were still many who would be unwilling to answer this clarion call until they were certain of safety for themselves and their families.

There was reason to worry. To be sure, for a time after the Civil War Nebraska had escaped widespread violence. It had been so quiet, in fact, that Lt. Gen. William T. Sherman believed Fort Kearny to be worth less than the money it would take to tear it down. "If a fire could accidentally burn up Fort Kearney," he wrote, almost bordering on suggestion, "it would be a good thing."[12]

It was another story, however, along the Bozeman Road in Montana, where the army, after enduring conditions of almost constant siege in 1866 and 1867, at last agreed to evacuate. In Nebraska the campaigns soon resumed, and they would last until the 1870s. Once again, the Republican River Valley became the focal point for military operations. In 1867, for example, Lt. Col. George A. Custer led a detachment of the Seventh Cavalry from Fort Hays, Kansas, into the Republican Valley, then to Fort McPherson and then back into the valley again. He skirmished with Indians on several occasions and had a particularly sharp conflict with the Sioux near present-day Haigler, Nebraska, on June 24.[13]

Most significant to Nebraska history, however, were the campaigns of 1868 and, especially, 1869 in the Republican Valley. The work of a congressional commission had failed to bring peace to the Plains, and 1868 saw many bands of Indians once again on the warpath. In the fall of that year, Maj. (and Bvt. Maj. Gen.) Eugene A. Carr led his Fifth cavalrymen through the Republican Valley on a scout that developed into a five-day running battle with the Sioux and Cheyennes.[14] Presumably Carr had driven the Indians—or at least a fair number of them—to the south, where they were being awaited by Maj. Gen. Philip H. Sheridan. Sheridan began his campaign against the Cheyenne and other southern Plains tribes in the winter of 1868–69 and ended it in victory at the Battle of the Washita in Indian Territory.[15]

Many of those Cheyennes who had escaped Sheridan's trap now retraced their steps to the Republican, joining several bands of Sioux in the valley that for so long had served as a refuge for central Plains Indians. But in the following summer of 1869 Carr's Republican River Expedition wrested the valley permanently from the red man in one of the most shattering Indian defeats in the history of Great Plains warfare—the Battle of Summit Springs, Colorado, just west of the Nebraska border.[16] Several months later, in a joint resolution of thanks, the legislature of the state of Nebraska credited the expedition with "driving the enemy from our borders and achieving a victory . . . by which the people of the State were freed from the ravages of merciless savages."[17]

Although this was the last major campaign in the state of Nebraska, the 1870s brought both continued scouting and skirmishing and several noteworthy incidents. In 1876, delaying their march to Brig. Gen. George Crook's Big Horn and Yellowstone Expedition, Col. Wesley Merritt's column struck the Cheyennes at Warbonnet Creek, near Montrose, Nebraska, where William F. Cody killed Yellow Hair. And in 1878 a wandering group of Cheyennes under Dull Knife, attempting to return to their traditional home, spread an Indian "scare" throughout western Nebraska. But such incidents occurred with less frequency by the end of the 1870s. As white population began to fill the prairies and valleys around the military posts, Nebraska's involvement in the Indian wars was diminishing.

The campaigns in western Nebraska were carried on by many military units, the Second Cavalry, the Eighteenth Infantry, and the Seventh Cavalry, for example. But if there is any regular army regiment that deserves to be called "Nebraska's Own," it is the Fifth United States Cavalry. More than any other regiment, either regular or volunteer, the "Dandy Fifth" was identified with the pacification of western Nebraska. Usually headquartered at Fort McPherson, the men of this regiment, after ending organized Indian resistance on the High Plains, remained through much of the next decade as a police power to insure the safe and orderly settlement of the state.

The Fifth Cavalry, like many other frontier regiments, resembled a foreign legion in the cosmopolitan background of its personnel. There was Capt. Thomas E. Maley, for example, born in Ireland and a veteran of the Civil War and of the Indian wars of the 1850s.[18] There was Capt. Gustavus E. Urban, who was born in Prussia, served in the Civil War and the Plains Indian wars, and died on duty in Nebraska in 1871. The Fort McPherson cemetery is the last resting place of Capt. Jeremiah C. Denney, born in Ireland. The list could be continued almost indefinitely: Capt. Robert Sweatman, born in England; Capt. John H. Kane, born in Ireland; Capt. Emil Adam, a stolid, good-humored German; Capt. John M. Hamilton, a Canadian; and the remarkable 1st Lt. Jules C. A. Schenofsky, a Belgian with French military training who was appointed a captain in the Union Army during the Civil War, accepted a reduced rank to engage in the Plains Indian wars, resigned to serve as a captain of French cavalry in the Franco-Prussian War, was captured by the Paris Commune, had a hairbreadth escape from death, and then retired to the quiet of his ancestral estate in Belgium. Schenofsky's service in Nebraska included posts at Fort McPherson, the Little Blue River, Meridian (in present Jefferson County), the Republican River Expedition, and several battles with the Indians.[19]

The field-grade officers of the regiment—each of whom seems deserving of a niche in Nebraska history—could list impressive qualifications and experience. The colonel of the Fifth Cavalry during much of its time in Nebraska was William H. Emory. Graduated from West Point in the class of 1831, Emory was one of the best-known officers of the Civil War army. In 1848 he completed the earliest reliable scientific account of the American Southwest, based on his notes from the march of the Army of the West in 1846–47.[20] After service in the Plains in the 1850s and a distinguished Civil War career, Colonel Emory served several of his last years in the army at Fort McPherson in command of the District of the Republican.[21]

A second noteworthy figure is Maj. William Bedford Royall, who served as a volunteer in the Mexican War, was a newspaper correspondent in the California gold fields, and then became an officer in the Fifth Cavalry when the regiment was organized in 1855. His service in Nebraska included the command of Fort Sidney in the 1870s and of an expedition known as the Niobrara Pursuit, which followed the Battle of Summit Springs.[22]

Nebraskans of the late 1860s and the early 1870s were well acquainted with the exploits of Maj. Eugene A. Carr, who commanded at various times the District of the Republican, Fort McPherson, and, as mentioned earlier, the Republican River Expedition. Like Royall and Emory a veteran of the Plains Indian wars, Carr had served on the early expeditions into the Republican Valley in 1858 and 1860.[23]

And no list of figures of Nebraska's military frontier should fail to include the Fifth Cavalry's chief of scouts, William F. Cody. Although his involvement in show business and his numerous ghost-written "autobiographies" have led scholars to doubt much of the Cody legend, the fact remains that "Buffalo Bill" was one of the finest of the military scouts and evidently deserving of the high praise bestowed upon him by such commanders as Carr and Sheridan.[24]

Cody was still practically unknown when Carr first met him in 1868.

In a reminiscence found in Carr's papers after his death, he described his first meeting with Cody. Upon arriving at a Kansas Pacific station called "Buffalo Tank," en route to take command of the Fifth Cavalry, Carr caught sight of "a man in buckskin, with broad-brimmed hat, sitting on a horse on some rising ground not far from the station."[25] In his years in the West Carr had been exposed to the nineteenth-century equivalent of the drugstore cowboy, or, as he put it, "so-called scouts who masqueraded around railroad stations, mostly fakes and long-bow storytellers to tenderfeet," and he adds, "I thought to myself, 'There is one of those confounded scouts posing.'" But Cody behaved in a businesslike fashion, offered to report Carr's presence to Maj. Royall, the temporary commander, and to have a horse sent back for him. Still entertaining some doubts, Carr answered, "You may if you want to." Cody did. Carr soon found that "Buffalo Bill" was the chief scout for his regiment, and in the months that followed Cody earned his new commander's highest respect and admiration. In evaluating Cody's character and services, Carr wrote several years later that "He is a natural gentleman in manners as well as in character, and has none of the roughness of the typical frontiersman. . . . His eyesight is better than a good field glass; he is the best trailer I ever heard of. . . . He is a perfect judge of distance, and always ready to tell correctly how many miles it is to water, or to any place, or how many miles have been marched."[26] Cody campaigned with the regiment until 1872, and the meeting at "Buffalo Tank" was the beginning of a friendship that was cemented in Nebraska, to last until the general's death in 1910.

Also deserving of mention is a unit unique in the annals of the military frontier—the famous Pawnee Scouts—recruited from the Pawnee Agency near Columbus and officered by its major, Frank J. North, his brother, Capt. Luther H. North, and other Nebraskans. The ethnologist and historian George B. Grinnell once stated that the North brothers "were in the class with Bridger and Carson, and the value of their services in the work of opening and developing the western country can hardly be overestimated."[27]

The Pawnee Scouts began their service towards the end of the Civil War, enlisted first as Nebraska volunteers, then as scouts for the regular army.[28] Perhaps their best known service in Nebraska was with the Fifth Cavalry and Carr's Republican River Expedition. Carr shared the regular army officers' mistrust of Indian abilities and was appalled when the Pawnee Battalion was assigned to his command. During the expedition he complained that they were "lazy and shiftless." But by the end of the campaign Carr declared the scouts to have been "of the greatest service to us."[29] And in 1876, while assembling his command to march with General Crook, he attempted unsuccessfully to obtain the services of a detachment of Pawnees.[30]

The military men who were serving on the Nebraska Plains and their families often found the country marvelous and strange. Custer waxed almost poetic in describing the Plains, "this boundless ocean of beautiful living verdure."[31] Mrs. Eugene Carr used a similar metaphor, stating that until her arrival at Fort McPherson she had not really "understood what that comprehensive word [Plains] meant. It was like the sea. As far as the eye could reach, vast stretches of vacant land, bleak and nothing in sight." She seemed especially impressed, as were many others, at the absence of trees and by the air, which she found "clear and bracing."[32]

There were some, however, who were less appreciative. Mrs. Frances Carrington, for example, quoted with some approval J. H. Beadle's description of the Platte River. "The broad Platte," Beadle had written,

[is] a dirty and uninviting lagoon, only differing from a slough in having a current, from half a mile to two miles wide, and with barely enough water to fill an average canal; six inches of fluid running over another stream of six feet or more of treacherous sand; too thin to walk on, too thick to drink, too shallow for navigation, too deep for safe fording, too yellow to wash in, too pale to paint with—the most disappointing and least useful stream in America.[33]

Somewhat more terse was the comment of General Sherman, who was told when he was serving on the Plains that "it was a fine country and all that it needed was plenty of water and good society"—and the general growled, "That is all hell needs."[34]

The fact remains, however, that, as frontier military service went, Nebraska was one of the more desirable places to hold station. Even Sherman's comment, it might be noted, is at least a shade more favorable than Sheridan's similar indictment of Texas: "If I owned both hell and Texas," he asserted, "I'd rent out Texas and live in hell."[35] The Fifth Cavalry always welcomed a return to its Nebraska station, and Fort McPherson was palatial in its accommodations when compared to the ramshackle exile of Fort Apache or Fort Abraham Lincoln. Contrary to the Hollywood stereotype, the typical western post was not surrounded by a log stockade and high battlements; most frontier forts were rather more like Fort McPherson, with buildings gathered into a rude rectangle around a central parade ground. By 1869 Fort McPherson had become a substantial and attractive post. Homes for the officers were as comfortable and stylish as any to be found on the military frontier, and the native Nebraska red cedar woodwork, polished to a deep sheen, was the pride of many an army wife.[36]

But military accommodations in Nebraska varied widely. Camp Mitchell, near Scottsbluff, was unenthusiastically described by one army wife as "peculiar and compact."[37] Still less comfortable was the camp at Plum Creek that held a small detachment, usually one company, in temporary structures of logs and sod.[38] Perhaps least attractive of all was Camp Ogallala, a one-company tent post near the railroad station. The wife of Capt. Andrew S. Burt, shortly after her arrival at Ogallala, was horrified to find "two soldiers carrying a tent pole from which was hanging a line of horrible rattlesnakes—yes, veritable rattlers that had been killed on the site where our tents were to be placed." Mrs. Burt added that the major solved the snake problem at Camp Ogallala by surrounding their tent with a hair rope which, presumably, the snakes did not care to cross.[39]

There were many kinds of frontiers in the American West, including those of the cattleman, the farmer, and the miner, but alone of all of them, the military frontier had its own extinction as its goal. It existed for the purpose of ending the conditions that made it necessary.[40] By the decade of the 1880s, those conditions had been ended in Nebraska, and the military frontier in the state was drawing to a close. One by one, the forts were abandoned and left to the elements—or to the settlers, who often used the materials for their new homes. There would be one more flurry of activity in 1890 at Wounded Knee, South Dakota, and for a few months the activity in Nebraska recalled the past years of the military frontier.

Nevertheless, the military exodus continued. In post after post, whether Fort Sidney or Camp Ogallala or Fort Kearny, the scene was the same: the last retreat was sounded, the last salute was given, the flag was drawn down the staff for the last time. The garrisons marched out once again into the Nebraska prairies, but this time they would not meet the proud Indian warrior of the Plains; their rendezvous now was with history. Where the Pony Express had once carried the mail, there were now railroads and telegraph lines. Where columns of blue-coated soldiers had marched, there were now cornfields, cities, and cattle ranges. The Indian wars in Nebraska had ended.

Notes

[1] Henry Putney Beers, *The Western Military Frontier, 1815–1846* (Philadelphia: Privately printed, 1935), 172–73. Other posts in the line were Forts Jessup, Towson, Washita, Smith, Gibson, Scott, Leavenworth, Des Moines, Snelling, and Wilkins.

[2] See James C. Olson, *History of Nebraska* (Lincoln: University of Nebraska Press, 1955), 134–40.

[3] Col. Samuel Cooper to Gen. Winfield Scott, Washington, D.C., Mar. 25, 1855, Letters Received (LR), Adjutant General's Office, Records of the Adjutant General's Office, Record Group (RG) 94, National Archives, Washington, D.C.

[4] Col. Edwin V. Sumner, "Report of Excursion into Indian Country," St. Louis, Mo., Oct. 5, 1858, LR, RG 94.

[5] Capt. Samuel D. Sturgis, Fort Kearny, to assistant adjutant general, Department of Texas, Aug. 12, 1860, LR, RG 94.

[6] Harvey J. Zabel, "History of Fort McPherson" (Master's thesis, Colorado State College, Greeley, 1954); Louis A. Holmes, *Fort McPherson, Nebraska: Guardian of the Tracks and Trails* (Lincoln: Johnsen Publishing Company, 1963), chaps. 1,2.

[7] See, for example, the letters in *The War of the Rebellion: A Compilation of the Official Records of the Union and Confederate Armies*, ser. 1, vol. 41, pt. 2 (Washington: Government Printing Office, 1893), 626, 722, 734. Olson, *History of Nebraska*, 141–42.

[8] *Official Records*, ser. 1, vol. 48, pt. 1 (1896), 568–69.

[9] D. Alexander Brown, *The Galvanized Yankees* (Urbana: University of Illinois Press, 1963), chaps. 2,6,7. [In this survey of the second phase of Nebraska's Indian wars, the author did not mention the engagements at Mud Springs and Rush Creek in February 1865. In terms of numbers of combatants, these were two of the largest pitched battles ever fought in the state.–Ed.]

[10] J. H. Beadle, *The Undeveloped West; or, Five Years in the Territories. . . .* (Philadelphia: National Publishing Company, 1873), 63.

[11] *Nebraska City News*, Mar. 19, 1869.

[12] Assistant adjutant general, Division of the Missouri, St. Louis, Mo., to Col. Christopher C. Augur, Mar. 23, 1867, LR, Division of the Missouri, Records of United States Army Commands, RG 98, National Archives, Washington, D.C.

[13] George Armstrong Custer, *My Life on the Plains* (Norman: University of Oklahoma Press, 1962), 66–112.

[14] De B. Randolph Keim, *Sheridan's Troopers on the Borders: A Winter Campaign on the Plains* (Philadelphia: David McKay, 1885), 78–80.

[15] *Report of the Secretary of War* (Washington: Government Printing Office, 1869; Serial 1412).

[16] James T. King, *War Eagle: A Life of General Eugene A. Carr* (Lincoln: University of Nebraska Press, 1963), 94–119.

[17] Joint Resolution of the Legislature of the State of Nebraska, Feb. 23, 1870, found in "Manuscript Laws, Sixth and Seventh Sessions, 1870, General, Special Resolutions and Memorials," Nebraska State Historical Society, Lincoln.

[18] George F. Price, *Across the Continent with the Fifth Cavalry* (New York: D. Van Nostrand, 1883), 404–14.

[19] Ibid., 517–18, and passim.

[20] Lt. Col. William H. Emory, *Notes of a Military Reconnaissance, from Fort Leavenworth, in Missouri, to San Diego, in California* (Washington: Wendell and Van Benthuysen, 1848; Serial 517).

[21] Price, *Across the Continent*, 210–23.

[22] Ibid., 292–93.

[23] King, *War Eagle*, 26, 31.

[24] See Don Russell's excellent *The Lives and Legends of Buffalo Bill* (Norman: University of Oklahoma Press, 1960).

[25] Eugene A. Carr, "The Campaigns of 1868 and 1869," manuscript in the Carr Family Papers, in the possession of Mrs. Theodore (Virginia Carr) Van Soelen, Santa Fe, N. Mex.

[26] Letter of Carr, Fort McPherson, July 3, 1878, reprinted in William F. Cody, *The Life of Hon. William F. Cody, Known as Buffalo Bill, the Famous Hunter, Scout and Guide: An Autobiography* (Hartford, Conn.: Frank E. Bliss, 1879), vi–viii.

[27] Donald F. Danker, ed., *Man of the Plains: Recollections of Luther North, 1856–1882* (Lincoln: University of Nebraska Press, 1961), xx.

[28] Ibid., 32–37, 40–41, 71.

[29] Carr to Maj. George D. Ruggles, June 17, July 20, 1869, LR, Department of the Missouri, RG 98.

[30] Telegram, Carr to assistant adjutant general, Department of the Platte, June 6, 1876, LR, Department of the Platte, RG 98.

[31] Custer, *My Life on the Plains*, 5.

[32] Mary P. M. Carr, "Memoirs of Bvt. Gen. Eugene A. Carr," ca. 1915 manuscript, Carr Family Papers.

[33] Frances C. Carrington, *My Army Life and the Fort Phil Kearney Massacre* (Philadelphia and London: J. B. Lippincott Company, 1910),

[34] Carrington, *My Army Life*, 33.

[35] Mody C. Boatright, *Folk Laughter on the American Frontier* (New York: Macmillan, 1949), 156.

[36] Carrington, *My Army Life*, 212.

[37] Ibid., 43.

[38] Lt. Col. Henry W. Wessels, Fort Kearny, to assistant adjutant general, Dept. of the Platte, Aug. 19, 1866, LR, Department of the Platte, RG 98.

[39] Merrill J. Mattes, *Indians, Infants and Infantry: Andrew and Elizabeth Burt on the Frontier* (Denver: The Old West Publishing Company, 1960), 176–77.

[40] James T. King, "The Military Frontier—What Was it?" *The Westerners Brand Book* 21 (Chicago, 1965):89–91,95–96. [The author omitted mention of the Cheyenne Outbreak that occurred at Fort Robinson in January 1879. This volume's epilogue discusses this event.–Ed.]

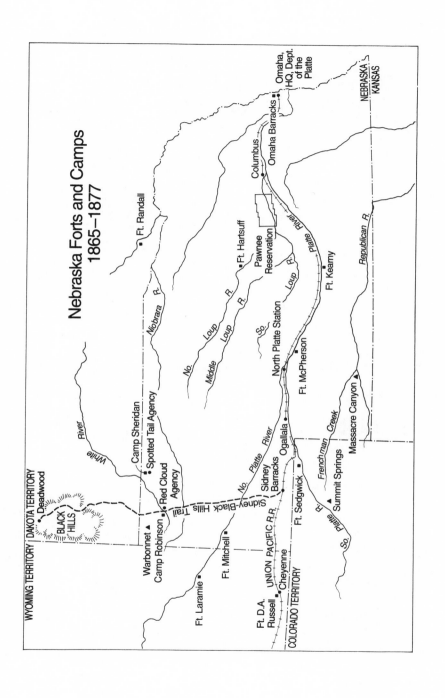

Nebraska Forts and Camps
1865–1877

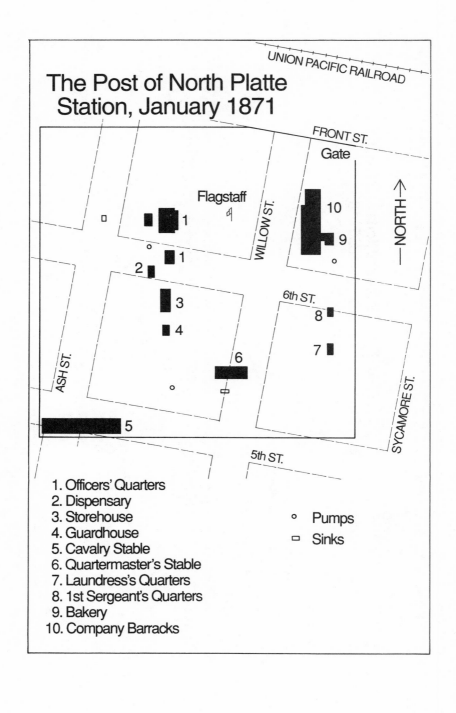

The Post of North Platte Station, January 1871

UNION PACIFIC RAILROAD

FRONT ST.

Gate

WILLOW ST.

Flagstaff

ASH ST.

6th ST.

SYCAMORE ST.

←NORTH→

5th ST.

1. Officers' Quarters
2. Dispensary
3. Storehouse
4. Guardhouse
5. Cavalry Stable
6. Quartermaster's Stable
7. Laundress's Quarters
8. 1st Sergeant's Quarters
9. Bakery
10. Company Barracks

○ Pumps
⬚ Sinks

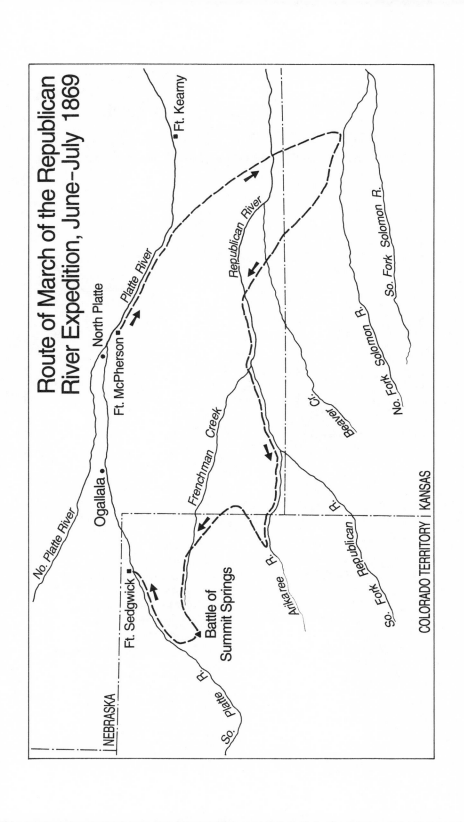

Route of March of the Republican River Expedition, June–July 1869

The Flagpole Incident
Red Cloud Agency, October 23, 1874
Witnessed and Described by Charles W. Allen

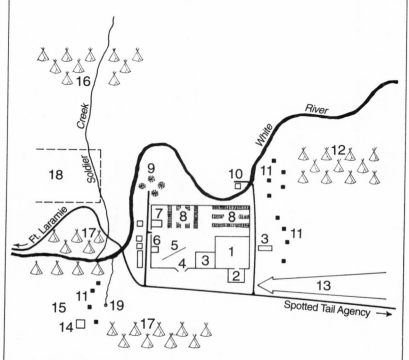

1. Agency office
2. Veranda (two stories high)
3. Trader's store
4. Gate
5. Flagpole
6. Clerk's house
7. Barn
8. Wood ricks
9. Haystack
10. Sawmill
11. Cabins
12. Sioux camp
13. Route of Sioux charge
14. Corral
15. Rocky Bear's camp
16. Cheyenne camp
17. Arapaho camp
18. Ft. Robinson reservation
19. Spring

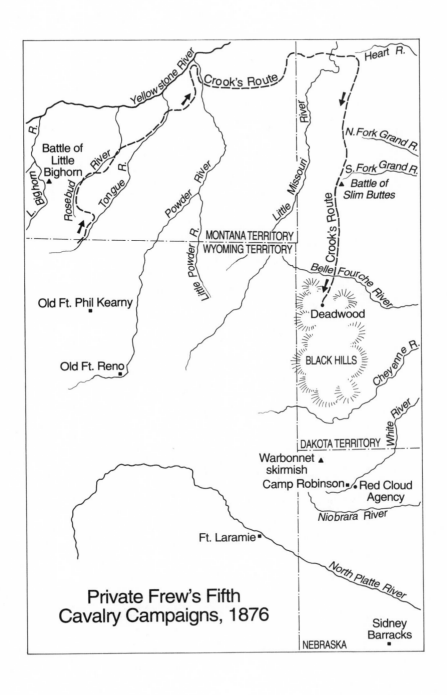

Heart R.

Yellowstone River

Crook's Route

Missouri River

N. Fork Grand R.

S. Fork Grand R.

L. Bighorn R.

Battle of Little Bighorn

Rosebud River

Tongue R.

Powder River

Little Powder R.

Little Missouri River

Battle of Slim Buttes

Crook's Route

Belle Fourche River

MONTANA TERRITORY
WYOMING TERRITORY

Old Ft. Phil Kearny

Deadwood

BLACK HILLS

Cheyenne R.

Old Ft. Reno

White River

DAKOTA TERRITORY

Warbonnet skirmish

Camp Robinson

Red Cloud Agency

Niobrara River

Ft. Laramie

North Platte River

Private Frew's Fifth
Cavalry Campaigns, 1876

Sidney Barracks

NEBRASKA

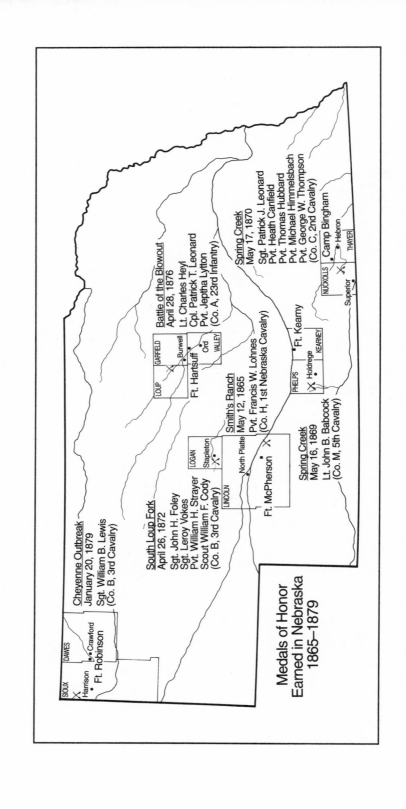

Medals of Honor
Earned in Nebraska
1865–1879

Part 1

Seizing Control of the Platte and Republican Rivers

After the Civil War, regular army units returned to the central Great Plains, replacing the volunteers who had manned the forts, stage stations, and road ranches of western Nebraska. The return of the "blue-coated soldiers" to Nebraska Territory portended a decade-long struggle that had been forestalled somewhat by the epic distractions to the south and east. The nation looked westward again, and it saw the Plains Indian as an impediment to its continued expansion.

Nebraska Territory before the Civil War modestly boasted of a population of just under thirty thousand, a somewhat misleading figure because the 1860 United States Census failed to enumerate its many long-time Native American residents. Looming large, though, in Nebraska's future were decisions made not on the battlefield but in the White House. In 1862 President Abraham Lincoln signed two bills of far-reaching consequences, one creating the Union Pacific Railroad Company, the second being the Homestead Act. The former made Omaha the railroad's de facto terminus, ensuring that town's economic success. The two pieces of legislation would help draw thousands of settlers to Nebraska and other western states with the promise of cheap land, agricultural bounty, and easy access to faraway markets.

By 1870 Nebraska's population exploded to more than one hundred twenty thousand, most of that increase coming since the war's end. Attracted by land and opportunity, veterans poured into the new state, beneficiaries of their martyred president's legislative foresight. And for a while Nebraska, today's Cornhusker State, was known as the soldier state.

Fertile farmlands along the Platte and Republican rivers, once the exclusive hunting grounds of the native tribes, fell open to settlement. The vast herds of buffalo were split by the new transcontinental ribbon of steel. The contest for this bounty continued between red and white and is detailed in the two chapters to follow.

Seizing Control

In "The Post of North Platte Station, 1867–1878," *Nebraska History* (hereinafter *NH*) 63 (Fall 1982):381–98, Thomas R. Buecker, long-time curator of the Fort Robinson Museum, Crawford, Nebraska, provided a capsule history of one outpost on the Plains. As a satellite operation, North Platte Station was neither as famous as Forts McPherson, Kearny, or Sidney nor as instrumental in wresting the Platte Valley from the Sioux and Cheyenne. Its career was typical, though, of how the U.S. Army established, manned, and used such posts to protect the country's transportation and communication lifelines.

The late James T. King was a frequent and valued contributor to *Nebraska History*, and it is appropriate that two of his articles appear in *The Nebraska Indian Wars Reader, 1865–1877*. "The Republican River Expedition, June–July, 1869," *NH* 41 (Sept.–Dec., 1960): 165–99, 281–97, documented the last major military campaign in Nebraska, one that originated from a Platte Valley base of operations. Because the Republican foray and its climax at Summit Springs involved "Buffalo Bill" Cody, arguably the West's most colorful personality, the events of 1869 inevitably passed from historical fact to theatrical fancy. Cody later added a depiction of the supposed events to his Wild West repertoire. King stayed the course, however, and kept the focus on expedition commander Eugene A. Carr, the North brothers and their Pawnee allies, and a mutual foe, the Cheyenne Dog Soldiers under Tall Bull.

Chapter 1

The Post of
North Platte Station,
1867–1878

Thomas R. Buecker

As the Union Pacific Railroad crossed western Nebraska in 1867, there were two military posts established for the protection of railroad employees and equipment: Fort Sidney (Sidney Barracks) and North Platte Station. The history of those two posts is little remembered today, though Fort Sidney is probably more familiar than North Platte Station. Troops were stationed at North Platte for eleven years from 1867 to 1878, but its role in the Indian wars has become blurred and its military significance forgotten. To better understand the decades of the 1860s and 1870s in central and western Nebraska, the history of this small army post needs examination.

By January 1867 the railroad reached North Platte, and, as the grade moved westward, Indian depredations increased. In recalling the construction of the Union Pacific, Chief Engineer Grenville M. Dodge said, "Every mile had to be run within range of musket, and there was not a moment's security."[1] The danger to employees necessitated military protection. North Platte, planned by the U.P.R.R. as a freight division point with shops and other facilities, was the location of the long railroad bridge over the North Platte River. Col. Christopher C. Augur, commanding officer of the Department of the Platte, decided that a company of soldiers should be stationed there. On January 29, 1867, Company I, Thirty-sixth Infantry, was sent from Fort McPherson, fourteen miles to the east, to "insure perfect security to the depot and bridge" at North Platte.[2] Its commanding officer was Capt. Arthur MacArthur, father of Gen. Douglas MacArthur of World Wars I and II fame.[3]

Until the Fort McPherson quartermaster could arrange supplies, the railroad furnished quarters and fuel for the troops. Company I camped on the north side of the railroad west of the new town. In addition to the main camp, ten enlisted men and a "trusty" noncommissioned officer were stationed on the east end of the bridge.[4] While the camp was established primarily for the protection of railroad property, it also served as a base of supplies for troops stationed along the railroad and for cavalry engaged in scouting the countryside. The post was designated "Camp at North Platte Station."

Winter, a time of few Indian forays, found soldiers pulling guard duty and trying to keep comfortable while living in tents. One night nine men deserted and headed east, intending to cross the frozen river. However, the river broke up, and the deserters were apprehended attempting to cross the railroad bridge. They were confined in a guardhouse of railroad rails formed into a twelve-foot-high triangle and covered. There they suffered through severe winter weather.[5]

In March 1867 Captain MacArthur reported quiet in the vicinity of the post and no rumors of Indian depredations. In early May Colonel Augur decided to make better use of MacArthur's company and transferred it to Fort Sedgwick, Colorado, some seventy miles to the west.[6] With spring sure to bring increased hostilities, many felt removal of North Platte soldiers ill-advised. Col. Henry B. Carrington, commander at Fort Sedgwick, urged the department commander to replace MacArthur's company with another. He wanted troops to remain at North Platte should it become the assembly point for friendly Indians, as the current Indian commissioners planned. Carrington felt the railroad line was in no immediate danger but was vulnerable to Indian aggression from Fort Kearny west.[7]

After Company I left North Platte on May 7, Indians began to roam the area. Attacks against the railroad began in earnest, and by summer opposition to construction reached its highest level. Attacks were frequent, particularly between North Platte and Julesburg, where grading was underway. At the same time Indians began coming to North Platte. The agent there requested a detachment of twelve to fifteen soldiers to assist in managing them and to provide security against hostiles.[8] Fear and apprehension of attack in the North Platte vicinity grew, even though Fort McPherson was close by.

Finally the need for more military protection was underscored by the derailment and burning of a train near Plum Creek (east of modern-day Lexington) and the death of six workmen nearby. Realizing the danger to the immediate vicinity of North Platte, Colonel Augur telegraphed Fort Sedgwick to send one company by special train to that place. They arrived field-equipped and went into camp at the station to protect railroad employees and property and to assist the Indian agent. In addition, a company was ordered out from Fort McPherson, along with a detachment of Pawnee Scouts.

Under the command of Maj. Richard I. Dodge, the force was to strike in retaliation for the Plum Creek incident.[9] Several days later the Pawnee detachment successfully attacked a group of Cheyennes and inflicted heavy losses. The brief affair saved the railroad from further molestation.

In the ensuing weeks the troops served as guards to stations on the railroad east toward Fort Kearny. In late August Company B, Fourteenth Infantry, was ordered to remain at North Platte and make it a permanent station. The new post was actually a subpost of Fort Sedgwick, which furnished troops and supplies. The new post was briefly named Camp Sargent [*sic*] in honor of William Sergeant, a Twelfth Infantry officer who died of wounds received at Gravelly Run during the Civil War.[10]

For several weeks the troops lived in tents on the north side of the tracks across from the depot. In October Major Dodge removed the post four hundred yards west of the railroad depot and two hundred feet south of the tracks. Although the post was to be permanent, no reservation was declared, and the land occupied was on the townsite owned by the Union Pacific. The railroad land commissioners were cooperative and with few exceptions declined to sell the lots occupied by the post.[11] The designation Camp Sargent was soon dropped, and by winter the post was officially known as North Platte Station.

In the latter part of the month materials for the first buildings were received, and construction of quarters began. Four structures were erected from portable white pine frames made in Chicago. The post took on a hurriedly-built appearance, but quarters were better than the tents in which the soldiers formerly lived. All buildings were constructed alike, the walls of upright boards and battens and the roofs of so-called "composition"—boards covered with tar paper secured by means of battens. The buildings were arranged around a parade ground with an officers' quarters, a storehouse, and a guardhouse on the west side and the company barracks on the east. The officers' quarters, a two-room, twenty-six by forty-four-foot building with attic, housed two officers most of the time. To the south and in line with the officers' quarters was a storehouse with a capacity for the supplies of one company. The third building on the west side was a small guardhouse, twelve by twenty feet, containing a guardroom and prison room. Across the parade ground was a one-story barracks building, thirty by ninety-six feet, with adjoining kitchen and mess room. The building was heated by three stoves, with one end of the dormitory partitioned into a washroom. To take care of the sick, a hospital tent was used when needed; the seriously ill were sent to the post hospital at Fort McPherson. A flagstaff was installed midway between the officers' quarters and the barracks, and the buildings and grounds (about eight acres) were surrounded by a fence.[12] Built to house but one company, the post never was taxed beyond its limit.

Before winter was over, several more buildings were added. South of the barracks two small quarters were soon constructed, one for the first sergeant, the other for a laundress. A stable holding eight horses was built, a larger stable being unnecessary until cavalry troops formed the garrison. In 1869 a one-story officers' quarters was erected just south of the existing unit to house a post surgeon. Only infantry soldiers served as the garrison for the first three years. Because the post was laid out square with the cardinal directions, it did not align with town streets running parallel to the railroad, which angled through the city.

One of the post buildings, the guardhouse, was frequently used by the town. North Platte in its earliest years had no jail. When civilian culprits were arrested, they were kept in the guardhouse. The army billed the county for boarding and tending the prisoners. The guardhouse, adequately warm but imperfectly ventilated, had a capacity of six prisoners, but there was a tendency to overload it with civilian offenders. The structure was built principally of adobe brick, making it necessary to post a sentry inside to keep the prisoners from cutting their way to freedom. After the town built a jail, soldier guards were requested several times by the sheriff to help when mobs threatened to seize prisoners. Such an event occurred in 1871:

> Sheriff Woodhurst . . . comprehending the situation, went to the Commander of the Post and asked for a guard to protect the jail. This was granted, and the leaders of the mob changed their tactics and presented a petition asking him to turn Manning over to them, and censuring him for protecting a murderer. His reply to this was that, being sheriff, it was his duty to protect the prisoners, and he would do so. Not to be foiled and lest Manning should be spirited away, the citizens put a guard at the jail to prevent him being removed without their knowledge. This state of affairs continued for five days, to the annoyance of Captain Brown and the sheriff, but the sheriff was equal to the occasion and, procuring a soldier's uniform, caused Manning to put it on in the morning and march to the post with the guard when it was relieved. The scheme worked, and he was taken to Fort McPherson, guarded by soldiers, to be kept until called for.[13]

On occasion prisoners in the guardhouse escaped and hid in town while avoiding patrols. In one incident a deserter hid in the kitchen of a Mrs. McConnell, much to the consternation of the ladies present. Eventually

captured, he was "presented with certain heavy jewelry consisting of brace-
lets and ball and chain and entered on the register of the barracks jail."[14]

The spring of 1868 brought an increase of Indian activity in the North
Platte area. Most of the Indians were in small bands on their way to the
Republican Valley to hunt; however, there were enough depredations to
warrant additional military guards. With Second Cavalry companies from
Fort McPherson patrolling east of North Platte, soldiers from the post
were sent out as guards to small railroad stations. O'Fallon's, Ogallala,
and Maxwell stations were usual duty points for five-man details.[15] Guards
were also sent with section crews doing routine maintenance. Besides
giving a feeling of security to railroad employees, soldiers could observe
Indian movements. A typical incident of Indian harassment occurred at
O'Fallon's Station when a section crew rushed into the station pursued
by Indians. When soldiers returned with section men to recover tools,
about seventy-five Indians on the bluffs fired on the party. The men
again retreated to O'Fallon's to telegraph for help. A lieutenant and ten
enlisted men arrived from North Platte to assist the detachment, but the
Indians had disappeared.[16] For several years guarding small railroad stations remained the main activity of infantrymen at North Platte.

The abandonment of the Bozeman Trail in Wyoming and Montana in
1868 freed a regiment and a half, and Colonel Augur spread its complement of men along the Union Pacific Railroad. In June Company D,
Eighteenth Infantry, arrived at North Platte for duty, and by October
companies of the Eighteenth were found at every station between Fort
Kearny and Cheyenne. When hostilities with Indians were reported west
of North Platte, soldiers were hurried to investigate. Usually they returned without sighting Indians, friend or foe, but the presence of soldiers reassured settlers and railroad employees. By 1870 it was determined that a cavalry company should occupy North Platte Station. Although infantry detachments continued as station guards, cavalry units
were mobile and more effective for scouting and pursuit. That fall the
garrison, Company I, Ninth Infantry, was replaced by Company F, Fifth
Cavalry.[17] A stable to hold eighty-five horses and a small grain storehouse
were constructed in the spring of 1871 as the cavalry period at North
Platte Station began.

Another change took place in 1871 as Fort Sedgwick was abandoned
and its men and material moved to Sidney Barracks. Afterwards Fort
McPherson furnished troops and supplies for North Platte Station until
it was declared an independent post four years later. The post took on an
improved appearance with the addition of gravel walks and a carriage
way. Trees were also set out around the parade ground.[18]

Scouting was the main occupation for the cavalry garrison. Shortly after Company F arrived at North Platte, most of the men were sent with several companies of Pawnee Scouts to the Republican River country. They returned a month later having found no Indians, a common result of scouting expeditions. In March 1871 one officer and twenty-seven men of the company scouted three days toward Ogallala for Oglala Sioux without a sign.[19] It was not uncommon for most men to be absent on scout for days or weeks. On March 12, 1871, Capt. William H. Brown, post commander, and thirty men moved against Indians who were driving off stock within three miles of town.[20] The detachment chased the Indians forty miles through "swamps and over sand hills," but failed to overtake them. The troops returned the next day after traveling about eighty miles.[21]

In May 1872, Company M, Third Cavalry, Capt. Anson Mills commanding, arrived for duty and remained for three years.[22] Lt. Frederick Schwatka, later famous as an Arctic explorer, served with the company.[23] Besides regular scouting patrols and other routine duties, Company M provided escorts for hunting excursions. Because North Platte was the closest railroad point to buffalo ranges of the Republican Valley, parties of businessmen, politicians, and high ranking military officers from the East made the post a staging area. As a courtesy and for security, escorts for the hunters were provided from the garrison. In the autumn of 1872 William F. "Buffalo Bill" Cody arrived with a group of businessmen from Omaha to hunt. Lieutenant Schwatka provided equipment and a squad of cavalrymen as their escort.[24] In another instance Lt. Gen. Philip H. Sheridan was at North Platte with a party planning a hunting expedition toward Fort Hays, Kansas, to the south. Company F, Fifth Cavalry, then stationed at the post, and a detail from Fort McPherson under the command of Captain Brown provided escort.[25]

Besides serving as guards for hunting parties, the men themselves hunted in the Dismal and Loup valleys to the north. In October 1873 Lieutenant Schwatka and a twenty-nine-man detail hunted for a month and returned with a large quantity of game to supplement the garrison's diet over the winter. The party covered a distance of more than 475 miles.[26] As a result of another hunt troopers returned with eleven elk calves, which they corralled. The newspaper stated, "it would pay anyone for the time spent visiting the barracks to see the trophies of the hunt." When the company changed stations, the elk were sent to a park near Cincinnati.[27]

While Captain Mills was the commanding officer, he attempted to improve the buildings and grounds. A new fence replaced the one put up in 1867. The dilapidated old fence allowed wandering livestock, particularly hogs, to roam the post to the annoyance of the garrison.[28] It was also proposed to align post streets with those of the town, but the plan was never totally carried out. A hospital containing a wardroom, kitchen, and dispensary was erected in 1874 from lumber salvaged from Fort Kearny (abandoned in 1871).[29] Mills's request for remodeling buildings in 1873 was denied because of a lack of quartermaster funds. Although the buildings presented a generally neat appearance, a few were still unpainted. An article in the *North Platte Enterprise* of May 23, 1874, commented:

> We wish Uncle Sam would have the barracks and the residences of the officers painted a brighter and more colorful color than [that] which now covers them. To do so would add greatly to the otherwise handsome and beautiful grounds of the military and be more in keeping with the cheerful spirits and deportment of the officers and their fair and charming ladies.

Between August 17 and October 2, 1874, Company M participated in an expedition into the Sweetwater country of Wyoming. Captain Mills commanded four hundred enlisted men and officers, thirty teamsters, and five scouts (headed by "Buffalo Bill" Cody). The expedition's objective was to search out Sioux then raiding miners and settlers near the South Pass. In the absence of the cavalrymen, an infantry company from Omaha Barracks served as a temporary garrison at North Platte. The soldiers in west-central Wyoming encountered no warriors and marched back to North Platte. The local newspaper reported, "[T]he hearty cheers of Company M could be heard for miles as they neared the town."[30]

Duty at western military posts often put soldiers in remote locations, but the troops at North Platte Station were near a growing frontier town on the railroad. North Platte in the middle 1870s had a population of 1,500 and probably a dozen saloons. Besides being the location of major Union Pacific shops, the town served as a center for the growing number of ranching operations. Proximity of civilians and soldiers frequently benefited both parties. Talented musicians of Company M formed a string quartet that entertained locally. Their music at one fair "enlivened the occasion with some choice selections" and raised money for a Catholic congregation.[31] Recreational activities for officers and civilians included dinner parties, croquet, and holiday festivals.

At other times the interaction of soldier and civilian brought hard feelings and occasional violence. Bimonthly paydays found scores of soldiers from the post and Fort McPherson in town for a spree. After payday Front Street saloons on occasion became boisterous. After a May 1874 payday a local paper commented:

> The soldiers at Fort McPherson were paid off Wednesday and at this point on Thursday last, since such time a number of them industriously sampling "bock" beer and "anti-crusade juice." As a result of their too frequent libations several of them came very near to receiving marching orders to that country where cremation is the order of the day.

> Quite a row took place on front street last evening between soldiers and citizens, a soldier named Kaiser severely cut on the head and otherwise seriously bruised. Our city has been remarkably quiet for months from rows, and citizens approve promptness of the sheriff to repress attempts at renewal of disgraceful scenes.[32]

Although troops were generally well behaved, drinking incidents, brawls in bars, and a dislike of Captain Mills by a small group of civilians caused a deterioration in the civil-military relationship that nearly resulted in abandoning the post.

A scandal surfaced in the winter of 1874–75 when Post Commissary Sergeant Page was arrested for selling government coal and oats to civilians. Page was put in the guardhouse but escaped the night of January 30. He was pursued by patrols, which fired reckless shots that struck several North Platte houses and which stopped and questioned citizens on the streets. The conduct of the patrols was not well accepted in North Platte. Captain Mills surmised that the escape was too well planned to have been carried out without civilian collaboration and that someone was harboring Page in the town. Guards were posted at intervals on North Platte streets.[33]

Knowing that Page faced a court-martial, some civilians made it known they hoped he would escape to avoid the exposure of their involvement with illegal sales of government supplies. Captain Mills reported the incident to Maj. Nathan A. M. Dudley, his superior at Fort McPherson.[34] When word of the incident reached Washington, Secretary of War William W. Belknap ordered Dudley to abandon the subpost of North Platte until the citizens learned "to respect the soldiers sent to protect them."[35]

Commissary and quartermaster supplies were to be moved to Fort McPherson, and an infantry detachment of fourteen men was sent from Omaha to take charge of the public buildings. Faced with abandonment of the post, citizens who realized the post was an asset to the town took action to convince the military not to withdraw the troops. Two representatives of the town, bearing a petition of more than one hundred names, hurried to Omaha to try to convince department commander Brig. Gen. Edward O. C. Ord to intercede on behalf of North Platte and not abandon the post. On February 5 a telegram to suspend the abandonment was received at Fort McPherson. The people of the town felt that Captain Mills had exaggerated the state of affairs and denied there was a citizen conspiracy to conceal Page. Major Dudley arrived in town to make peace and later reported to Secretary Belknap that the citizens and the military were reconciled, and the post was ordered saved. Later Page was captured and sentenced to military prison, and, as the *North Platte Republican* remarked, the hatchet was buried and "peace reigns in the breast of all."[36]

In March 1875 North Platte Station was declared an independent post, and Captain Mills and his cavalrymen were transferred to Camp Sheridan near the Spotted Tail Agency in northwest Nebraska. Afterwards infantry troops were again used as the garrison of the post.

The new commander, Capt. James Henton, improved relations between town and post by entertaining civilians and parading the soldiers through the streets on holidays.[37] During the winter of 1875–76 when prairie fires threatened the town, troops were dispatched to put out the flames. In another instance Captain Henton's company fought a fire in a stable in North Platte.[38]

Fire, a constant danger to the town and post, burned the post stable on September 11, 1875, and gave North Platte a spectacular display of fireworks. With the cavalry no longer at the post, the stable had been used to store forage and ammunition. At 8:45 P.M. the building was struck by lightning, and fifteen minutes later the magazine blew up. In the building were 12,000 rifle cartridges and eighty twelve-pounder howitzer shells. A hail of bullets clattered against the fence and buildings of the post, and from a distance the passing of shells presented a magnificent sight. Luckily no one was seriously injured, but a hundred tons of hay, several hundred bushels of corn, stoves, ten mules, harness, and ordnance material were lost.[39]

With the discovery of gold in the Black Hills, North Platte and other towns along the Union Pacific trumpeted their advantages as "jumping off" points for the gold fields. In addition, the establishment of the Spotted Tail Agency and Camp Sheridan in 1874 led businessmen to realize the benefit of having a trail start north at their city. Townsmen believed that a larger military post at the start of the trail would encourage increased government use of the route.

In 1874 meetings were held to encourage the government to enlarge the post and move the Department of the Platte headquarters to North Platte.[40] Businessmen were confident that they would get a route and could then demand a railroad line to the north. The declaration of North Platte Station as an independent post, they reasoned, meant abandonment of Fort McPherson, after which North Platte would become the most important military town in Nebraska.[41]

The plans of the North Platte citizens were further encouraged when they learned that, as Captain Mills and his company were traveling to Camp Sheridan, they had orders to determine the practicality of a road for the transportation of government supplies. The land commissioner of the Union Pacific, sensing the possible sale of land to the government, wrote the army that the railroad extended "every possible facility in the way of grounds or whatever needed for their use."[42] Regardless of the elaborate planning, by late 1875 it was evident that Sidney would be the starting point for government supplies bound for the north. North Platte Station remained as originally built, a one-company post on the railroad.

By the time of the major Indian campaigns of 1876, the only Indian activity in North Platte was an occasional rumor. The *Republican* noted that summer:

> Indian rumors on our streets dwindled down to the fact that two Indians were seen on Birdwood Creek a few days ago. . . . Rumors of a massacre near Julesburg. One Redskin in the eyes of some magnifies itself into a hundred.[43]

The decline of Indian activity brought a new duty to the troops. As cavalry companies from nearby posts were ordered to the field, infantry detachments from North Platte served as temporary guards at those posts. In June of 1876 one sergeant, one corporal, and eight privates performed guard duty at Fort McPherson during the absence of the cavalry. A similar detail served at Sidney Barracks and scouted along the South Platte River.[44]

With the major campaigns happening farther to the northwest, North Platte soldiers watched troop trains carry soldiers to active theaters. Companies changing station and heading east stopped at the post to draw rations or to rest their horses.[45]

With most men on detached duty at other forts, the post mustered only fifteen men—seven noncommissioned officers and eight privates. In the summer of 1877 guard mount, drill, roll call, and all bugle calls were suspended on account of the scarcity of men. In August the troops were mustered in undress uniform and without arms.[46]

The last major duty performed at North Platte was on September 19, 1877, when a detachment was called out to search for bandits that on the day before had robbed the Union Pacific express train at Big Springs, some seventy miles west of the post. Several days later the troops returned without finding any trace of the robbers, the legendary Sam Bass and five companions.

The few soldiers still at North Platte were able to raise the first successful post garden after years of failure by digging an irrigation lateral to the main water ditch running through the town. The post medical report for August noted that a quantity of sauerkraut and pickles were made up at the post.[47]

On October 19 fire struck a second time, destroying the quartermaster stable with a loss of three mules, one horse, harness, and forage. The blaze was thought to be the work of an arsonist, but this was never proved.[48]

With the Indian activity largely removed from Nebraska, and the larger military posts of Sidney Barracks and Fort McPherson also located on or near the railroad, the army decided to deactivate North Platte Station. The last company at the post, Company A, Ninth Infantry, left November 4, 1877, for Fort McPherson. Pursuant to orders, Capt. William H. Jordan, the company commander, remained at North Platte with ten enlisted men detached from Fort McPherson to take charge of public property. The next several months were spent packing and removing subsistence and quartermaster stores and other property to Fort McPherson. On January 31, 1878, almost eleven years to the day after the first troops arrived at North Platte, the detail finished its work.[49]

With the garrison withdrawn, the grounds and buildings received caretaker service from Fort McPherson soldiers until the army decided to sell the buildings in 1881. In his annual report for 1881 Brig. Gen. George Crook, department commander, reported the buildings were sold for "satisfactory prices."[50] Because the land used by the military was never declared a reservation and was regarded as such by occupancy only, it was given up to the private owners. Most of the land belonged to the Union Pacific, but three lots were owned by Anson Mills, who had purchased them in 1874 while he was the post commander. North Platte Station was officially abandoned on May 31, 1881.[51]

After the buildings were removed, the town expanded over the site of the post. Today the corner of Sixth and Willow Streets in west-central North Platte is the center of the old parade ground.

Appendix
Companies and Officers Stationed at North Platte, 1867–1878

• **First Garrison**
 Company I, Thirty-sixth Infantry
 Jan.–May, 1867
  Capt. Arthur MacArthur
  1st Lt. Henry H. Link
  1st Lt. Hugh G. Brown

• **Battalion of Troops at North Platte**
 Commanding Officer, Maj. Richard I.
 Dodge, Thirtieth Infantry

 Company H, Thirtieth Infantry
 Aug. 1867
  Capt. Eugene Wells
  1st Lt. Appleton D. Palmer
  2d Lt. Patrick H. Breslin

 Company B, Fourth Infantry
 Aug. 1867
  Capt. John Miller
  2d Lt. Edward L. Bailey

 Company C, Thirtieth Infantry
 Aug. 1867
  1st Lt. William H. Andrews
  2d Lt. John S. Bishop

 Company A, Pawnee Scouts
 Aug. 1867
  1st Lt. Isaac Davis

• **Camp Sargent**
 Company B, Fourth Infantry
 Sept.–Oct. 1867
  (same as above)

• **North Platte Station**
 Company C, Thirtieth Infantry
 Oct. 1867–June 1868
  (same as above)

 Company D, Eighteenth Infantry
 July 1868–Apr. 1869
  Capt. Richard L. Morris
  1st Lt. Alvan S. Galbreath (a)
  1st Lt. Thomas H. B. Counselman

**Company E, Twenty-seventh
Infantry** (b)
Apr.–July, 1869
 Capt. Isaac D'Isay
 1st Lt. Winfield S. Matson

Company K, Ninth Infantry
July 1869–Sept. 1870
 Capt. Campbell D. Emory
 1st Lt. Alpheus H. Bowman
 2d Lt. Thomas G. Tracy

Company F, Fifth Cavalry
Sept. 1870–Nov. 1871
 Capt. William H. Brown
 1st Lt. John B. Babcock
 2d Lt. William P. Hall

Company K, Second Cavalry
Nov. 1871–Apr. 1872
 Capt. James Egan
 1st Lt. Joshua L. Fowler
 2d Lt. James N. Allison

Company M, Third Cavalry
May 1872–Aug. 1874
 Capt. Anson Mills
 1st Lt. Henry W. Wessells, Jr. (c)
 1st Lt. Augustus C. Paul
 2d Lt. Frederick Schwatka

Company H, Thirteenth Infantry (d)
Aug.–Oct. 1874
 Capt. Ferdinand E. De Courcy
 1st Lt. Jesse C. Chance

Company M, Third Cavalry
Oct. 1874–Apr. 1875
 (same as above)

Company B, Twenty-third Infantry
Apr. 1875–Nov. 1876
 Capt. James Henton
 2d Lt. Calvin D. Cowles
 1st Lt. John F. Trout (e)

Company H, Fourth Infantry
Nov. 1876–Jan. 1877
   Capt. William H. Bisbee
   1st Lt. James H. Spencer
   2d Lt. Robert H. Young

Company A, Ninth Infantry
Jan.–Nov. 1877
   Capt. William H. Jordan
   2d Lt. Thomas S. McCaleb

*(a)Left post August 12, 1868, and
   replaced by Counselman.*

*(b)Consolidated with the Ninth
   Infantry in July 1869.*
*(c)Left post in April 1873 and
   replaced by Lieutenant Paul.*
*(d)Temporary guards while Company
   M accompanied the Sweetwater
   Expedition.*
*(e)Lieutenant Trout arrived for duty
   in July 1876.*

• **List of Known Surgeons Stationed
at the Post**
Assistant surgeons (a.s.) were regular army surgeons; acting assistant surgeons (a.a.s.) were civilian contractors. Contract surgeons received the same pay as their army counterparts but were required to serve only for the length of time specified in their contract. The following names come from the Medical History of North Platte Station, Nov. 15, 1875, Records of the Adjutant General's Office, Record Group 94, National Archives, Washington, D.C., and from Francis B. Heitman, *Historical Register and Dictionary of the United States Army* 1 (Washington: Government Printing Office, 1903). The post's medical officer at the time noted in this document the informational gaps: "There is no record, among the Post Medical papers, nor in the office of the Post-Adjutant, giving the early history of the Post."

A. L. Flint, a.a.s., June 1869–Apr. 1870; Aug. 1872–Jan. 1874; Oct. 1875–Nov. 1877.

Frederick W. Elbrey, a.s., Apr.–Aug., 1870.

Edward Lauderdale, a.a.s., Aug. 1870–Aug. 1872.

J. B. W. Gardiner, a.a.s., May 1873–Feb. 1874; June 1874–Oct. 1874.

Jno. W. Ridgeley, a.a.s., Feb. 1874–June 1874.

Dr. F. N. Dick, a North Platte citizen, performed fill-in medical duties at the post until Jan. 1875.

Charles L. Stephens, a.a.s., Jan. 1875–Oct. 1875.

Notes

[1] Archibald R. Adamson, *North Platte and Its Associations* (North Platte: *The Evening Telegraph*, 1910), 18.

[2] Special Orders, Department of the Platte, Jan. 29, 1867. Records of the Adjutant General's Office, Record Group (RG) 94, National Archives, Washington, D.C.

[3] Arthur MacArthur was born in Massachusetts and served through the Civil War with the Twenty-fourth Wisconsin Infantry, rising to the rank of colonel. He served as a captain in the Thirty-sixth Infantry for three years on the frontier and later in the Adjutant General's Office. He was promoted to major general on February 5, 1901. Francis B. Heitman, *Historical Register and Dictionary of the United States Army* 1 (Washington: Government Printing Office, 1903):652.

[4] Special Orders, Department of the Platte, Jan. 29, 1867, RG 94.

[5] "Experiences of Thomas O'Donnell while a Workman in Building the Union Pacific Railroad." O'Donnell Collection, MS1284, Nebraska State Historical Society, Lincoln.

[6] Fort Sedgwick Post Return, May 1867, RG 94.

[7] Col. Henry B. Carrington to Col. Christopher C. Augur, department commander, May 6, 1867, Telegrams Received, Department of the Platte, Records of the U.S. Army Commands, RG 98, National Archives, Washington, D.C.

[8] Ibid., Aug. 2, 1867.

[9] Richard I. Dodge, a graduate of the U.S. Military Academy in 1844, served in the Civil War, was appointed major of the Thirtieth Infantry in 1866 and was with the regiment for three years. He retired a colonel in 1891 and died in 1895. Heitman, *Historical Register*, 377.

[10] Camp Sargent Post Return, Aug. 1867, RG 94. The camp's name in the post returns is consistently spelled "Sargent," which differs from its namesake Sergeant.

[11] O. F. Davis, land commissioner, Union Pacific Railroad, to Capt. William S. Stanton, Omaha, Nov. 26, 1875, Letters Received, Chief Engineer, Department of the Platte, Records of the U.S. Army Continental Commands, RG 393, National Archives, Washington, D.C.

[12] Medical History of North Platte Station, RG 94.

[13] Adamson, *North Platte and Its Associations*, 51–53, 73.

[14] *North Platte Republican,* June 19, 1875.

[15] Fort Sedgwick Post Returns, June–July, 1868, RG 94.

[16] Report of 2d Lt. Thomas G. Tracy, North Platte Station, July 27, 1869, Letters Received, Department of the Platte, RG 98.

[17] Fort McPherson Post Return, Sept. 1870, RG 94.

[18] *Platte Valley Independent* (North Platte), Feb. 29, 1870.

[19] Fort McPherson Post Returns, Sept. 1870 and Mar. 1871, RG 94.

[20] William H. Brown enlisted in the Second Cavalry before the Civil War and served through the war as a captain in the Fifth Cavalry. He remained with the Fifth Cavalry until his death in June 1875. Heitman, *Historical Register*, 254.

[21] Comment of Captain Brown, Fort McPherson Post Return, Mar. 1871, RG 94.

[22] Anson Mills, who attended but did not graduate from the U.S. Military Academy, served in the Eighteenth Infantry until 1870, when he transferred to the Third Cavalry. He was promoted to major in the Tenth Cavalry in 1878 and retired a brigadier general in 1897. Heitman, *Historical Register,* 713.

[23] Frederick Schwatka, Galena, Illinois, graduated from West Point in 1871. He was engaged in frontier service with the Third Cavalry until he resigned in 1885. In 1878 he led an Arctic expedition that determined white men could survive in polar regions by adopting the native way of life. He engaged in other explorations and wrote several books. He died in 1892. Heitman, *Historical Register,* 867; Dumas Malone, ed., *Dictionary of American Biography* 16 (New York: Charles Scribner's Sons, 1943): 481–82.

[24] Ira L. Bare and Will H. McDonald, eds., *An Illustrated History of Lincoln County, Nebraska and Her People* (Chicago and New York: The American Historical Society, 1920), 365–70.

[25] Fort McPherson Post Return, Sept. 1871, RG 94.

[26] Ibid., Oct. 1873, RG 94.

[27] *North Platte Enterprise,* June 27, 1874; *North Platte Republican,* Apr. 10, 1874.

[28] Capt. Anson Mills to the chief quartermaster, Department of the Platte, Sept. 22, 1873, Consolidated Correspondence File, North Platte Station, Records of the Office of the Quartermaster General, RG 92, National Archives, Washington, D.C.

[29] Medical History of North Platte Station, RG 94.

[30] *North Platte Western Nebraskian,* Aug. 20, Oct. 2, 1874; *North Platte Enterprise,* Oct. 3, 1874.

[31] *North Platte Republican,* Jan. 30, 1875.

[32] *North Platte Enterprise,* May 20, 1874.

[33] *North Platte Republican,* Jan. 30, Feb. 6, 1875.

[34] Nathan Augustus Monroe Dudley entered the army as a first lieutenant of the Tenth Infantry in 1855. At the end of the Civil War he was a colonel of a Massachusetts regiment. A major in the Third Cavalry from 1870 to 1876, he retired a colonel in 1889. Heitman, *Historical Register,* 386.

[35] Telegram from William W. Belknap, secretary of war, to Brig. Gen. Edward O. C. Ord, Feb. 4, 1875, in the *North Platte Republican,* Feb. 6, 1875.

[36] *North Platte Republican,* Feb. 13, 1875.

[37] James Henton was born in England, enlisted in the army in 1853, and became a captain at the end of the Civil War. He served with the Twenty-third Infantry from 1866 to 1894. He was lieutenant colonel of the regiment at the time of his death in 1895. Heitman, *Historical Register,* 525.

[38] *North Platte Republican,* Feb. 5, 26, 1876.

[39] Ibid., Sept. 12, 1875; Medical History of North Platte Station, RG 94.

[40] *North Platte Enterprise,* Feb. 7, Apr. 18, 1874.

[41] Ibid., Sept. 5, 1874, Mar. 30, 1875.

[42] Davis to Stanton, Nov. 26, 1875, RG 393.

[43] *North Platte Republican,* July 15, 1876.

[44] North Platte Station Post Return, June 1876, RG 94.

[45] July 1877 papers accompanying the Medical History of North Platte Station, RG 94; North Platte Station Post Return, June 1877, RG 94.

[46] July and Aug., 1877, papers accompanying the Medical History of North Platte Station, RG 94.

[47] Ibid., Sept. 1877.

[48] Ibid.

[49] North Platte Station Post Return, Jan. 1878, RG 94.

[50] Brig. Gen. Richard C. Drum, adjutant general, to Lt. Gen. Philip H. Sheridan, commanding officer, Division of the Missouri, Jan. 14, 1881, Letters Sent, RG 94; "Report of Brigadier-General Crook," Department of the Platte, Omaha, Nebr., Sept. 29, 1881, *Report of the Secretary of War* (Washington: Government Printing Office, 1881; Serial 2010), 112.

[51] Davis to Stanton, Nov. 26, 1875, RG 393; National Archives data sheet on North Platte Station and its inventory of records.

Chapter 2

The Republican River Expedition, June–July, 1869

James T. King

Part 1. On the March

The Republican River Expedition, like other frontier task forces, was organized for a single specific purpose. In June and July 1869 the expedition operated in the area of the Republican River Valley in Kansas, Nebraska, and Colorado and was charged with the duty of driving the Indian out of this last stronghold on the central Plains.

In the years following the American Civil War the burden of protecting the advance of white population into the central Plains was borne primarily by the thin ranks of the United States Army. The units of this frontier army were often undermanned, overofficered, inadequately supplied, and beset by discouragement and adversity, and the Republican River Expedition was no exception. These and other aspects of a small-scale Indian campaign become apparent in the story of the five-week operations of this Fifth United States Cavalry detachment from the time of its departure to the eve of the victory at Summit Springs on July 11, 1869, which "forever secured to the white race the undisputed and unmolested possession of the Republican River and its tributaries."[1]

The situation that called the expedition into existence had become serious by late spring of 1869. A letter opened by the commanding officer of the military Department of the Platte, Brig. Gen. Christopher C. Augur, on the morning of June 1 bore the seal of the governor of the state of Nebraska. It was a desperate appeal for help. "I have just received news from the Big Sandy and Republican [rivers]," Governor David Butler had written to the general:

> The Indians are in arms again and are again threatening to repeat their former depredations in that region. The news which I have received is no idle rumor. . . . I would ask if you can send a company of soldiers to that region. If you can how soon can you do it? Can

you spare them for four months? Or if not how long can you spare them? If you cannot spare them at all can you furnish me with ammunition, subsistence and transportation for one hundred men immediately? Or if not with all, with what of these can you furnish me?[2]

General Augur doubtless was concerned, but he could have been little surprised, for the governor's hasty note was only the latest in a series of reports of actual and threatened Indian terrorism in the country surrounding the Republican River. Earlier in the spring, a particularly dangerous group of Cheyennes, a warrior society known as the Dog Soldiers, had taken refuge in the Republican Valley.[3] Led by the redoubtable Chief Tall Bull, the Dog Soldiers had managed to elude the dragnet that followed Lt. Gen. Philip H. Sheridan's winter campaign on the southern Plains. They had been joined by numerous Cheyenne stragglers and by Sioux, particularly the bands of Little Wound, Whistler, and Pawnee Killer. The Plains Indians were becoming more and more hard-pressed by the inexorable extinction of the buffalo and by the extension across the prairie of the Union Pacific Railroad.

Sullenly, through the spring of 1869, the warriors concentrated in the Republican Valley had watched white settlement move gradually closer to their stronghold. By the month of May they could restrain themselves no longer. Smearing on the war paint, the Dog Soldiers plunged into a series of depredations that brought terror and death to the Republican country. Storming across the Plains from the Saline River in Kansas to the Big Sandy in Nebraska, the Indians first struck a small hunting party, then levelled farms and homesteads in a series of lightning raids throughout the region. After nearly annihilating the crew of a Kansas Pacific railroad train, they had ended by destroying a German settlement in Kansas, killing thirteen settlers and carrying off Mrs. Susanna Alderdice, her baby, and Mrs. Maria Weichell to their Republican Valley stronghold.[4] It was apparent that Governor Butler's information was indeed "no idle rumor."

For the moment, however, General Augur could offer little more than token assistance. The frontier army had been left a skeleton force as a result of the great demobilization of 1865–66. "If I detach companies from my command," Augur had to reply, "which is the only mounted force I have to protect all exposed settlements, I will have none to operate against the Indians. . . . To enable settlers to protect themselves, I send you, as you request, fifty Spencer carbines and ten thousand rounds of ammunition for them." But the general could hold out some hope for more substantial aid in the very near future. "A command of cavalry will leave Fort McPherson on the 9th inst. against all Indians in the Republican country." If it was obvious that the root of the trouble lay in the concentration of Indians in the valley, the solution was just as obvious. "The only permanent safety to your frontier settlements," Augur noted, "is to drive the Indians entirely out of the Republican country. This is what I hope to do this summer."[5]

Even as Augur wrote, the cavalry command of which he spoke—the Republican River Expedition—was assembling at Fort McPherson. Under ordinary conditions command of an expedition of this sort perhaps would have gone to a captain, but, due to an abundance of high-ranking officers in the frontier army, Augur had assigned the task to Bvt. Maj. Gen. Eugene Asa Carr, major of the crack Fifth United States Cavalry.[6] The erect, dark-bearded General Carr was an experienced frontier officer. Described by one of his junior officers as "a master of the methods of Indian warfare," the general was a West Point graduate with almost twenty years' active service, much of it on the Kansas, Nebraska, and Colorado frontiers.[7] Carr had a splendid Civil War record of field command. For a time he had been commanding officer of the entire Army of the Southwest until he was forced from the field by an illness apparently brought on by wounds suffered in battle. Like hundreds of other officers left without commands after the great postwar demobilization, General Carr had accepted the sop of brevet rank with a reduced command rather than leave the army.[8]

Carr was not the only high-ranking officer to serve with this task force. The Republican River Expedition, like the rest of the frontier army, was noticeably rank-heavy. Second and third in command were, respectively, Maj. (Bvt. Col.) William Bedford Royall, another hero of the late war, and Maj. Eugene W. Crittenden, nephew of Sen. John J. Crittenden of Kentucky.[9] In command of the undermanned companies of the Fifth Cavalry (none was more than half its authorized strength) were a number of veteran officers, Majors (of regular and brevet rank) Thomas E. Maley, Gustavus E. Urban, Leicester Walker, and John B. Babcock; Captains Jeremiah C. Denney, George F. Price, Robert Sweatman, Philip Dwyer, John H. Kane, Edward M. Hayes, and William H. Brown; and Lt. Charles B. Brady.[10]

To supplement the thin regular army ranks, the famous Pawnee Battalion had been assigned to serve with the Fifth Cavalry. The Pawnee Battalion, a detachment under the command of Maj. Frank J. North made up primarily of Pawnee Indian troops, eventually contained three companies, led by Capt. James Murie, Capt. Sylvanus E. Cushing and by Major North's brother, Capt. Luther H. North.[11] General Carr, who had never commanded Indian troops, did not conceal his doubts about the "lazy and shiftless" natives. But manpower was at a premium, and Carr surely felt that Indian troops were better than none at all.[12]

Whatever the general's feelings about the Pawnees, there was no doubt in his mind about the competence of the chief of scouts of the Fifth Cavalry, the famous William Frederick "Buffalo Bill" Cody. Lauded by Gen. Philip Sheridan for his "endurance and courage," Cody had been assigned to Carr in the winter campaign of 1868.[13] So impressed was General Carr with Cody's "great skill . . . his fighting . . . his markmanship" that upon being placed in command of the Republican River Expedition, Carr had requested particularly that the scout be retained with the regiment "as long as I am engaged in this duty."[14]

In addition to the military the expedition included the usual complement of teamsters, wagoners, and herders—civilians picked up in frontier settlements—as a rule neither particularly ambitious nor especially reliable.[15] They were charged with the duty of maintaining and driving the cumbersome wagons of the expedition's supply train.

This, then, was the composition of the "task force" that was soon to penetrate the Indian country surrounding the Republican River. A detachment of eight to ten small companies of the Fifth Cavalry would be riding beside a battalion of dark-skinned warriors a few years removed from "savagery." They were accompanied by one of the most famous of frontier scouts and by an unruly group of civilian workers. Somewhat heavy in rank and more than a little light in enlisted men, the polyglot column would be led in its march by one of the noted Indian fighters of the frontier army.

On June 7, 1869, when Carr received his orders from headquarters to move out in two days, the command still was not completely prepared for the march. For the past two weeks the general had been working through army red tape to secure at least the bare essentials for a campaign into hostile Indian country.[16] Equipment, some of it of inferior quality, and personnel had been arriving daily, but the expedition still lacked vitally needed wagons and supplies.[17]

Whatever the state of preparation of the expedition, headquarters was explicit in the task it set before General Carr. "The object of your expedition," his orders read, "is to drive the Indians out of the Republican country, and to follow them as far as possible, and most of the details must be left to your judgment." In addition, Carr was asked to keep a journal, report regularly on his progress, and to prepare maps and make note of facts concerning the almost unknown country of the Republican Valley. "The Departmental Commander," the instructions concluded, "relies upon your known energy and skill to accomplish successfully a result so important."[18] Whether "energy and skill" could compensate for half-filled ranks and shortages of equipment may have appeared questionable to General Carr. But he had his orders. The column must move.

As a rule, there was little to brighten the dreary existence at a frontier post. The departure of the Republican River Expedition, however, brought some rare dash and sparkle to the routine life of Fort McPherson, and the garrison troops and their families took full advantage of it. General Augur and a number of his staff officers had arrived on June 8 to be present for the occasion. Welcomed by the post commandant, Lt. Col. Thomas Duncan, the departmental officials were conducted to the parade ground for a full-dress review of the expedition.[19]

Both the cavalry and the Pawnees performed on the hot, dusty McPherson parade ground. As the veteran Fifth Cavalry troopers went through the precise mounted drill, their blue and yellow uniforms and their sabers glistening in the bright July sun doubtless made a splendid show for the small audience gathered at the fort. And despite the bizarre dress of his Indian battalion, Major North was "highly complimented by the reviewing officers for the efficiency of drill to which he had brought the Pawnees."[20]

That evening, after the review, the Pawnee Scouts shed their uniforms. The white troops had had their ceremonial in the afternoon, and the Indians had cooperated, but the evening belonged to the Pawnees. Though a parade might satisfy the whites, the Indians were not about to begin a campaign against their enemies without their own traditional ceremonies, and the visiting officers and the ladies of the fort gathered near the campfires to watch the war dances of the Pawnee tribe.[21]

On June 9, with flags flying and the music of the regimental band echoing in the still summer morning, the Republican River Expedition marched out of Fort McPherson and moved ponderously across the prairie to the south.[22] "It was indeed a gallant command," remarks one author, "and General Carr had good reason to feel proud of his troops."[23]

Moving south and east along the Platte River, the long, winding column was led by the Pawnee Scouts, temporarily under the command of Capt. Luther North.[24] The scouts were followed at a close distance by eight companies of the Fifth Cavalry. Behind the cavalry, the fifty-four wagons of the supply train stretched out into the distance. And somewhere in the clouds of dust raised by the lumbering train was a wagon belonging to Scout Cody. With the business acumen that was later to make him a great showman, Cody had hired a teamster and loaded his wagon with groceries, canned fruit, and vegetables to sell to the soldiers.[25]

The first day's march was a short one. After laboring along the banks of the Platte for a short distance, the expedition went into camp after travelling only three miles from Fort McPherson.[26]

Before the march was a day old, it was becoming apparent that non-regular army personnel did not take military discipline very seriously. That evening Cody invited Captain North to dinner at his home in nearby North Platte, and they left camp without orders. As they were returning late that night, they were caught in a blinding rainstorm. "We waited until the storm was over," recalled North many years later, "and tried to figure out where we were but could not. Cody said, 'Well, we are fine scouts, lost within three miles of the fort.'" At daybreak they at last found the road to camp, but, rather than let the embarrassing facts be known, "We told them we had stayed at the fort overnight on account of the rain."[27]

Shortly after North and Cody returned, the column was ready to move. Just before six o'clock in the morning, June 10, the march was resumed. Entering Snell's Canyon, south of the Platte, the command followed "a practicable roadway through the large sandhills which run parallel to the Platte." To the expedition, a "practicable" road often meant that it was just possible to worry a wagon over it. Passing the sites of many wood-choppers' camps, the column emerged from the canyon and followed a winding route to the south out of the Platte Valley. Dark clouds began to gather on the horizon as the cavalry led the lurching wagons over the "quite rough" country of the Plains.[28] The troops had more to worry about than the approaching storm. Despite its jaunty departure from Fort McPherson, the command was already in serious trouble. General Carr described the situation to headquarters. "We left back six wagons as the corn [for the horses and mules] had not yet arrived; but more corn came at the last moment and was put on the fifty-four wagons and overloaded them." This was just the beginning. "The mules [pulling the wagons] were already tired from hauling across the Platte," and to make matters worse, "many teamsters were drunk." As a result of all this, Carr noted dismally, "Several wagons were overturned and most of the rations came in after dark."[29]

As the column approached Medicine Creek, the storm at last broke. After a day's march of twenty-seven difficult miles, the drenched, hungry soldiers pitched their tents on the banks of the river and went into camp.[30]

If the situation was bad on June 10, things were little better the next day, though this time the crisis was of an entirely different kind. The march had been resumed at 6:15 A.M. on June 11. After moving a little over five miles down Medicine Creek, Carr suddenly called the command to a halt and ordered it to camp. One of his veteran officers had

had a complete mental breakdown. The general appointed an escort of several troopers and placed the officer, Capt. Jeremiah C. Denney, in their care. Captain Denney, who had been grieving over the recent death of his wife, had served with the Fifth Cavalry since its organization in 1855. Carr must have been saddened as he wrote headquarters, "I send in Captain J. C. Denney who is not fit to command troops and utterly beyond recovery. He came to the doctor today and told him his wife had just informed him that he would die in an hour."[31] Tragically, the captain's premonition erred only in the time. Escorted back to Fort McPherson under guard, he was placed in the post hospital; the next day he seized a revolver and blew out his brains.[32]

From this camp on Medicine Creek, Carr made another in his series of attempts to obtain equipment for his command. He still needed ambulances. Optimistic authorities had allowed him only one, with, as the general noted, "worn-out wheel boxes. I wish that you would order two to be sent with the next train."[33] Many weeks—and many requests—later, Carr would still have too few.

Scouting operations began early the next morning, June 12. At 4:30 A.M., 1st Lt. Charles B. Brady, with Company L and a group of Pawnee Scouts, set out for the Republican to search for signs of Indian activity. At ten o'clock a second party was sent out under 2d Lt. William J. Volkmar to scout along Deer Creek. In the meantime the main force of the column continued south down Medicine Creek. Suddenly Volkmar's detachment stumbled onto "a hunting party of about 20 Indians." The first contact with the hostiles had been made. Before Volkmar could organize for a charge, the Indians dashed over a hill and were gone. The news was rushed to the main column. The alarm was given. Immediately going into camp, Carr sent out a company of cavalry and a group of Pawnees to follow the trail, while a courier was sent to call in Lieutenant Brady's detachment. Their action was in vain. Following in the Indians' path, the pursuit party discovered that the trail soon scattered off in different directions. They were forced to return with the news that the Indians had escaped. All was again quiet by midnight, when Lieutenant Brady's detachment, contacted by the messenger far down the Republican, at last rode into camp.[34]

The sun was high on the horizon when, at 5:30 A.M., June 13, the expedition broke camp and began again to move south, following the overgrown ruts of an old wagon road leading toward the Republican.[35] According to a story told by Capt. Luther North, General Carr had arranged to bring his pet greyhounds with the expedition and now decided to take them out for an antelope chase. Asserting, says North, that his greyhounds could catch "anything," the general assembled a group of officers and rode ahead until an antelope had been sighted. The dogs, Captain North related,

> saw [the antelope] at once and started for him. He saw them, and instead of running away, he trotted toward them. Then we rode up in sight. By this time the dogs were only one hundred feet from him, and he turned and ran the other way.
>
> The General said, "Oh, they will catch him before he gets started. . . ." When we came into sight of them they were running across a big flat, and as our horses were pretty well blown we stopped and watched them. The antelope soon went out of sight over a hill about a mile away, with the dogs about two or three hundred yards behind, and when they reached the top of the hill they stopped for a minute, looked, then turned and came trotting back. No one had said a word up to this time, when Cody spoke. "General," he said, "if anything the antelope is a little bit ahead."

From that time on, North states, it was the adjutant who took out the greyhounds.[36]

At last the command struck the Republican, reaching its banks about five miles below the mouth of Medicine Creek. Just a few yards from this point stood the decaying remains of an old log stockade, "by whom built, or when, was unknown." Fording the river here, the column moved down stream to the mouth of Deer Creek and at the end of the day's march of almost twenty miles went into camp on a "very sandy" site.[37]

Luckily there was enough timber near the campsite to build a bridge over Deer Creek. The next morning the wagons were pulled across the bridge, and the column pushed steadily on down the "bottom" of the Republican Valley. It was an uneventful day. After urging the wagons over twenty miles of the soft soil and grassy gullies of the Republican bottomland, the column reached the mouth of Prairie Dog Creek. Moving five miles beyond the mouth of the Prairie Dog, the expedition halted for the day and went into camp.[38]

If the troopers were hoping for a break in the monotony of the march, they found it the next day. Breaking camp early in the morning on June 15, Carr sent out scouting parties to look for Indian signs. Though detachments had been out every day, no Indians had been seen since Lieutenant Volkmar's contact on June 12. It was certain that Indians were present somewhere in the area. But after several hours of operations the scouts returned to the column with only negative results to report. About mid-day the general called the expedition to a halt and ordered camp made on the banks of the river.[39] The Pawnees were encamped about half a mile below the cavalry, and the wagon train was strung out in the center. Cody had drawn up his grocery wagon and made camp near the Pawnee Scouts. Taking advantage of the good grass near the river, the wagon boss had sent two teamsters out to graze the mules. The camp settled down for supper. Suddenly a war whoop broke the stillness of the late afternoon, and seconds later a teamster galloped into camp with an arrow in his body. The Indians had made their presence known.[40]

The Indians, who apparently had hidden in the underbrush when the column went into camp, doubtless had assumed that there would be plenty of time to drive off the mule herd while the cavalry was preparing itself for action. If successful, it would have been a serious blow to the expedition, for without mules the wagon train was unable to move.[41] But while the cavalry was sounding "boots and saddles," the Pawnees had shed their uniforms and, without bothering with saddles or bridles—or orders—had set off in hot pursuit of the hostile war party.[42] Cody, whose horse had not been unsaddled, was the first to cross the river, but he was soon overtaken by Captain North and the Pawnees. Before the cavalry was able to leave the camp, Cody, North, and the Pawnees had engaged the warriors in a running fight. Soon Major Royall and several companies of cavalry joined in the pursuit. Though the chase lasted until nightfall, only two of the marauders were killed. After losing the war party's trail in the darkness, the tired, hungry pursuers halted and returned over the moonlit prairie to the camp.[43] The search could wait until tomorrow.

The next morning Captain North rode over to the cavalry camp to report the action to General Carr. "I thought," North wrote to his uncle, "I had done pretty well to get all the mules back." But the general was unimpressed by the spur-of-the-moment charge, and he was not about to compliment an officer who had violated military protocol by leaving camp and engaging in an action without orders. According to North:

> I went up to his tent and there before all of his Officers he reprimanded [*sic*] me for leaving camp to pursue the Indians without orders from him. I answered as civilly as I could that the only way to fight Indians was to go for them as fast as possible whenever they were found. He said that he understood his business and that all I had to do was obey orders. I told him that I expected to obey orders but that when the Indians attacked a camp that I was in I intended to go for them and that I shouldn't wait for orders from him nor any other man. Having spoke my little piece I touched my pony with the spurs and dashed away to the head of my company.[44]

"I expected," North remarked, "that I would be placed under arrest but was not." Surely the general was itching to arrest such an upstart captain of volunteers who presumed to lecture him on "the only way to fight Indians!" But Carr was in a poor position to arrest any officer, whatever his breach of discipline or insubordination. With the already small command deep in Indian country any further reduction in numbers might be dangerous. The general probably also took into account that the captain and his men were irregular volunteers almost completely unaccustomed to army discipline, and that, however unmilitary their procedure, they had, after all, saved the mules.[45] But the result could have been much less happy; in Indian territory, Carr's experience told him, isolation could often mean annihilation. North's behavior was a courting of disaster. The incident could not be allowed to pass without reprimand.

The incident did little to dispel Carr's earlier doubts about the reliability of Indian troops. "The Pawnees," the general wrote to headquarters, "are rather lazy and shiftless; but I hope to make their Indian qualities useful. I would however like to exchange all but thirty of them for good cavalry soldiers."[46] But for the time being, the problem could rest, for the Indians who had attempted the stampede could not be far away, and, if immediate action was taken, there was still a chance of catching them.

Reveille sounded at 3:00 A.M. After bolting down breakfast, the sleepy soldiers placed five days' rations on pack mules and prepared to move out. Assigning one company to remain as protection for the slow-moving wagon train, the general ordered the command forward at daybreak. The raiders' trail was at first quite clear, and soon became so heavy that the Pawnees were certain that a village must be near. At seven o'clock the command halted briefly at the swollen waters of Prairie Dog Creek. The stream was obviously too full for the wagon train to cross without bridging. Carr could waste no time; the wagon train, which until now had managed to remain close to the cavalry column, had to be left behind. Turning to the south, the troops followed the marauders' path for twenty-five miles. The trail led straight to the North Fork of the Solomon River. The column marched down into the bottom land, splashed through the stream, rode up the bank—and found to their dismay that the Indians' tracks scattered in all directions. The trail was lost.[47]

Even the Pawnees were confused. There was little hope now of finding the raiders. For want of anything tangible, the general turned the column off to the west, "followed some scattered pony tracks" for a short distance and then went into camp.[48] Nature added a fitting end to a day of discouragement. Evening brought a torrential thunderstorm that lasted most of the night.[49]

The ground was still wet when reveille sounded at three o'clock the next morning. Camp was broken at 5:30, and, again sending out the usual scouting parties, Carr moved the column to the southwest. During the day, Maj. Frank North, who had been delayed by the thunderstorm, joined the column with the newly recruited Company C of the Pawnee Scouts and again assumed command of the battalion.[50]

Difficulties apparently had not been confined to the main column for Major North had found his share. His company had drowned four horses in crossing the Platte on June 13. Striking out across the Plains, they had encountered such withering heat—"Oh what a long dry march," the major had written, "mules horses and men nearly perished"—that the thunderstorm had seemed a relief.[51]

More frustration awaited General Carr. Major North had been given a message from the departmental adjutant, Maj. George D. Ruggles, to deliver to the expedition's commander. Carr must have been incredulous when, upon opening the letter, he found orders to detach Captain Sweatman's company from the command. "He is to go for the summer," the orders read, "to cover and protect settlements on the Little Blue."[52] Carr was to exchange his "good cavalry soldiers" for the newly arrived company of "lazy and shiftless" Pawnees!

As he sat down to acknowledge receipt of the orders, the general may have reflected briefly upon the many regiments under his command when he had led the mighty Army of the Southwest in the Civil War. Now, the loss of a single company made a considerable difference. There was a note of exasperation in General Carr's reply:

I detach Captain Robert Sweatman's Company "B" in compliance with orders.

It is very disheartening to me for my command to be reduced; it was already too small, (companies not half full) and there are a good many men whose terms will soon expire.

I have to escort my supply trains; and when I go on a trail I do not feel justified in leaving less than a company. And then, if I wish to divide my command for pursuit, or any purpose, the parties are too small to act with confidence and vigor.

Custer's smallest command last winter was eleven full companies with, I believe, Infantry train Guards. I send with this, official application for four full companies of Infantry.[53]

Carr had little prospect of getting four full companies—or even one company—of infantry, and doubtless he was quite aware of it. But an official request was one certain way to point up his dissatisfaction with the size of his force and perhaps would discourage a further reduction of his command.

With Company C of the Pawnees filling the gap left by the departure of Sweatman's company, the numerical strength of Carr's column had not been reduced. But the general, still unconvinced of the soldierly qualities of Indian troops, noted that the Pawnees were not as well mounted as the regular cavalry. Indeed, Carr reported, the scouts were so "miserably mounted" that "their ponies can hardly keep out of the way of the troops on an ordinary march," and would "require fifty good ponies to mount them properly."[54] Carr's mind could hardly have been at ease as he watched Captain Sweatman's company leave the column for the east. Regardless of the loss of the company, the campaign continued. The general moved the column to the southwest a few miles and then ordered it into camp.[55]

From this camp near the North Fork of the Solomon River in Kansas, Carr made out his regular report to headquarters. After recounting the actions of the previous day, the general again pointed out to departmental officials some of the most pressing problems of his command. The expedition seemed to be suffering more from the difficulties of the march itself than from any hostile Indians. "I hope," wrote Carr, "you will order a sufficient number of wagons so that our train may not be overloaded, and thus delay us." There were far too few vehicles even to adequately "carry our twenty days supplies and baggage," and Carr requested "fifteen additional wagons" for the wagon train accompanying the column. But those fifteen were by no means enough to meet the needs of the entire operation. A supply train was to meet the column in two weeks at "Thickwood," a point on the Republican south of Fort McPherson. Underequipped himself, Carr could hardly provide wagons enough for such a supply unit. "We also need fifty wagons to carry the twenty days supplies from Fort McPherson to meet us, not including the baggage wagons of the Escort, which should be two per company."[56]

With the train hardly able to carry the bare necessities of the campaign, there had been no room for luxuries. Hoping to avoid as much hardship to his men as possible, Carr brought the situation to the attention of headquarters. "Being out constantly," the general wrote, "the troops should be provided with some comforts, or it will be more than humane [*sic*] nature can and will stand."[57] The few "comforts" in Cody's wagon doubtless had long since been exhausted.

Despite Carr's requests during preparations at Fort McPherson, a supply of hobbles to keep the mules in camp had been overlooked. He now asked that they be made at Fort McPherson and then sent to him, "as they have facilities, old blankets, etc. for making them there, and we find it very difficult to make them in the field." Troops could not easily be spared for such tasks, and, the general added with a note of disgust, "it is almost impossible to get the teamsters to make them."[58] The ambulances requested earlier had not yet arrived, and the commander gently reminded headquarters that "I attended to ambulances in my last."[59]

There was little to cheer the general as he affixed his sprawling signature to the report and prepared to send it off. During the day the scouting parties sent out that morning had rejoined the column and could report finding no more than a trail left by a detachment of the Seventh Cavalry operating out of Fort Hays. At three o'clock in the afternoon the expedition's wagon train, left far behind during the cavalry's gallop to the banks of the Solomon, lumbered into the quiet camp.[60] Carr may have ruefully surveyed the creaking, overburdened wagons as he summed up the events of the day's difficult thirty-mile march: no sign of the Indians, the loss of an entire company to guard duty in the east, its replacement by a group of "miserably mounted" Indian troops, short supplies, requests that seemed to be completely ignored—and all this with a small command of hardly four hundred troops in the heart of Indian country.

The next day the general moved the command only a little more than a mile, then went into camp to send out scouts to continue the search for traces of Indian activity. To avoid a repetition of the Pawnees' reckless charge at Prairie Dog Creek several days earlier, Carr was careful to see that each scouting party was made up of both a group of Pawnees and one or two companies of cavalry. But the reports differed little from those of the day before. There were no fresh Indian signs. The scouts could claim to have found only old wagon trails, a dilapidated log stable of uncertain date, a broken wagon, and the remains of a cavalry camp of the previous winter.[61]

On June 19 the column moved north back toward the Republican. The next ten days were spent in a wandering march through the rolling hills of the Republican Valley. For the most part conditions were similar from day to day. The Indians were staying out of sight. The rugged country continued to wreak havoc with the wagons. There was still a shortage of supplies. New misfortune now beset the expedition. Illness and injury began to take such a toll of soldiers that "at one time our two ambulances overflowed so that a sick Officer could not find a place." The general's plea for more ambulances had been only partially heeded, and at last he was forced to carry sick and injured men in the gradually emptying wagons.[62]

There were some compensations for the difficulties of the march through the Republican Valley, for the territory at least was more pleasant than the plains crossed on the march to the south. The route of travel lay cross-country from the Prairie Dog to the rendezvous at "Thickwood" in the southwest corner of Nebraska. Although the units of the command were forced to make some journeys as far as twenty-five or thirty miles without water, they could always depend upon striking a reasonably comfortable, well-watered campsite before nightfall.[63] Major North noted these conditions in his diary. On June 21 the expedition "marched 28 miles without water. Have a very good camp tonight on Short Nose" [Prairie Dog Creek]; on June 22 "we march[ed] 25 miles. . . . I have a fine camp here," and on June 24 "came across the country to big Beaver [Creek] here we find splendid fuel and water."[64]

The long days were relieved by diversions that probably came naturally to a command of this sort. Their recreation was simple, if somewhat rough. Despite one day's long, dry march, Major North and several others were not too weary to have "some fun riding one of our bucking horses. It threw [Sgt. Sam] Wallace 3 times. Finally a lieut. [of the regulars] rode it."[65]

Buffalo hunting, a pastime born of necessity, was a regular part of the days' activities. Killing buffalo was good sport, and it produced a welcome addition to the rations of the troops as well. "Killed lots of Buffalo," recorded Major North in his diary one evening, "had lots of ribs."[66] The buffalo hunt was traditional with the Pawnees, and the regiment's chief of scouts was soon to become the most famous buffalo hunter of all time. In one day's incident related by a biographer of Major North, the major and Cody had left the column to watch the Pawnees "make a surround." After they had encircled one herd and killed thirty-two buffalo, the Pawnees were preparing to surround another herd when Cody asked North to "Let me show your Pawnees how to kill buffalo." The Pawnees withdrew, and Cody, it is told, "in a run of about half a mile . . . dropped thirty-seven buffaloes, killing one at nearly every shot and stringing them along on the prairie about fifty feet apart."[67] Such slaughter, however, was evidently uncommon on this expedition for the usual number of buffalo killed seems to have been only a few at any particular time.

There was a quieter kind of entertainment as well. It perhaps was left only to the regulars to enjoy the time-honored tradition of gathering around the campfire for singing. On this expedition the troops may have sung some of the songs that Major North hastily pencilled in his notebook, such as, for instance, this lusty ballad:

I'm just as fond of beauty/as any one can be

With pretty eyes and rosy cheeks/I always love to see

But none of us have got them/except myself and you

For I know a little fellow/and he's got the money too.

Cho: Oh, don't I love my honey/and won't I spend his money

I am happy as a flower/that sips the morning dew

For I know a little fellow/and he's got the money too.

Or the lament that North must have heard from one of the many displaced rebels in the frontier army:

Oh the old home aint what it used to be/The banjo and the fiddle has gone

And no more you hear the darkies singing/among the sugar cane and corn.

Great changes have come to poor old [land]/But this change makes [me] sad and forlorn

For no more we hear the darkies singing/among the sugar cane and corn.[68]

Some members of the command, particularly young Lieutenant Volkmar, who kept the command's journal, often rode a short distance from the command to investigate the hitherto largely unexplored countryside. Upon returning he made careful notations of his findings in the "Journal of the March." On June 21, for example, the lieutenant wrote:

Passed a rising mound, lying about two miles to the north. This mound has upon its top the figure of a man, spread upon his back, with spear and shield; a medal is attached to his neck;—all made, in outline, from small pieces of limestone. This mound is about three miles south of the Beaver Creek and is about three miles west of the mouth of that creek. It is supposed to be an Indian place of worship. The mound was named by Lieut. Volkmar, 5" Cavalry, who discovered the image, the 'Homo Calcis' mound.[69]

The journal and General Carr's reports added a great deal of information to the little yet known about the Republican Valley. Including in his reports both corrections and suggestions for improvement of the "very

meagre as well as incorrect" information on army maps, Carr noted especially the correct courses of both known and previously unknown streams,
including the one which yet bears the name he gave it, the Driftwood.[70]

On June 29 still in the Republican Valley, the column went into camp
on "Buffalo Head Creek," near Thickwood on the Republican, to await
the arrival of the supply train from Fort McPherson. As usual, scouting
parties were sent out in several directions. Ordering the troops to prepare
for a muster and mounted inspection to be held the next day, the general
prepared to write another report of his operations to headquarters.[71]

Not a single hostile Indian had been seen since the raid on the mule
herd on June 15, but Indian signs had been appearing with increasing
frequency. In recent days it had seemed to be almost too quiet, and the
hoofprints around the column's line of march were occasionally too fresh
for comfort. Innocent objects had begun to take on suspicious characteristics as an "Indian fever" at last crept over the command. Major
Crittenden and his escort, for instance, came into camp with the wagon
train at two o'clock on June 29 and reported that a large number of
Cheyennes had been seen lurking near the McPherson road. Carr immediately ordered two companies to equip themselves for a three days' march
and sent them out to investigate. They returned hours later with the
news that the "Cheyenne" were only a herd of grazing buffalo.[72] Meeting
with only slightly more success was a detachment under Sergeant Wallace
that had been sent out earlier and in a different direction. Wallace had
been able to report a trail that was "pretty fresh," but that was all.[73]

Meanwhile the general was finishing his report. Again he had launched
a barrage of requests—more ambulances, some expressmen to carry dispatches to the fort, two good horses for Cody—but Carr apparently was
beginning to question the wisdom of his incessant hammering for supplies. "I hope," he wrote, "the General will not think me too persistent
in these applications. I know he is inclined to supply me with everything
in his power which he deems necessary, and I will rest content with what
I receive, but still," Carr added hopefully, "I feel it my duty to report
deficiencies, in case they may have been overlooked, or orders may have
been given and not obeyed." General Carr, still vexed by the loss of Company B, made it clear to headquarters that he wanted no such thing to
happen again. Noting that he had sent Major Crittenden with two companies to follow a "promising" trail, Carr added somewhat testily that
"Should the trail take Major Crittenden [north] to the [Union Pacific]
railroad & beyond, I will be left with only five companies with which I
suppose I must make some sort of a scout up the Republican. I hope that
you will bear this in mind."[74]

The Indian troops, the general could report, had caused no trouble of late. He felt even that "the Pawnees are improving somewhat in discipline and general usefulness; and [I] hope to get good service out of them."[75]

The eagerly awaited supply train from Fort McPherson had arrived, and as Carr sat writing in his tent, the troops were busy "transferring the supplies to the train of the command," while the officers were "busy . . . getting ready to muster." The "lots of stores" brought in from McPherson bolstered the spirits of the weary command. As Major North put it, "we will live high again for a while."[76] The next morning, June 30, the column was mustered and the mounted inspection held. Later in the day the McPherson train, its empty wagons carrying the expedition's wounded and injured, set off for the north. The column remained in camp for the remainder of that day and all of the next, resting, organizing supplies, and sending out scouting detachments. Carr informed the command that the march would resume in the morning.[77]

Moving out at dawn, July 2, the column continued up the Republican "bottom." The timber along the river, which had been heavy in the eastern part of the valley, began to thin by July 3, as the command moved steadily toward the west. There was little wood near the campsite as the column halted to make camp on the Frenchman River (North Fork of the Republican). In the afternoon, July 3, a scouting party returned with the most promising news so far. A fresh trail had been found, and a Cheyenne camp that had not been "abandoned more than thirty-six hours" had been located. The numerous mule shoes found around the camp indicated that these Indians had recently stolen a large number of animals from the frontier settlements.[78] This, perhaps, was the trail of the Dog Soldiers themselves!

The Indian signs grew even more promising as a more extensive investigation was made. "The trail," reported the general, "seemed to follow the general course of the North Fork of the Republican, keeping, however, about ten miles away from that stream and encamping on the heads of small tributaries." These Indians, apparently about thirty lodges with three hundred animals, were moving very cautiously up the river, attempting to disguise their trail. "They would scatter," Carr noted, "when leaving camp; then come together on the high, hard prairie and drive their animals in every direction to confuse the trail; then scatter again and not reassemble till near their night camp."[79]

This party was too large and too careful to be simply a casual hunting party; it must almost certainly be an important part of Tall Bull's village. The Indians, believed General Carr, must surely be near. The situation called for immediate action. Carr detached three companies of cavalry along with Lt. Gus Barclay's company of Pawnee Scouts and gave them pack mules to carry three days' rations. Major Royall was placed in charge of the small unit. Ordering Royall to "try to surprise them, kill as many warriors as possible and capture their families and animals," the general sent the detachment out to follow the trail.[80]

As Royall set off to the west, the main column forded the Republican. It was still early in the morning as they entered the rugged, sandy, treeless country north of the river. At four o'clock in the afternoon the command found a site near a "clump of trees, the only timber on the river worth mentioning," and encamped to await word from the scouting party.[81]

Soon dispatches from Royall's unit began to arrive. They contained no news of any real success. Though he "had passed several camps lately abandoned," Royall on July 5 had not overtaken the Cheyennes. Major North, for one, was disappointed. "I [should] think," he wrote, "that he has found the Indians before this time." Carr, too, must have been disappointed as he read in the message brought by Royall's courier that, after following the trail for forty-eight miles, the tracks appeared to be four days old.[82]

Little could be accomplished by remaining here. On July 6 the main column broke camp and began slogging through the barren sand hills of the High Plains. It was a trying march. "Sand till you can't rest," wrote Major North in his diary, and still "no news from Royal today." The sky was cloudless. With the hot sun beating down on the shifting sand, it is not surprising that tempers began to grow short. "Sam and Bart walked about ten miles for disobeying the q[uarter] m[aster]."[83] Water was becoming scarce. The Frenchman River did not extend as far west as the inaccurate army maps had indicated, and Carr was forced to turn the command toward the headwaters of the Black Tail Deer Creek to go into camp.[84]

Meanwhile, Major Royall was still on the trail of the Cheyennes. Moving to the north from his camp of July 4, Royall had led his detachment eighteen miles across the country. Suddenly his Pawnees sighted a group of horsemen. It was a war party of twelve, carrying one wounded warrior on a litter. This was enough for the Pawnees; once more discipline was broken. "The Pawnee reported that the 'Whole Party' was there," General Carr later reported, "and started in pursuit, and the troops had no choice but to follow."[85]

The small group was no match for Royall's detachment. The scouts rode the Cheyennes down, took three scalps, and captured eight horses, two with an army brand. The chase had led the small command almost back to their starting point. Because they had only one more day's rations, and because the main band of Indians would probably be warned by the small party that the Pawnees had impetuously charged, Royall decided to return to the column.[86]

The cavalry camp was thrown into confusion about two o'clock in the afternoon, July 7, as the soldiers sighted a party of Indians streaking across the empty sand hills, yelling and brandishing scalps on poles. The cavalrymen at first believed it to be a Sioux raiding party. But as the Pawnees who had remained behind were making no preparations for battle, it was apparent that the approaching Indians were not hostile, and Captain North assured General Carr that it was just some of his own troops celebrating a victory. Lieutenant Barclay's Pawnees, leading Royall's detachment into camp, were bringing news of their skirmish.[87] The Pawnees' commander was jubilant. "Today," wrote the major, "has been a great day for the Scouts." That night, the Pawnee Scouts, no less jubilant than their major, celebrated with a victory dance.[88]

The gaiety of the Pawnees was in sharp contrast to the gloom in the general's tent. Despite the fact that this was the first real victory of the campaign, the affair gave General Carr little cause to rejoice; the Indians who had escaped the Pawnees' rash charge doubtless had already alerted the main body of hostiles. Already following a trail four days old, the lumbering column could now only fall farther behind the fleet Cheyennes.[89]

Nevertheless, the trail had been the first of any importance, and there was still little else to do but continue to follow it. "I had little hope of overtaking the Indians," said Carr, "but thought I could at least hunt them out of the country." There seemed little need now to travel light—"the trail being reported so old, and the Indians being alarmed, and, it being probable that it would require a chase too long for rations to be carried without wagons"—the general determined to take the entire command on the trail. It was impossible to get the heavy equipment through the sand hills to the present camp, so the discouraged commander moved his column back down the Frenchman River to find a good route to the Indians' trail.[90] Sharp Cheyenne eyes were watching, apparently, as the column reversed direction and began to retrace its tracks.[91]

During the day, while the main body of the expedition was moving through the inhospitable country, three men under Cpl. John Kyle of Company M left the column to bring in a straying cavalry horse. They were several miles from the column when, suddenly, eight Indians swooped down on them. Corporal Kyle led the little party to a sheltering rock, and, killing the horse for a defense, opened fire on the hostiles, managing to wound two before the Indians retreated. Apparently the Cheyennes had indeed been aroused by the July 5 attack.[92]

That evening the command encamped at the same spot they had used on July 4 and 5 on the Frenchman, a few miles east of the Colorado border. Fighting off mosquitoes, the regulars and scouts made camp beside each other on the banks of the river and settled down for the night. Suddenly, about eleven o'clock, the silence was shattered by the rattle of gunfire. Galloping past the sentry at the east end of the camp, several mounted Cheyennes charged through the horses in an attempt to stampede them, then spread confusion into the middle of the camp itself. Yelling, and firing in all directions into tents and wagons, they dashed out of the west end of the camp and disappeared into the night. The attack was over as quickly as it had begun.[93]

The swift raid had left the column with only one casualty, and that one was not wounded by the Cheyennes. Completely unprepared for such an unusual nighttime attack, the troops had fired at anything that moved. Mad Bear of the scouts, who had dashed forward into the hail of bullets to reach a fallen Cheyenne, had been hit by a wild shot from the cavalry.[94]

There could now be little doubt that Major Royall's skirmish had warned the Cheyennes. The presence of Cheyennes in numbers enough to attempt a raid made it likely that there were perhaps even more in the vicinity. The trail, then, seemed to be getting warm, but the whereabouts of Tall Bull's main force was unknown. While skirmishes might hamper the Indians' activities, their main village must be found and destroyed to achieve a really decisive victory.

Only by a series of forced marches was there any possibility of overtaking the Cheyennes. Therefore, despite the oppressive heat, General Carr decided to push on at once. At dawn the next day, July 9, Carr changed the direction of the march and set out to the north. It was, as the general noted, "a very long, hot and tiresome day's march" through the barren expanses of northeastern Colorado.[95] "The country," wrote Lieutenant Volkmar in the journal, "is a succession of sand hills, and a hot blast which blew all day, rendered the march very trying."[96] The tired, thirsty column pushed on through the shifting sand and at last, about four o'clock in the afternoon, went into camp on "Bechers [sic] Battle ground," over thirty miles north of their starting point on the Frenchman. "March 30 miles without water," wrote Major North in his diary, "and oh how hot and dry. We have nothing . . . but standing rainwater."[97] The column was now not far from the point where Major Royall had left the Cheyennes' trail.

It was already warm at five o'clock the next morning, July 10, when the command doggedly resumed the march. A "thick growth of cactus" covered the ground "for miles" along the winding route of the march, and the sun beat down unrelentingly on the little column pushing its way through the sand hills. The rigorous thirty-two-mile march was worth the effort. Crossing the winding Frenchman River "some eight times," the troops discovered an abandoned Indian camp, then another, and then still another. The command was fast approaching the Cheyennes; they had covered in one day the territory the Indians had traveled in three![98] And the last camp apparently had been abandoned only that morning.[99] Prints of a white woman's shoe had been seen along the trail; there could be little doubt now that these were Dog Soldiers, the band that had terrorized the settlements of Kansas and Nebraska.[100] Carr halted on the site of the third camp and began making preparations for swift action.

In the meantime the Cheyenne Dog Soldiers under Tall Bull had struck out from the Frenchman River across the sand hills toward the South Platte. Finding the Platte and other streams too full for safe crossing, Tall Bull, perhaps against his better judgment, made the fatal mistake of going into camp on White Butte Creek, near Summit Springs, Colorado.[101] Why Tall Bull felt secure enough to allow camp to be made with the cavalry so close behind is not clear. Perhaps, since he had scattered his village, as Carr had found the previous week, into many small parties, he felt that this would throw the cavalry off his trail.[102] Such a belief would have seemed to be confirmed by the apparent withdrawal of the column as it turned back to the east to find a better way to the Cheyennes' trail.[103] Whatever the reason for Tall Bull's carelessness, it was to result in disaster for the Dog Soldiers.

In his camp some twenty miles to the south, General Carr was hurriedly preparing for the next day's march. The adversities of the last four weeks, and especially of the past few days, had taken their toll on the command. Carr's inadequate wagon train had had no room for proper forage for the horses, and the grass of the valley had been replaced by the yucca and cactus of the sand hills. The troops were tired, but their horses were exhausted. Assembling his command, Carr selected for duty all available men, "that is, all those whose horses were fit for service." The outlook was bleak; out of seven companies of the Fifth Cavalry (almost 400 men) and three companies of the Pawnee Scouts (150 men), the general could muster only 244 cavalry and fifty scouts for the next day's forced march.[104]

There was no way of knowing the number of warriors in the Cheyenne village, but, even with the expedition's force reduced by half, speed and strategy might compensate. General Carr ordered three days' rations placed on pack mules. The heavy wagon train would be left behind under guard of those unable to make the march. Major North and his fifty scouts would precede the command at a short distance. The column would march at daybreak.[105]

The campaign was approaching its climax. Behind the expedition lay over a month of hard marching with, until now, most disappointing results. Equipment had been meager and often defective; supplies had been short. But they had sufficed. The country itself had been an adversary, but it had been conquered. The ranks of the command were thin, but, despite the general's fears, there would be soldiers enough for the task at hand; even the unpredictable Pawnees would gain Carr's approval.

There was little doubt on that evening of July 10, 1869, that the next day would bring a conflict. "We will have a fight tomorrow sure," wrote Major North in his diary; "I hope we may come out victorious. I shall be careful for the sake of the dear ones at home."[106]

The command bedded down for the night to await the morning's forced march that would lead them to victory at the Battle of Summit Springs.

Part 2. The Battle of Summit Springs

The Battle of Summit Springs was one of the most celebrated conflicts between the white man and the Indian in the history of the American frontier. It received national notice at the time, and its reenactment was the climax of William F. Cody's Wild West Show in Madison Square Garden as late as 1906.[107] But little of the glamour of Buffalo Bill's show was to be seen in the tired little column pushing through the sand hills of northeastern Colorado early in the morning of Sunday, July 11, 1869.

Maj. Frank North's fifty Pawnee Scouts had moved out by five o'clock and were followed shortly by the cavalrymen Carr had selected the day before. The supply wagons and their escort quickly fell behind as the smaller detachment moved across the hills. By 7:30 A.M. Carr's column had splashed through the twisting Frenchman River "some six or seven times" and was heading directly west.[108] During the early morning there were two reports from the Pawnees that hostile Indians had been seen, and the command had taken up the gallop only to find that the "Indians" were just wild horses.[109]

At about 10:30 A.M., as the column reached the rough country at the breaks of the Platte bluffs, the scouts again sent back a message, reporting that two horsemen had been seen and recommending that the entire command be taken into a concealing ravine.[110] This, perhaps, was another herd of horses, but there was too much at stake to risk discovery by the Dog Soldiers. "Great caution" therefore, "was observed by the column, everybody dismounting and leading the horses quickly over the ridges, and down through steep ravines to the 'bottom'" to continue the march.[111]

Soon the trail divided into two; one small one led to the right toward the Platte, while the other, considerably larger, struck out across the hills.[112] It was apparently a ruse. Carr reasoned that the Indians were as badly in need of water as was his own column and that they would hardly set off across the dry sand hills to get it. Consequently, the general gambled on the lighter trail leading to the Platte and "moved directly toward that stream." The column labored on for several more miles through deep, loose sand, nearing the vicinity of Summit Springs.[113] The scouts again sent in reports. One party had sighted "a herd of animals in the valley near the stream to the right, while at the same time came a report from the left of Indians seen."[114]

Either might prove to be the Cheyenne camp. Carr decided to detach three companies under Major Royall, accompanied by Scout William F. Cody, to move toward the "animals." In the meantime the general would lead the rest of the command along the main trail toward the point where the Indians had been reported. Now even pack mules were too great an encumbrance, and Carr sent them back to the wagon train, which was still barely visible in the distance.[115]

Both parties took up the gallop. In a few minutes the detachment of scouts in advance of General Carr's group sent back word that tipis had been sighted. This would have to be the Cheyenne village.[116]

Briefly, Carr halted. He seemed very pleased at the prospect of at last meeting the elusive Cheyennes for battle.[117] Any victory over the Cheyennes would loosen their hold on the valley. But if this should prove to be the village of Tall Bull himself, the power of the Dog Soldiers perhaps could be broken with a single powerful blow. The general quickly sent a messenger to Major Royall to ask for a company "as soon as he could spare one." Royall immediately sent his strongest company. Again Carr's command set out on the gallop.[118]

For an hour the column traveled at a wearing pace through the hot, loose sand. Still nothing was to be seen of the hostiles. The old doubts began to creep into the general's mind. "I began to think the whole thing was a humbug, and that I would have to follow them across the Platte and across the Railroad to the north"—in which case the chances for a decisive victory would be small indeed. "With little hopes of finding anything," Carr moved his tired, thirsty command forward toward the place where the scouts had reported seeing Indians. At about two o'clock in the afternoon several Pawnee Scouts signalled to the general to come up with them. Carr galloped up to the advance party. The Pawnees pointed out a herd of animals about four miles away among the hills. The scouts were sure that they were horses belonging to hostile Indians, but Carr, "having been so often disappointed," was skeptical. "I thought it very possible," he later reported, "it might be buffalo, but, of course, [I] determined to go and see."[119]

Despite his doubts, the general could not risk a mistake. He ordered the command to prepare for battle. While the sweating cavalry tightened girths, the Pawnees began stripping for action, wearing only enough of their uniforms to identify themselves as soldiers. Major Royall's detachment rejoined the command as it was preparing for battle; after a difficult twenty-mile journey he had found that the "animals" reported were only bushes.[120]

Their preparations made, the column moved on. Keeping well hidden in the depressions and ravines between the sand hills, the small command moved rapidly to a position northwest of the point named by the Pawnees. It soon became apparent that this time there had been no error. This was indeed Tall Bull's village.[121]

As the troops approached within about a mile of the Dog Soldier camp, concealment was no longer possible. Carr called the command to a halt and ordered a battle formation of two ranks. The general placed three companies in the first rank and divided them into three parallel columns, double file, with the Pawnees on the left. As a rising wind stirred clouds of dust around the tensely waiting ranks, Carr directed Major Crittenden to take command of the first line and ordered the bugler to sound the charge.[122]

Lt. [Bvt. Capt.] George F. Price, in command of Company A on the right in the front rank, describes that moment:

> Only those who were near him could hear the short, sharp notes, but every man saw him going through the motions. That was enough. All knew that there was only one call to sound then; and away dashed the gallant troopers in one of the most superb charges ever made by the Fifth Cavalry. The spurs sunk deep in the flanks of the good but jaded horses, who, seeming to understand the necessity of the occasion, responded with a magnificent burst of speed.[123]

While the leading companies were traveling "at speed" the second rank was following at a fast gallop. Almost a mile had to be covered in the long charge, and the advance became ragged as some of the poorer horses fell behind. The irregular blue line was unnoticed almost until it burst into the long valley that held the Dog Soldiers' camp.[124]

The surprise was complete as the regiment "with ringing cheers" struck the village.[125] Some of the cavalry "reached the village so quickly that the Indians had little time to saddle or bridle their horses, and many could not even get on horseback."[126] Historian Carl Coke Rister presents this picture of the havoc caused by the charge:

> [P]andemonium reigned. The thunderous approach of the cavalry, screaming women and crying children running here and there to mount ponies or to save some treasured possession, the war whoops of the Cheyennes and the counter-challenges of the soldiers caused great confusion while dust from an approaching storm drove through the village.[127]

Captain Price's unit, according to Price's own account, "turned the enemy's left flank, and, dashing to the rear, killed seven warriors and captured three hundred animals," while Captain Walker, "endeavoring to turn the enemy's right flank, encountered an ugly side-ravine, which delayed his progress and permitted a number of the enemy to escape."[128]

As the first line of cavalry spread destruction through the village, General Carr signaled in the remaining companies. The Cheyennes broke. Those lucky enough to have reached their horses streamed out of the camp in an effort to escape the vicious onslaught of the cavalry. The troops swept back through the camp; one detachment pursued the panic-stricken escapees for about four miles, with "some of their horses giving out at every step, until finally none were able to raise a gallop." Of the thirteen horses lost in this chase, only one was killed by the Indians; the rest died of exhaustion.[129]

In the meantime hot fighting still raged in the village. It was certain that there were white prisoners in the camp, and they must be found. The Pawnee Scouts were all over the village, fighting singly and in groups. They were joined by cavalrymen to hunt down those individuals firing from the ravines that led off from the valley.[130] The Cheyennes, though fewer in number than had been anticipated, put up a stout, last-ditch resistance.

Tall Bull himself, though he could have escaped, determined to die with his tribesmen. "He saw," says Vestal, "that the day was lost—and through his own fault," and had decided to atone for his mistake.[131] According to General Carr, Tall Bull "had a little daughter on his horse and one of his wives on another. He gave the daughter to his wife, and told her to take the white woman who was prisoner, and she might use her to make terms for herself when peace was made. The wife begged him to escape with her, but he shut his ears, killed his horse, and she soon saw him killed, fighting."[132]

The exact way in which Tall Bull met his death has long been a subject of controversy. Credit for killing the chief has been given to Scout Cody, Major North, and 1st Lt. George F. Mason. Of the three, North's claim is the strongest. In all probability the story related by Sorenson is essentially correct:

> Upon reaching the ravine, [Tall Bull] placed his squaw and child inside where he thought they would be safe, and he then returned to the mouth of the ravine and shot his magnificent steed rather than see him fall into the hands of his enemies.

> [The Cheyennes in the ravine] kept Major North and his party at bay for some time. . . . While [the fighting] was still going on, one of the Indians climbing to the top of the bank nearest the soldiers, and raising his rifle slowly over the top of the bank he laid it down on top of the ground, and then poking it up sufficiently to take a sight along the barrell [*sic*] of the weapon he fired directly at Major North but missed him [and disappeared into the ravine]. . . . Major North marked well the spot where the Indian had dropped his head out of sight, . . . dropped down on one knee . . . and awaited the reappearance of the Indian's head. Soon the Indian raised his head up to take aim. Major North instantly fired, and the Indian dropped dead without firing. . . . Later in the day the dead chief, Tall Bull, was found in the ravine, directly under the spot where he had climbed up to fire at Major North.[133]

The importance of the incident lies not so much in who killed Tall Bull as in the significance of his death. There is considerable truth in Stanley Vestal's statement that "when Tall Bull's body fell backwards into that gulch, the power of the Dog Soldiers crashed down with him."[134] The passing of their strong leader broke the back of the Dog Soldiers' resistance.

After Tall Bull had been killed, his wife and daughter came out of the ravine and surrendered themselves to Major North, who ordered them to the rear where they would be out of danger. The scouts continued to pour gunfire into the ravine until it was no longer returned; then, cautiously peering over the side of the little canyon, they found eighteen dead Cheyennes. All had fought to the end.[135]

Meanwhile a search of the camp had revealed two white women captured by the Dog Soldiers from the Kansas settlement they had raided in May. One was dead, murdered by the vengeful Indians during the heat of the battle. The other, Mrs. Maria Weichell, was painfully wounded.[136] Mrs. Weichell had been cowering in a lodge, fearing when she saw the

Pawnees that she had been freed from the Cheyennes only to become the prisoner of another tribe.[137]

General Carr posted pickets and made camp to include the entire village as the troops slowly returned from the hillsides and from the futile chase.[138] Captain North was among the exhausted soldiers who stopped for water at the little creek that flowed through the middle of the camp. "I will never forget that creek," recalled the captain years later:

> When we came to the village after the fight was over I sat down on the east bank and dipped up a cup of water and drank it. There was a storm coming up. This must have been about five or six o'clock, and just as I was drinking the sun shone through the clouds straight in my face. I dipped up another cup full, when one of my Pawnee boys said "Don't drink that," and pointed up the stream to my left and there about ten feet above me was a dead Indian. His head was crushed in and the water was running right through the wound and down to where I was dipping it up. If you ever saw a sick man I was one.[139]

With the exception of one soldier slightly scratched by an arrow, the command had not suffered a single casualty. All men were present or accounted for.[140]

General Carr immediately organized his camp. He sent a courier to call in the wagon train and appointed a board to make a preliminary count of captured and dead Cheyennes. Mrs. Weichell was made as comfortable as possible in one of the ambulances.[141]

The long-approaching storm finally broke in the late afternoon. The "terrible thunder and hail" and the "lightning striking frequently near the command" made a fitting climax to the chaos of the battle. Throughout the evening, troops straggled in through the raging storm; one bolt of lightning struck "a horse while a trooper was astride of him," killing the horse but leaving the rider unharmed. Rain still fell as the wagon train lumbered into camp late that night.[142] In his tent Major North summed up the day in his diary:

> Marched this morn at 6 a.m. with 50 of my men and 200 whites with three days rations. Followed trail till 3 p.m. and came up to the village. Made a grand charge and it was a complete victory. Took the whole village about 85 lodges. Killed about 60 Indians, took 17 prisoners and about 300 ponies and Robes etc. innumerable. Rained pretty hard tonight.[143]

The rain of the previous night had turned to mist as reveille sounded early the next morning. At five o'clock a detachment was sent out across the hazy hills to "see if any Indians were hovering about," while other units were detailed to "count dead bodies and drive in stray animals."[144]

The warm morning sun had dispersed the mist by eight o'clock, when services were held for the dead captive. She had been identified by Dr. Louis S. Tesson, the command's surgeon, as Mrs. Susanna Alderdice of the raided Kansas settlement. Mrs. Alderdice was wrapped in lodge skins and robes and placed in a deep grave, away from wolves and coyotes, on the battlefield. The command was assembled at the graveside, and an officer "who was a religious man"—there was no chaplain with the command—read the burial service. The grave was filled, and a wooden headboard "with an inscription stating what we knew of her" was placed over it.[145]

After the conclusion of the service Carr turned his attention to the disposition of the Indian camp. The village, of course, could not be left for further use by hostile Indians. Directing the troops to load everything moveable on the wagons, the general ordered that the torch be put to everything that remained. "There were," reported General Carr, "160 fires burning at once to destroy the property."[146]

The proportions of General Carr's victory became apparent as the work of destruction progressed. The command had seized a tremendous amount of supplies and equipment, of which the following is only a part: 274 horses, 144 mules, 9,300 pounds of dried meat, eighty-four complete lodges, fifty-six rifles, twenty-two revolvers, forty bows and arrows, fifty pounds of gunpowder, twenty boxes of percussion caps, seventeen sabers, nine lances, and twenty tomahawks. "The above," Carr observed drily, "will materially reduce their means of killing white people."[147]

Besides these weapons the soldiers also had found such things as scalps of white women, household furniture, clocks, quilts, and "papers captured which certify to the high character of certain Indians, who must have degenerated since they were written." Perhaps the most grisly find was a necklace made of human fingers.[148]

The general's board reported that fifty-two Indians had been killed on the field, seventeen women and children captured, and twenty-five Indian horses killed.[149] The board's statement served to underscore a fact which by now had become obvious. The general's fears for the smallness of his command had been unnecessary. Even with half his column unable to make the charge, the element of surprise and the forcefulness of the attack had made the battle a complete rout.

Sending ten men off to Julesburg station with dispatches telling of the victory, Carr ordered the bugler to sound the "general call," and the troops

assembled for their departure.[150] The general had little choice in his desti-
nation. The horses were in such poor condition that a march to a place as
far away as Fort McPherson could hardly be considered. And he had captured so many Indian horses, mules, and supplies that he had to reach the
nearest point to turn them in. Consequently Carr determined to march
for Fort Sedgwick, Colorado Territory, planning "to remain for two or
three weeks to rest my animals and cure [their] sore backs."[151]

Moving in an easy four-hour march along the South Platte, the command halted for the day on the banks of the river, about sixty-five miles
southeast of Julesburg. On the way the hotheaded Captain North, for
some unknown reason, had again "had words with Gen. Carr," and had
decided that he would resign when the command reached the fort. Marching slowly along the river, the weary expedition at last reached Fort
Sedgwick on July 15.[152]

Here at Fort Sedgwick Carr made out the last of his reports of the
operations of the Republican River Expedition. The general sent in his
list of captured goods, a report on the events of the past few days, and
the names of those men who had distinguished themselves in action: his
adjutant, 1st. Lt. Jacob Almy, 1st Lt. Edward P. Dougherty, the acting
quartermaster, Lieutenant Volkmar, Corporal Kyle, Sgt. Mad Bear (although meaning Traveling Bear), and Major North.[153]

The general's attitude toward Indian troops had changed in the past
few weeks. He could now state that the scouts had been "of the greatest
service to us throughout the campaign . . . and the result has shown their
value."[154]

General Carr was the man of the hour. While the command was coming into Fort Sedgwick, the *New York Times* gave front page notice to the
Battle of Summit Springs:

THE INDIANS
Operations of General Carr
A Cheyenne Village Broken Up
The Indians Routed

"A dispatch from Omaha," said the article, "gives reports from General
A. E. [sic] Carr of his operations against the Indians. On the 11th instant
he surprised a village of 'dog soldiers' and Cheyennes, under command
of Tall Bull." Listing the amount of supplies captured and the number of
Indians killed, the Times noted that the Cheyennes "had murdered one
[captive] whose first name is said to be Suzanna."[155]

Carr's superior, General Augur, wrote "with great pleasure" of "my
own sense of the importance of your success. . . . I add my own congratu-

lations, and express my entire and perfect satisfaction with the whole conduct of your expedition."[156] Later, in his more official general orders, Augur again tendered "his thanks to General Carr and his command, for their patient endurance of the privations and hardships inseparable from an Indian campaign, and for the vigor and persistency of their operations, so deserving the success achieved."[157]

The commanding officer of the Fifth Cavalry, Col. (Bvt. Maj. Gen.) William H. Emory, penned a glowing endorsement on the outside of Carr's report to headquarters:

> I beg to express my highest appreciation of the gallant and brilliant services rendered by Bvt. Major General E. A. Carr, 5th U.S. Cavalry, and the troops under his command, . . . and of the Pawnee Scouts under Major North.[158]

Plaudits came from sources other than the military. The purpose of the expedition had been the relief of frontier settlements, and, as soon as the legislatures of Colorado and Nebraska were in session, they passed resolutions of thanks.

By the joint resolution of the Nebraska state legislature, the "thanks of the people of Nebraska" were

> tendered to Brevet Maj. Gen. Carr and the officers and soldiers under his command of the 5th United States cavalry, for their heroic courage and their perseverance in their campaign against hostile Indians on the frontier of this State in July 1869, driving the enemy from our borders and achieving a victory at Summit Springs, Colorado Territory by which the people of the State were freed from the ravages of merciless savages.

Thanks were offered also "to Maj. Frank J. North and the officers and soldiers under his command."[159]

The legislature of the Territory of Colorado was no less laudatory in its resolution of January 25, 1870. Pointing out that "the prosperity of this territory has been greatly retarded during the several years past by Indian warfare, preventing immigration; . . . defenseless women and children of our pioneer settlements have been murdered by savages, or subjected to captivity worse than death," the assembly resolved "that the thanks of the people of Colorado, through the Council and House of Representatives of the Legislative Assembly of the Territory of Colorado, be extended to Brevet Major General Eugene A. Carr, of the United States Army, and the brave officers and soldiers under his command for their victory thus achieved."[160]

General Carr, of course, was pleased by these expressions of gratitude for the end to Indian terrorism that had so long held back settlement. But the expedition and its victory held for him another significance:

> It is a source of extreme gratification to the 5th Cavalry after all our hardships and exposures for ten months in the field, we have at last met with an undisputed success. . . .

> We spent a most miserable and depressing winter on the Canadian River, watching our base, and we chased these same Indians in May and fought them twice, losing (4) four killed and several wounded. It may be imagination, but there is a general feeling that the services and hardships of the regiment have not been appreciated for want of any brilliant list of killed and wounded. We have, however, no pleasures in killing the poor miserable savages, but desire, in common with the whole army, by the performance of our duty, to deliver the settlers from the dangers to which they are exposed.[161]

Carr, then, viewed with disfavor such slaughter as the Sand Creek Massacre and the Battle of the Washita. Moreover, he felt that such spectacular operations gathered more than their share of credit for a general campaign in which many units had cooperated. The victory at Summit Springs was sweeter because recognition had at last been gained by work long well done but long unnoticed.

General Carr's hour of triumph was marred by personal tragedy. As the victory at Summit Springs was being greeted with commendation from all quarters, Carr received a telegram reporting the death of his child. The grief-stricken general turned his command over to Major Royall and left Fort Sedgwick on July 25 on the morning train.[162]

Colonel Emory, at Fort McPherson, had planned to visit the expedition's camp at Fort Sedgwick to pay his respects to General Carr. When he received a telegram from Carr informing him of what had happened, Emory attempted to see him as the train from Sedgwick passed through but arrived at the station just in time to see the cars moving off into the distance.[163]

On this unhappy note General Carr's Republican River Expedition came to an end. There would be two subsequent campaigns, one led by Major Royall, the other by Colonel Emory. But the results of both would only emphasize the completeness of the victory at Summit Springs. The Dog Soldiers, having fled far to the north of their valley, now had no stomach for battle.[164]

The Republican River Expedition must be credited with two achievements. First, it was largely responsible for changing the Republican Valley from an Indian-held wilderness to a region ready for settlement. And, second, it had succeeded in overcoming a multitude of difficulties, perhaps not unknown to many such operations, to achieve its goal.

The campaign of the Republican River Expedition was but one facet of the inexorable westward advance of the American frontier. White settlement in the fertile Republican Valley was inevitable. The Indians eventually would have been dispossessed had the expedition never existed. But in the course of history, the causative factor always has some significance, and it was the Republican River Expedition that removed the Indian threat from the Republican country.

General Carr had been apprehensive of the dangers that might lie in the weaknesses of his command. But he accepted them, by no means gracefully, and hoped to make the best of it. As events were to show, however, Carr's greatest fear—that of too small a force for the task at hand—was unfounded, and it proved surprisingly easy to carry the day at Summit Springs.

Within a decade after the campaign had ended, the Republican country was no longer a frontier. The rapidly growing farms and cities of the Republican Valley stood as a monument to the weary little column of cavalry in the sand hills.

Notes

[1] George F. Price, *Across the Continent with the Fifth Cavalry* (New York: D. Van Nostrand, 1883), 141.

[2] Gov. David Butler to Brig. Gen. Christopher C. Augur, May 31, 1869, Selected Documents, Letters Received, Department of the Platte, 1867–69, Records of United States Army Commands, Record Group (RG) 98, National Archives, Washington, D.C. This microfilm, as are all manuscripts and microfilms unless otherwise noted, is at the Nebraska State Historical Society.

[3] George Bird Grinnell, *The Cheyenne Indians: Their History and Ways of Life* 2 (New Haven: Yale University Press, 1923):71. According to Paul I. Wellman, *Death on Horseback: Seventy Years of War for the American West* (New York: J. B. Lippincott Company, 1947), 93, membership in the Dog Soldier band was restricted to "the fiercest and most dangerous of all the Cheyenne Warriors." The group "had its own dances, songs, ceremonial costumes and insignia, besides special medicines and taboos." Carl Coke Rister, *Border Command: General Phil Sheridan in the West* (Norman: University of Oklahoma Press, 1944), 147–48.

[4] Marvin H. Garfield, "Defense of the Kansas Frontier, 1868–1869," *Kansas Historical Quarterly* 1 (Nov. 1932):468–69; Carl Coke Rister, *Border Captives: The Traffic in Pris-*

oners by the Southern Plains Indians (Norman: University of Oklahoma Press, 1940), 162. The Alderdice baby, notes Rister, was strangled by the Indians on the way back to the Republican.

[5] Augur to Butler, June 1, 1869, RG 98.

[6] Rister errs in his statement that Carr was sent out by Col. (Bvt. Maj. Gen.) William H. Emory at Fort McPherson. General Carr's orders were issued by General Augur, commanding officer of the Department of the Platte. Although Emory was colonel of the Fifth Cavalry, the companies serving in the Republican River Expedition were on detached service and therefore not under regimental direction. Rister, *Border Command*, 149; cf. Emory to Maj. (Bvt. Brig. Gen.) George D. Ruggles, July 10, 1869, RG 98.

[7] Price, *Across the Continent*, 135.

[8] Ibid.; Francis B. Heitman, *Historical Register and Dictionary of the United States Army* 1 (Washington: Government Printing Office, 1903):285.

[9] Price, *Across the Continent*, 292–93; Heitman, *Historical Register*, 338, 849.

[10] Report of Maj. (Bvt. Maj. Gen.) Eugene A. Carr to Ruggles, June 17, 1869, RG 98, hereafter cited as Report, Carr to Ruggles, with appropriate date; Fort McPherson Post Return, June 1869, Records of the Office of the Adjutant General, RG 94, National Archives, Washington, D.C.

[11] Pawnee Battalion Muster Rolls, Companies A, B, and C., October 1869, RG 98. The North Brothers and their famous scouts are the subject of George Bird Grinnell, *Two Great Scouts and Their Pawnee Battalion* (Cleveland: The Arthur H. Clark Company, 1928), and numerous newspaper and magazine articles. Grinnell, well known for his extensive research and publications on the Plains Indians, in this book has used almost word for word several manuscripts now in the archives of the Nebraska State Historical Society. One of these manuscripts (Alfred Sorenson, "A Quarter of a Century on the Frontier, or The Adventures of Major Frank North, the 'White Chief of the Pawnees'," Frank Joshua North Collection, MS448, Nebraska State Historical Society Archives, Lincoln) was written in collaboration with Major North and appears to be reasonably accurate in its coverage of the Republican River Expedition. But when accounts conflict, Grinnell has accepted the other (Luther Hedden North, "Recollections of Captain L. H. North," Luther Hedden North Collection, MS449, Nebraska State Historical Society Archives, Lincoln). Parts of this manuscript are unreliable, due no doubt to the fact that it was written some fifty years after the events, and Captain North's failing memory is reflected in errors in Grinnell's book.

[12] Report, Carr to Ruggles, June 17, 1869; cf. Report, Carr to Ruggles, July 20, 1869.

[13] Philip H. Sheridan, *Personal Memoirs of P. H. Sheridan* 2 (New York: Charles L. Webster and Company, 1888):300–301.

[14] Report, Carr to Ruggles, May 22, 1869. In a letter on the same date Carr also requested that a $100 bonus be paid to Cody "for extraordinarily good services."

[15] Report, Carr to Ruggles, June 11, 1869. According to the account of one J. E. Welch, there was a group of "volunteers to serve without pay" accompanying the column. J. E. Welch, Edith, Texas, to Col. Henry O. Clark, June 16, 1891, reprinted in Cyrus T. Brady, *Indian Fights and Fighters: The Soldier and the Sioux* (New York: McClure, Phillips and Company, 1904), 173–79. This letter, almost totally unreliable, presents a badly confused picture of the march of the column and the concluding Battle of Summit Springs. Unfortunately this letter comprises almost the whole of Brady's treatment of the expedition.

[16] Among those things most needed, the general had written, were medical men, teamsters, a signal officer, "colored servants," remounts, wagons, and pack mules. Letter, Carr to Ruggles, May 22, 30, 1869, RG 98.

[17] Report, Carr to Ruggles, June 11, 1869. Some of the supplies intended for the expedition were still arriving a month after the column had left. Lt. Col. Thomas Duncan, commanding Fort McPherson, to Ruggles, July 8, 1869, RG 98.

[18] Orders, Ruggles to Carr, June 7, 1869, RG 98.

[19] Sorenson, "Quarter Century," 133.

[20] Reports on the appearance of the Pawnee Battalion do not agree. Sorenson, whose source of information was Major North himself, states that the Indian troops "turned out in all sorts of styles—some with their overcoats on and some without, and some with pantaloons and others with only breech-cloths, some with hats and others without; some with pantaloons changed into leggings by having the seat cut out; some with boots and others with moccasins; some with spurs on their moccasins and others wearing them on their bear [*sic*] heels; and a few appeared in full uniform," Sorenson, "Quarter Century," 134. Grinnell, however, has made a point of stating that "fanciful and quite untrue stories have been told of this occasion," and that "at this review, the Pawnees appeared in full uniform." Grinnell's information apparently came from the "Recollections of Capt. Luther H. North," Grinnell, *Two Great Scouts*, 183.

[21] Sorenson, "Quarter Century," 134.

[22] Lt. William J. Volkmar to 2d Lt. William C. Forbush, acting assistant adjutant general, District of the Republican, Fort McPherson, Nov. 19, 1869, transmitting Carr's report, "Journal of the March of the Republican River Expedition," entry for June 9, 1869, RG 98. Hereinafter cited as "Journal of the March," with date of entry.

[23] Sorenson, "Quarter Century," 134.

[24] Major North had left for Columbus, Nebraska, to enlist a third company of Pawnees. Frank North diary, June 9, 1869. North's diary has been printed in Donald F. Danker, ed., "The Journal of an Indian Fighter: The 1869 Diary of Major Frank J. North," *Nebraska History* 39 (1958):87–177.

[25] Luther North, "Recollections," 66.

[26] "Journal of the March," June 9, 1869.

[27] Luther North, "Recollections," 67.

[28] "Journal of the March," June 10, 1869.

[29] Report, Carr to Ruggles, June 11, 1869.

[30] "Journal of the March," June 10, 1869.

[31] Report, Carr to Ruggles, June 11, 1869.

[32] Fort McPherson Post Return, June 1869, RG 94. Captain Denney was buried at Fort McPherson with the full garrison in attendance. Price, *Across the Continent*, 409–11. Such an incident was hardly unique to this expedition. At almost that exact spot, for instance, just two years before, a colonel in Custer's detachment of the Seventh Cavalry had committed suicide "while," wrote Custer, "in a fit of delirium tremens." Quoted in Marguerite Merington, ed., *The Custer Story: The Life and Intimate Letters of General George A. Custer and His Wife Elizabeth* (New York: Devin–Adair, 1950), 204.

[33] Report, Carr to Ruggles, June 11, 1869.

[34] "Journal of the March," June 12, 1869.

[35] Ibid., June 13, 1869.

[36] Luther North, "Recollections," 67.

[37] "Journal of the March," June 13, 1869.

[38] Ibid., June 14, 1869; Report, Carr to Ruggles, June 17, 1869.

[39] "Journal of the March," June 15, 1869.

[40] Sorenson, "Quarter Century," 135.

[41] "Journal of the March," June 15, 1869.

[42] Sorenson, "Quarter Century," 135; Luther North to Jacob C. North, Nov. 28, 1874, MS449.

[43] "Journal of the March," June 15, 1869; Price, *Across the Continent*, 136; Report, Carr to Ruggles, June 17, 1869.

[44] Luther North to Jacob C. North, Nov. 28, 1874, MS449.

[45] Ibid. Years later, however, Captain North insisted that General Carr "put me under arrest, and put Captain Cushing in charge." The next morning, North claimed, Carr sent his adjutant ahead with orders to Captain Cushing to send out a scouting party. When told that Captain North was the only officer who knew enough of the Pawnee language to give orders, North claimed, "the adjutant laughed and rode away, but was soon back with word from the General that I was released from arrest, that I should take command again and send the scouting party as directed. This I did, and that was the end of the matter," Luther North, "Recollections," 71–72. This later account is wholly unsubstantiated by the records of the expedition.

[46] Report, Carr to Ruggles, June 17, 1869.

[47] "Journal of the March," June 16, 1869; Report, Carr to Ruggles, June 17, 1869.

[48] Report, Carr to Ruggles, June 17, 1869; "Journal of the March," June 16, 1869.

[49] "Journal of the March," June 16, 1869.

[50] Ibid., June 17, 1869; Frank North diary, June 17, 1869.

[51] Frank North diary, June 13–17, 1869.

[52] Orders, Ruggles to Carr, June 11, 1869, RG 98.

[53] Report, Carr to Ruggles, June 17, 1869.

[54] Ibid.

[55] "Journal of the March," June 17, 1869.

[56] Report, Carr to Ruggles, June 17, 1869; "Journal of the March," June 29, 1869.

[57] Report, Carr to Ruggles, June 17, 1869.

[58] Ibid.

[59] Ibid.

[60] "Journal of the March," June 17, 1869.

[61] Ibid., June 18, 1869.

[62] Ibid., June 19–29, 1869; Report, Carr to Ruggles, June 30, 1869. One of the most seriously ill was Capt. James Murie, Company C, Pawnee Battalion. Major North, wor-

ried by Murie's illness, wrote later that "I am real sorry I did not send him home with the train," Frank North diary, July 2, 1869.

[63] "Journal of the March," June 19–29, 1869.

[64] Frank North diary, June 21–24, 1869.

[65] Ibid., June 21, 1869.

[66] Ibid., June 23, 1869.

[67] Sorenson, "Quarter Century," 136.

[68] Frank North notebook, MS448.

[69] "Journal of the March," June 21, 1869.

[70] Report, Carr to Ruggles, June 30, 1869.

[71] "Journal of the March," June 29, 1869.

[72] Ibid., June 28, 1869; Luther North, "Recollections," 72; Report, Carr to Ruggles, June 30, July 20, 1869.

[73] Frank North diary, June 29, 1869.

[74] Report, Carr to Ruggles, June 30, 1869.

[75] Ibid.

[76] "Journal of the March," June 29, 1869; Frank North diary, June 29, 1869.

[77] Frank North diary, June 30, July 1, 1869; "Journal of the March," June 30, July 1, 1869.

[78] "Journal of the March," July 2–3, 1869.

[79] Report, Carr to Ruggles, July 20, 1869.

[80] Ibid.; "Journal of the March," July 4, 1869.

[81] "Journal of the March," July 4, 1869.

[82] Ibid., July 5, 1869; Frank North diary, July 5, 1869; Report, Carr to Ruggles, July 20, 1869.

[83] Frank North diary, July 6, 1869. "This reference," says Danker, "possibly referred to Samuel Wallace, first sergeant, and Barton Hunt, a teamster, both of Company B of the Pawnee Scouts. Danker, "Journal of an Indian Fighter," 137n.

[84] Report, Carr to Ruggles, July 20, 1869.

[85] Ibid.

[86] Frank North diary, July 7, 1869; Report, Carr to Ruggles, July 20, 1869.

[87] Sorenson, "Quarter Century," 137.

[88] Frank North diary, July 7, 1869.

[89] Report, Carr to Ruggles, July 20, 1869.

[90] Ibid.

[91] Luther North to Jacob C. North, Nov. 28, 1874, MS449.

[92] Ibid. Corporal Kyle was commended in Carr's report for this action, "Journal of the March," July 8, 1869; cf. Price, *Across the Continent*, 136. Price is mistaken in stating that Kyle's party was attacked by thirteen Indians.

[93] Frank North diary, July 8, 1869; Price, *Across the Continent*, 36. There were five

Indians in the raiding party, according to Major North. Captain North says there were not more than "six or seven." Carr reports only that there were "a number" of them. But impressionable young Lieutenant Volkmar insists that there were thirty; cf. Luther North, "Recollections," 74; Report, Carr to Ruggles, July 20, 1869; "Journal of the March," July 8, 1869.

[94] Report, Carr to Ruggles, July 20, 1869; Frank North diary, July 8, 1869. Luther North and Grinnell both state that it is unknown how Mad Bear was injured; cf. Luther North, "Recollections," 74; Grinnell, *Two Great Scouts*, 191.

[95] Report, Carr to Ruggles, July 20, 1869. Luther North and Grinnell both claim that the command remained in camp the next day. It did not. Cf. Luther North, "Recollections," 75; Grinnell, *Two Great Scouts*, 192; "Journal of the March," July 9, 1869.

[96] "Journal of the March," July 9, 1869.

[97] Frank North diary, July 9, 1869. This campsite was in the vicinity of Major Royall's skirmish on July 6. "It is not to be mistaken," warns Danker, "for the better-known site of the Beecher Island battle of 1868," some thirty miles to the south. Danker, "Journal of an Indian Fighter," 138n; "Journal of the March," July 9, 1869.

[98] "Journal of the March," July 10, 1869. Grinnell, once again repeating North, states that the command remained in camp this day to await a wagon train from Fort McPherson. It did not. The train, in fact, was not due for several days. It is difficult to account for North's statement; it may be that he confused the command's own wagon train, which was left behind the next day (see below) with the McPherson train. Luther North, "Recollections," 76; Grinnell, *Two Great Scouts*, 194.

[99] Report, Carr to Ruggles, July 20, 1869.

[100] Sorenson, "Quarter Century," 137.

[101] This, at least, is Captain Price's belief. He stated that the delay was made "at the suggestion of the medicine man and against the advice of Tall Bull." Price, *Across the Continent*, 140.

[102] This explanation is accepted by Stanley Vestal, *Warpath and Council Fire: The Plains Indians' Struggle for Survival in War and in Diplomacy* (New York: Random House, 1948), 170.

[103] This opinion is offered by Captain North: "They had seen us turn back and thought we were going straight to Fort McPherson." North adds that "When he [the Indian] knows that an enemy is after him it is impossible to take him unawares, but let him think himself safe and he is the most careless being on earth." Luther North to Jacob C. North, Nov. 28, 1874, MS449.

[104] Report, Carr to Ruggles, July 20, 1869.

[105] Ibid.; Luther North to Jacob C. North, Nov. 28, 1874, MS449.

[106] Frank North diary, July 10, 1869.

[107] *New York Times*, July 15, 1869; Clarence Reckmeyer, "The Battle of Summit Springs," *Colorado Magazine* 6 (Nov. 1929):218.

[108] "Journal of the March," July 11, 1869.

[109] Report, Carr to Ruggles, July 20, 1869.

[110] Ibid.

111 "Journal of the March," July 11, 1869.

112 Report, Carr to Ruggles, July 20, 1869. Both Luther North and Grinnell claim that there were three trails and that the cavalry column was here divided into three parts. Cf. Luther North, "Recollections," 76; Grinnell, *Two Great Scouts*, 194. This same error is found in, among others, Reckmeyer, "Battle of Summit Springs," 213.

113 Summit Springs is located about twelve miles south and four miles east of present Sterling, Colorado.

114 Report, Carr to Ruggles, July 20, 1869.

115 Ibid. This incident was recalled in garbled form by Luther North. He stated that Carr, "with a part of the cavalry and five or six of our scouts under Sam Wallace took the trail toward the northwest. Col. Royal [*sic*] with the rest of the cavalry and Cody as guide took the righthand trail toward the northeast, and my brother with myself and Capt. Cushing and thirty-five of our scouts took the middle trail, leading straight north." Luther North, "Recollections," 76. Apparently Major North's advance column was a good distance ahead, and Captain North perhaps assumed that he was following a separate trail. This account is repeated by numerous secondary sources, especially Grinnell, *Two Great Scouts*, 194.

116 Report, Carr to Ruggles, July 20, 1869.

117 Sorenson, "Quarter Century," 139.

118 Report, Carr to Ruggles, July 20, 1869.

119 Ibid.

120 Ibid. Grinnell, Vestal, Reckmeyer, and others accept Captain North's statement that Royall and Cody did not return in time for the battle. According to North's recollections many years after the incident, Carr "said he would wait for a while for Colonel Royal to join him, before making a charge on the village. After waiting for perhaps half an hour the General said he would wait no longer . . . and we started." Cf. Luther North, "Recollections," 77; Grinnell, *Two Great Scouts*, 201; Vestal, *Warpath and Council Fire*, 270; Reckmeyer, "Battle of Summit Springs," 213. However, there can be little question that, as General Carr states, Royall had rejoined the column before the battle.

121 Report, Carr to Ruggles, July 20, 1869.

122 Ibid. Captain Price states that the Pawnees were in the center. Price, *Across the Continent*, 138. According to Brady, the bugler was "so excited that he was unable to produce a note. Twice Carr gave the command. Finally, Quartermaster Hayes snatched the bugle from the agitated musician and sounded the charge himself," Brady, *Indian Fights and Fighters*, 171. Though this story also appears in many other secondary works, it seems to have no basis in contemporary records.

123 Price, *Across the Continent*, 138–39. Even the usually sedate and factual "Journal of the March" (entry for July 11) breaks into flowing prose to describe the charge. "All being ready, the trumpets rang out the 'charge' and with hurrahs the column and reserve dashed over the hill."

124 Report, Carr to Ruggles, July 20, 1869.

125 Price, *Across the Continent*, 139.

126 Report, Carr to Ruggles, July 20, 1869.

127 Rister, *Border Command*, 150.

[128] Price, *Across the Continent*, 139.

[129] Report, Carr to Ruggles, July 20, 1869.

[130] Sorenson, "Quarter Century," 139.

[131] Vestal, *Warpath and Council Fire*, 172.

[132] Report, Carr to Ruggles, July 20, 1869.

[133] Cody was first given credit for killing Tall Bull by the sensationalist writer E. Z. C. Judson, or "Ned Buntline," and the story was perpetuated by those who wrote under Cody's name. There is even a statement attributed to General Carr, published after his death, which says that Tall Bull, "firing as he charged . . . [was killed] by Cody's unerring rifle fire" and that when Cody led a horse into camp, "Mrs. Tall Bull said that was her husband's horse" (quoted in Elizabeth Jane Leonard and Julia Cody Goodman, *Buffalo Bill: King of the Old West* [New York: Library Publishers, 1955], 196). But the accuracy of Carr's recollection becomes dubious in light of the statement in his report of the battle that the chief had "killed his horse." Report, Carr to Ruggles, July 20, 1869. Mason's claim is found in the highly questionable account in Brady, *Indian Fights and Fighters*, 173–79. Sorenson's account, giving Major North the credit, is the only one that does not conflict with known facts. Sorenson, "Quarter Century," 140–41.

[134] Vestal, *Warpath and Council Fire*, 173.

[135] Sorenson, "Quarter Century," 142.

[136] Report, Carr to Ruggles, July 20, 1869.

[137] Sorenson, "Quarter Century," 143.

[138] Report, Carr to Ruggles, July 20, 1869.

[139] Luther North, "Recollections," 82.

[140] Report, Carr to Ruggles, July 20, 1869.

[141] Ibid.

[142] "Journal of the March," July 11, 1869.

[143] Frank North diary, July 11, 1869.

[144] "Journal of the March," July 12, 1869; Report, Carr to Ruggles, July 20, 1869.

[145] Report, Carr to Ruggles, July 20, 1869; Sorenson, "Quarter Century," 143.

[146] Report, Carr to Ruggles, July 20, 1869.

[147] Ibid.

[148] Ibid.

[149] Ibid.

[150] "Journal of the March," July 12, 1869.

[151] Report, Carr to Ruggles, July 20, 1869.

[152] Ibid.; Luther North to Jacob C. North, Nov. 28, 1874, MS449; "Journal of the March," July 13, 14, 15, 1869.

[153] Report, Carr to Ruggles, July 20, 1869. Carr should have written Traveling Bear as the Pawnee Scout who distinguished himself in battle. Luther North thought the confusion arose when earlier in the campaign a scout by the name of Mad Bear had been shot during a skirmish. This mix-up has persisted to the present.

[154] Ibid.

[155] *New York Times*, July 15, 1869.

[156] Letter, Augur to Carr, July 17, 1869, RG 98.

[157] General Orders No. 48, Headquarters, Department of the Platte, Aug. 3, 1869, RG 98.

[158] Report, Carr to Ruggles, July 20, 1869.

[159] Sorenson, "Quarter Century," 147–48.

[160] Quoted in Dean F. Krakel, *South Platte Country: A History of Old Weld County, Colorado, 1739–1900* (Laramie: The Powder River Publishers, 1954), 132.

[161] Report, Carr to Ruggles, July 20, 1869.

[162] Maj. William B. Royall, Fort Sedgwick, to 2d Lt. William C. Forbush, July 25, 1869, RG 98.

[163] Letter, Emory to Ruggles, July 26, 1869, RG 98.

[164] Capt. William H. Brown, commanding Company F, Fifth Cavalry, to Capt. George F. Price, Oct. 3, 1869; Lt. Col. Thomas Duncan to Forbush, District of the Republican, Oct. 7, 1869, RG 98.

Gen. George Crook and his Department of the Platte staff.
Courtesy of the Nebraska State Historical Society (A741-148).

The headquarters of the Department of the Platte was located in downtown
Omaha, Nebraska. Courtesy NSHS (054-253).

In 1868 Gen. William Tecumseh Sherman (*third from left*), fresh from his many Civil War victories, came West at a diplomatic disadvantage. Sioux warriors had closed the Bozeman Trail and forced the government to a treaty council at Fort Laramie. Courtesy NSHS (R539:11-2).

A Sioux Indian grave stood as a lonely sentinel outside Fort Laramie. Courtesy NSHS (L323-5).

The Union Pacific railroad bridge over the Platte River at North Platte, a strategic point in western Nebraska. Courtesy Union Pacific Museum Collection (2-40).

A Union Pacific roundhouse sat near its protector, the post of North Platte Station. Courtesy Union Pacific Museum Collection (7-203).

Maj. Nathan Augustus Monroe Dudley, one of Fort McPherson's commanding
officers, oversaw the affairs of his subpost at North Platte.
Courtesy NSHS (P853).

Once stationed at North Platte Station, Lt. Frederick Schwatka (*right*) saw later duty in the Sioux War of 1876–77. He posed with the Seventh Cavalry guidon recaptured at the Battle of Slim Buttes. Courtesy National Anthropological Archives, Smithsonian Institution (3711-N-3).

Gen. Eugene F. Carr, Fifth U.S. Cavalry, whose command attacked Tall Bull's village at Summit Springs in 1869. Courtesy NSHS (C311-8).

William F. "Buffalo Bill" Cody, Nebraska's premier scout.
Courtesy NSHS (c671-6).

A cavalryman from "Nebraska's Own" Fifth U.S. Cavalry at Fort McPherson,
staging area for the Republican River Expedition.
Courtesy NSHS (MI71-24).

Site of the Summit Springs battlefield and the canyon where
Chief Tall Bull died. Courtesy NSHS (R298-10).

Luther North, who fought at Summit Springs and whose brother
Frank shot Tall Bull, returned to the site in the late 1920s.
Courtesy NSHS (N864-232).

Scouts Blue Hawk (*seated*) and Coming Around with the Herd wore a mixture
of U.S. Army–Pawnee garb. Courtesy NSHS (M613-3).

Bull Thigh and his son Tall Bull, brother and nephew of Tall Bull, the
Cheyenne Dog Soldier leader killed in 1869. Photo taken at Lame Deer,
Montana, in 1915. Courtesy NSHS (R298-12).

(*Above left*) Maj. Frank North
of Columbus, Nebraska, leader
of the Pawnee Scouts. Courtesy
NSHS (N864-3).

(*Above right*) Younger brother
Luther North, a captain in the
Pawnee Battalion. Courtesy NSHS
(N864-9).

(*Opposite*) White Horse, a Pawnee
Scout. Courtesy NSHS (1396-6).

Rattlesnake with his wife. Note the corporal's chevrons on this Pawnee Scout's army issue clothing. Courtesy NSHS (1396-124).

Petalesharo, a Pawnee chief, posed in the Sioux headdress he had captured in battle. Courtesy NSHS (1396:2-4).

(*Above*) Pawnee men swelled the crowd around a Union Pacific train in 1867. Courtesy Union Pacific Museum Collection (R152).

(*Left*) Sky Chief, a leader of the Pawnee tribe, died at the Battle of Massacre Canyon, 1873. Courtesy NSHS (1396:5-29).

Brulé Lakota warrior-leader Pawnee Killer surprised his traditional enemies
during the Pawnee seasonal buffalo hunt in the Republican River area.
Courtesy NSHS (B774-27).

Massacre Canyon in 1911. Courtesy NSHS (M414:8-1).

In 1925 Sioux and Pawnee participants of the Battle of Massacre Canyon held an uneasy reunion. John William Williamson, who accompanied the Pawnees on their 1873 buffalo hunt and proved ineffectual as a trail agent, stood in this group's center. Courtesy NSHS (M414:10-4).

Part 2

Pawnee Triumph,
Pawnee Tragedy

When Eugene Carr's Fifth Cavalry and the Pawnee Battalion crushed the Cheyenne Dog Soldiers and cleared the Republican country, they essentially made the area safe for white settlement. The same degree of safety did not exist for the Pawnee tribe, which traveled to the Republican Valley for communal, semi-annual buffalo hunts. Only four years after the triumphal defeat of one set of enemies at Summit Springs, the tribe suffered a major setback from another. In 1873 a superior force of Brulé and Oglala Sioux surprised and attacked a hunting party of Pawnee men, women, and children, and dozens of Pawnees were killed. The southwest Nebraska site of their destruction came to be known as Massacre Canyon.

The struggle for diminished resources was not confined to the buffalo ranges of western Nebraska. The Pawnee reservation in east-central Nebraska had once been an isolated enclave; now it was hemmed in by advancing homesteaders, who scared away game and cleared scarce stands of trees. Drouth and grasshoppers devastated Pawnee crops. The Pawnee way of life was clearly threatened, and a viable solution seemed to be to live where neither Sioux enemies nor white settlers were present. The decision of the tribe to "go south" came in 1874, and soon the first Pawnee emigrants left for Indian Territory, now Oklahoma.

They did not leave defeated. Pawnee warriors had compiled an impressive record against their Sioux, Cheyenne, and Arapaho enemies. Donald F. Danker's "The North Brothers and the Pawnee Scouts," *NH* 42 (Sept. 1961):161–80, traced the sterling record of one of the most successful and longest serving units of Indian auxiliaries in the U.S. Army. The Pawnees' ability to overcome their army superiors' initial apprehension and succeed beyond all expectations was well documented by historian Danker, then the archivist for the Nebraska State Historical Society. His article reveals not only the military prowess of the Pawnees, but also their ability to adapt and to thrive in changing cultural conditions.

Pawnee Triumph, Pawnee Tragedy

In "The Battle of Massacre Canyon," *NH* 54 (Summer 1973):221–50, the late Paul D. Riley, then a respected Historical Society researcher, provided the best, most concise synthesis of the events leading to and following the massacre. These two chapters remind us that the "Indian wars" can refer equally to intertribal conflicts.

Chapter 3

The North Brothers
and the Pawnee Scouts

Donald F. Danker

The Plains Indian wars of the 1860s and 1870s left their mark on America's traditions and literature as well as on its history. From them have emerged an array of fighting men around whose names legends have clustered from their day to our own. Not the least of these were the North brothers and their famous scouts.

The use of white frontiersmen and of Indian scouts and auxiliaries by American military forces was not uncommon. From colonial times on they had figured in campaigns where their talents in wilderness warfare were useful. Thus the service of Frank North and the Pawnee Scouts was in keeping with American frontier tradition.

The Pawnee was one of the important Plains tribes. In a sense it was a transitional group between the agricultural and sedentary tribes along the Missouri and the nomadic hunters of the prairie. Pawnees lived in earthlodge villages along the Platte, Republican, and Loup rivers in Nebraska and were primarily engaged in agriculture. However, they took two extended buffalo hunts each year and were excellent horsemen and hunters. They had a tradition of friendship for the whites, and, when the Kansas–Nebraska Act opened Nebraska to white settlers, the tribe did not resist the loss of its land. In 1857 the Pawnee tribe was assigned a fifteen-by-thirty-mile reservation along the Loup River with the agency at Genoa.[1]

Although the Pawnee had a record of peaceful relations with the whites, they had long waged almost constant warfare with the more nomadic tribes to the west. They were enemies of the Lakota and the Cheyenne with whom they competed for the buffalo and exchanged horse stealing raids. Service with the U.S. Army gave them a welcome opportunity to strike at their longtime foes with the aid and approval of the powerful whites.

The man most responsible for the success of the Pawnee Scouts was Frank Joshua North. He was a restless, intelligent person who had a great distaste for the humdrum of ordinary activity. He had come to Nebraska in 1856 as a boy of sixteen. The next year his father died in a spring blizzard, leaving the mother on the frontier with five children. Frank and an older brother, James, went west along the Platte to the new settlement of Columbus. There he farmed a little, trapped and hunted, and freighted to Fort Kearny and Denver. He became acquainted with the nearby Pawnee, learned the language, and in 1861 was hired by the post trader as a clerk and interpreter. As a friend and associate of the Pawnee he came to share the tribe's hatred for the Sioux, who frequently raided the reservation, stealing horses and killing the women in the cornfields.[2]

Luther Hedden North was six years younger than Frank, and the fatherless youth enjoyed a boyhood of hunting and riding. Among his companions were Pawnees, and his hero to the day of his death, at the age of eighty-nine, was his brother Frank.

In the summer of 1864 Sioux and Cheyenne raiders had reduced most of the stations and road ranches along the overland trail to ashes, travel had almost ceased, and settlers were abandoning their homes. Maj. Gen. Samuel R. Curtis, commander of the Department of Kansas, requested that a company of Pawnees be hired to serve with the army. Over two hundred volunteered, but only seventy-six were accepted, partially because the agent did not want the reservation left undefended.[3]

Joseph McFadden, an army veteran and a clerk at the agency store, was hired as captain at five dollars a day. He had a Pawnee family and could speak the language. Frank North was second in command. This first group of Pawnee Scouts did no fighting. After a march to the Solomon River in Kansas the force split and Brig. Gen. Robert B. Mitchell returned to the Platte with McFadden and the main body of Pawnees, and Curtis proceeded to Fort Riley. Neither group encountered hostiles. Curtis, while favorably impressed by North, did not believe that McFadden had proper control of the men.[4]

When the scouts were discharged in October, Frank North, at the direction of General Curtis, organized a new company with himself as captain. He and his officers were commissioned by the territorial governor of Nebraska, and the company was accepted as Nebraska Civil War volunteers. This marked the real beginning of the services of the Pawnee Scouts. They were in the field in 1865, 1867, 1868, 1869, 1870, and finally in 1876–77.

The reputation of the Pawnee Scouts began on the Powder River Expedition in the summer of 1865. A three-columned offensive under Brig. Gen. Patrick E. Connor moved against the aroused Sioux, Cheyennes, and Arapahos in central and northern Wyoming. A force under Col.

Nelson Cole was to march from Columbus, Nebraska, through the Sand Hills into Dakota and Wyoming. Lt. Col. Samuel Walker was to join him from Fort Laramie with about six hundred men, and Connor himself commanded the third column, which also started from Fort Laramie.[5]

Connor's orders to Cole and Walker, his column commanders, reflected his determination to break the Indians if possible: "You will not receive overtures of peace or submission from Indians but will attack and kill every male Indian over twelve years old."[6] The Pawnees, numbering ninety-five in all, marched with Connor's column. The several reports of the operations reveal that the Pawnees welcomed the chances for action more than did the war-weary, semimutinous veterans who found themselves exposed to new dangers several months after Lee had surrendered at Appomattox.

Connor's forces left Laramie about August 1 and proceeded to a point on the Powder River where they constructed Fort Connor, later known as Fort Reno.[7] From there the Pawnees scouted the area and discovered the trail of a party of Cheyennes. North and forty-eight Pawnees followed the trail all night and at dawn came upon the Cheyennes. North, to avoid being a conspicuous target, painted his face like a Pawnee warrior. When the fight was over, they had killed the whole party of twenty-four Cheyennes, including one woman. The Pawnees were jubilant. This was their first big victory in many years, and they credited North with their change of fortune. They had not lost a man and had captured twenty-nine horses and mules. In a triumphant return to camp they entered brandishing scalps and singing. Their war dance lasted two nights, interrupted only by speeches and a name-changing ceremony during which they christened North "Pani Lasher" (Pawnee Chief). The only casualty they suffered came when one of them, while demonstrating how bravely he had fought, accidentally shot and killed North's orderly.[8]

Four days later the Pawnees discovered another party of Cheyennes, and North's career came near being ended. In the running fight he outdistanced his men, and the Cheyennes turned and attacked him. He led his wounded horse, keeping it between him and the Indians, until he was rescued by his first lieutenant, Charles Small. The two men then retreated until they came upon the Pawnee Scouts, who had a wounded old Cheyenne trapped in a log corral. The scouts were seeing how many times they could shoot him in the legs without killing him. North ordered, "Stop, don't fire another shot. Kill him with a sabre." A mixed-blood scout, Nick Janis, identified the Indian as Red Bull, a Cheyenne chief.[9]

Eleven days later the Pawnees came upon a large village of Arapahos under Chief Black Bear on Tongue River. North sent word back to Connor, who came up with the main body of troops. The Arapahos were routed and an undetermined number killed. Reports range from thirty-five to one hundred and sixty-three. More might have been killed had not the troops, Indian and white, stopped to plunder. Connor was infuriated and caused most of the booty to be destroyed, to the dismay of the Pawnees.

The column under colonels Cole and Walker did not appear at the rendezvous point on the Tongue River. Connor sent North and twenty Pawnees to look for them. They found several hundred dead horses, many of them shot. North thought a battle had taken place and reported back to Connor. The whole force followed Cole's trail for several days, and then North was sent out again with several Pawnees. This time he came upon the combined Cole and Walker commands in a destitute condition. They had shot their own starving mounts, been reduced to walking, and, harassed by Indians, were close to disaster. Cole, in marching through the Nebraska Sand Hills and the Black Hills, had run short of supplies and lost his way.[10] The entire expedition returned to Fort Connor, where General Connor found orders relieving him of the command, and the Powder River Expedition of 1865 ended with goals unachieved and the Indians undefeated. The Pawnee Scouts, however, had made a favorable impression and were destined for further service.

The Union Pacific Railroad had been pushed west along the Platte River in 1866. The work season of 1867 would place the crews in an area exposed to Indian attack. Grenville M. Dodge, chief engineer, wrote to Lt. Gen. William T. Sherman asking for protection for the workers. Campaigns against the hostiles were not enough; patrols along the road were needed. Dodge stated:

> I believe the moment you get into the Indian country with troops for the campaign the Indians will leave the Platte route . . . but what you and I may know it is hard to make a lot of Irishmen believe. They want to see occasionally a soldier to give them confidence and that is all we need to get the labor on the road.

Sherman sent the letter on to Gen. Ulysses S. Grant with the endorsement that help should be given to Dodge because the road finished into Wyoming would be of great importance to the army. Grant concurred that "Every protection practicable should be given by the military both to secure the rapid completion of the road and to avoid pretext on the part of the builders to get further assistance from the Government."[11]

Col. Christopher C. Augur, commander of the Department of the Platte, asked North to organize a battalion of four companies of Pawnees to help protect the road. North did not wish to give up his position of post trader at the agency, and Augur secured a leave of absence for him from the commissioner of Indian affairs.[12] North was major of the battalion, and each company was led by a white captain and a first lieutenant. The officers, for the most part, were men drawn from North's acquaintances who were familiar to a degree with the Pawnee tribe and the frontier. In 1867 the captains were Albert W. Arnold, a friend of the North family; Charles Morse, who had married North's sister Alphonsene; James Murie of Scotch ancestry who founded two families, one Pawnee and one white; and Luther North. The noncommissioned officers were Indian. There were four sergeants, four corporals, a bugler, a farrier, and forty privates in each company.[13] The officers were hired by the Quartermaster Department as civilian employees and given rank and pay corresponding to their counterparts in regular army units. The men enlisted into the United States service with the same pay as white soldiers.

Horses were purchased in Columbus and vicinity at prices of from eighty to one hundred dollars, and the Pawnee Battalion entrained for Fort Kearny. Urgent requests were submitted to the army for subsistence pay because the Pawnee chiefs made the scouts leave all food on the reservation for use by the tribe.[14]

Dodge had been mistaken about the Indians leaving the Platte Valley when troops arrived, and the scouts had a busy summer. The records of the Department of the Platte reveal that they were shuttled back and forth between Fort Kearny, Plum Creek, Fort McPherson, and the ever more distant "end of track." Their errands were varied. Col. John Gibbon at Fort McPherson reported, "Brought up forty Pawnee who might be advantageously used here for a few days in unearthing certain red and white scoundrels who are engaged in horse stealing and murdering in the vicinity."[15] Dodge wrote from the end of track that three of his workers had been killed and twenty-seven head of stock run off. The country between the Plattes was filled with hostiles. "They strike us at some point daily."[16]

The Pawnee Battalion was distributed at different points along the road and could be moved quickly. The railroad itself was proving an important factor in the defense of the workers and in military operations. Augur reported it "essential to the interest of the Department in the way of moving troops and supplies at great saving of time and money . . . its completion to the Black Hills in its effect upon Indian affairs is equivalent to a successful campaign."[17] The scouts were well armed with revolvers and Spencer carbines. When their officers had difficulty obtaining what they considered adequate equipment or treatment from the commanders of various posts, they did not hesitate to appeal directly to

Augur, who backed them up. It was apparent that the colorful Pawnees and their leader had the support of the commander of the Department of the Platte. He realized that the battalion of Pawnee Scouts differed from the regular army units, and he did not treat it as such. Soon the scouts proved their worth to Augur.

In August a party of Cheyennes under Spotted Wolf derailed a freight train a few miles west of Plum Creek, killing several of the crew. The Cheyennes frequently appeared across the Platte River from the station, and Frank North eventually received a call to arms:

> The operator at Plum Creek reports Indians now in sight of his office and the line out beyond that station. Please see what the matter is.[18]

North dispatched the nearest company of scouts to the scene. The report of the officer in charge of the small garrison at Plum Creek indicates why Colonel Augur supported the Pawnees:

> The party of soldiers in charge of the telegraph station at Plum Creek ran off shamefully at the approach of the Indians. They appeared here at about ten p.m. badly scared. . . . The operator has not been heard from. They report he ran off before they did. The Indians destroyed a half mile of line cutting down the poles. They then encamped. . . . On the approach of Captain Murie with the Pawnee Company the Indians advanced coolly to meet him thinking his command white men, as soon as they were near enough to recognize the Pawnee they broke in every direction with wild cries of Pawnee Pawnee. The fight was a complete success. Captain Murie and Lieutenant Isaac Davis and all the Scouts deserve the greatest credit.[19]

Murie brought back fifteen scalps and two prisoners, a woman and a boy. The boy was a nephew of Turkey Leg, the Cheyenne chief. The Cheyennes offered an exchange of prisoners, and the Pawnees' captives were traded at North Platte for two white girls and their twin brothers who had been captured near Grand Island on July 24, 1867.[20]

Augur gave the Pawnees all the stock they had captured that was not branded "U.S.A." and expressed regret because he did not feel authorized to give them government property.[21] In his report on the activities of the Department of the Platte he praised the scouts:

> I have never seen more obedient and better behaved troops and they have done most excellent service. . . . They are peculiarly qualified for service on the Plains. They are unequalled as riders, know the country thoroughly, are never sick, never desert and are careful of their horses. . . . I have never seen one under the influence of

liquor. . . . [A]s the season for active operation closes they can be discharged to go home and look after their families for the winter. This they prefer.[22]

He asked permision to raise three more battalions for future service.

In September the Pawnees were scheduled to accompany Capt. Lewis Merrill on an inspection tour of Forts Reno, Phil Kearny, and C. F. Smith. Geminien P. Beauvais, special Indian commissioner, protested that their presence would destroy all efforts of the commission to make peace with the Sioux. Sherman wrote to Augur:

I rather think it best not to send the Pawnee up there at present. Let us give these Indian men a fair chance to settle this matter. They have as many notions of propriety as an old maid.[23]

Augur soon proved his friendship for North and his knowledge of Indians. The scouts were sent to Fort Kearny to await muster out. They soon tired of inactivity. North attempted to discipline one of them, and most of the Pawnees went home to the reservation without the formality of discharge. Messages were exchanged in which the word "mutiny" was used. Augur, however, instructed his adjutant:

Issue orders to this effect: "The service of the Pawnee Scouts being no longer required, they will be sent to Fort Kearny to turn in their horses, arms, ammunition and equipment and then to their reservation to be paid and discharged." Send a clerk with blank discharges and final statements and let him remain and make them out correctly. . . . Have the Paymaster ready to pay them off.[24]

And the affair ended.

The next spring Union Pacific officials urged the army to re-employ the Pawnees, even though the road had attempted to charge the government for transporting the scouts the previous year. North was instructed to raise two companies of fifty men each, though the railroad had requested twice that number.[25] The Pawnees were assigned to patrol the road from Wood River to North Platte.

Early in July a warning came up from Maj. Gen. Philip H. Sheridan in Kansas that a large body of Cheyennes and Arapahos was heading north after the Pawnee and that if any of that tribe were out hunting they had better get out of the way.[26] It happened that most of the tribe was hunting on the Republican. North, apparently without direct orders, picked twenty men from each company, went down, and joined the tribe on their hunt. Inquiries as to his whereabouts drew only rumors that North was going for the Cheyennes, and the entire Pawnee nation was on the move.[27] North took with him four civilians in search of excitement. One of them, J. J. Aldrich, published an account of the trip when he returned, which is the best record of the episode. North joined the large Pawnee hunting party, and they had a successful hunt on the Republican in which North and the scouts joined with gusto, North stating that he was going to bring some meat up to the railroad. Then they were attacked by a large party of Sioux, who evidently did not know that the scouts were present. In probably the most severe fight of his career Major North lost two men and almost lost his own life, but succeeded in his apparent mission—to protect the bulk of the tribe from an attack.[28] North simply reported when he returned, "Arrived here last night. Lost two of my men on the Republican in skirmish with Sioux while out hunting."[29]

In February 1869 Luther North led one company on Capt. Henry E. Noyes's winter campaign on the Republican. The expedition was caught in a severe ice storm. The men's breath froze on their whiskers, their eyes froze shut, and the column seemed in danger of disaster. Noyes reported that the Pawnees cut a ford across the Frenchman River and "were of material assistance to us."[30] It is revealing that of the eighty-three men reported suffering from frostbite the only members included from the Pawnee Scouts were the two white officers.

The summer of 1869 saw the Republican River Expedition, under command of Col. Eugene A. Carr, organized for the purpose of driving the Indians from the Republican River country, their favorite buffalo hunting grounds. Carr's command consisted of eight troops of the Fifth Cavalry and three companies of Pawnee Scouts. They left Fort McPherson on June 9, and on June 16 hostiles made a raid and ran off some mules. Luther North and his Pawnees pursued the Indians and recovered the mules only to be reprimanded by Carr for leaving camp without orders.[31]

Frank North with Company C of the scouts joined Carr on June 17. He found the commander in a depressed state of mind. The expedition seemed to have gotten off to an unfortunate start in hot, dry weather. Carr wrote to Maj. George D. Ruggles that the troops should be provided with some comforts or "it will be more than humane [*sic*] nature can and will stand. We now find it almost impossible to get colored servants to go with us on account of the hardship." He had never before had Indians under his command and was not impressed by the Pawnees. He found them poorly mounted, shiftless, and lazy, and, while he hoped he could make their Indian qualities useful, he reported that he would like to trade all but thirty for good cavalry soldiers.[32]

As the campaign progressed, he became better pleased and noted that the Pawnees were improving. Perhaps the arrival of Frank North had helped the situation. Carr recommended one scout, Traveling Bear (whom he mistakenly referred to as Mad Bear), for a Medal of Honor for action in a skirmish with the Cheyenne, though he still believed the scouts prone to rush to the attack without proper orders and feared that their attack on a small party of hostiles had alerted the whole tribe. However, on June 11 the village of Tall Bull, a Cheyenne chief, was discovered and destroyed in the Battle of Summit Springs. Tall Bull was killed by Frank North, a captive white woman rescued, $1,500 in gold and bank notes found, fifty-two Indians killed, seventeen captured, and an immense quantity of equipment destroyed. The campaign was a success. Carr's report indicated the considerable part the Pawnees played in locating the village and in the subsequent battle, and he concluded:

> The Pawnee under Major Frank North were of the greatest service to us throughout the campaign. This has been the first time since coming west that we have been supplied with Indian Scouts and the results have shown their value.[33]

The Battle of Summit Springs was the climax of the expedition. However, scouts took part in a fruitless pursuit of the fleeing survivors of the fight through the Sand Hills of Nebraska to the Niobrara River.[34]

In September Companies A and B went out again to the Republican, this time attached to a force of Fifth and Second Cavalry under the command of Lt. Col. Thomas Duncan. It was on this expedition that North and his friend "Buffalo Bill" Cody, who was along as a scout, were attacked by Sioux while hunting ahead of the column. Much has been written about this episode and the rescue of the two men by 1st Lt. George F. Price and 2d Lt. William J. Volkmar. North's diary contains the laconic entry:

> Today we marched 24 miles and I and Cody came ahead to the Creek and 6 Indians got after us and gave us a lively chase you bet. I got my men out and they killed one Indian and got ponies a mule and lots of trash.[35]

Lieutenant Colonel Duncan reported that the Sioux abandoned a village of fifty-six lodges and lost material, including nine thousand pounds of meat. He especially commended a private, Clay Burford of the Fifth Cavalry, who kept up with the Pawnees in pursuing the hostiles several miles after the other soldiers had halted.[36] An old woman, the mother of the Sioux leader, Pawnee Killer, was captured six days later and was questioned by a Ponca who was with the scouts. He could translate her Sioux into Pawnee, and then North translated the Pawnee into English.[37] The expedition ended without a decisive action. The Battle of Summit Springs had cleared the area of any substantial group of hostiles. Duncan reported that he wished especially to commend the Pawnees and Major North and noted that "no portion of the command has manifested more willingness to come into contact with hostile Indians."[38]

The scouts were mustered out at the end of the expedition. In August 1870 two companies were raised for patrol duty along the railroad. The duty was uneventful, and they were discharged in December.[39] Frank North served as a scout and interpreter at Fort D. A. Russell and Fort Sidney and also maintained a home in Columbus. He and Luther served as guides for scientific parties and for the army.[40] The Pawnee tribe was moved from Nebraska to the Indian Territory in 1874–75.

The summer of 1876 saw the Plains Indian wars reach a climax. The Sioux in defending the Black Hills had fought Brig. Gen. George Crook to a standstill on the Rosebud River and had annihilated Lt. Col. George A. Custer's command. The hostile bands then separated, and the army set into motion the operations which, in effect, crushed the Indian resistance. The Pawnee Scouts played a part in this effort. Gen. Phil Sheridan believed that the hostiles would never fight a decisive battle. To be thoroughly defeated they would have to be fought in their own manner and surprised.[41]

To help achieve this end an unprecedented number of Indian scouts was raised, almost four hundred, including Sioux, Arapahos, Shoshones, Bannocks, a few Cheyennes, and a final two companies of Pawnees. North, in the excitement following the news of the Custer massacre, had offered to raise a regiment of Pawnees and frontiersmen to fight the Sioux. The offer was refused. However, in August he was authorized to proceed to the Pawnee reservation in Indian Territory and enlist one hundred scouts.[42] Frank and Luther North found the Pawnees more than willing to serve and had to post guards on the train to prevent more than the regularly enlisted one hundred from boarding. The Pawnees furnished their own horses, for which the government paid them forty cents a day, and they received regular army pay. North got $150 per month, his first lieutenant $130, and his second lieutenant $120, and all were furnished horses and equipment. The company was armed at Fort Sidney.[43]

On October 22, while on their way to Fort Robinson, the scouts received word to join Col. Ranald S. MacKenzie in a march on the Lakota villages of Red Cloud and Red Leaf, who were off the Red Cloud Agency against orders. Both villages were captured without bloodshed and the captives marched back to the Red Cloud Agency. To the joy of the Pawnees 722 horses were taken, and the Pawnees were each given one. The horses caused a good deal of controversy, and in 1889 Congress passed a law approving payment to Sioux who could prove they lost horses.[44]

The Powder River Expedition of 1876–77 was under the command of General Crook. It reached Fort Fetterman on November 12 and left on the fourteenth with the objective of moving against Crazy Horse and Sitting Bull, but found these leaders wary and their bands scattered.[45] As a target of opportunity Crook decided to attack a Cheyenne village on Crazy Woman Creek that had been discovered by the Indian scouts.[46] MacKenzie was placed in command of the attack, and the village was struck. The North brothers and a portion of the Pawnees took part in the attack, charging into the center of the village, which consisted of 173 lodges. Six soldiers were killed, and twenty-five Cheyenne dead were positively accounted for. The bitterly cold weather probably killed more of the Indians, especially the children. Luther North, who shot the son of Chief Dull Knife, wrote years later to a friend:

> The thermometer never got higher than 25 below. . . . Those poor Cheyennes were out in that weather with nothing to eat, no shelter, we had burned their village, and hardly any clothing. It was said many children died. It makes me sort of sick to think about it.[47]

The Cheyennes had scattered in all directions. The fight had alerted the whole area, and it was not likely that another engagement could be fought. After some fruitless scouting along the Belle Fourche River the expedition was ended. The scouts were mustered out at Fort Sidney in May and moved home to Oklahoma with a herd of about 250 horses, 125 of which they had captured.[48] The North brothers went with them to shepherd the Pawnees through the settled area of Nebraska and Kansas. While camped near Hays, Kansas, several of the Pawnees went into town, and one of them was fatally wounded by a quick-triggered deputy after the scout had broken a store window. His angry comrades mounted their ponies and came into town stating that if the wounded boy died there would be trouble. The local newspaper reported the citizens turned out the lights and went for their sidearms, and added, "as to the necessity of shooting the Indian we shall not venture our opinion . . . but our citizens certainly owe Major North a debt of gratitude for holding the revengeful and bloodthirsty savages in check."[49]

A few days later the Pawnees and the North brothers parted for the last time, and the Pawnee Scouts became a part of the history of the West. Their strong points had been their eagerness for action, their native ability as trailers and riders, and their endurance and toughness. Their weak points were their tendency for impetuous action and their obsession with plunder, especially the capture of horses; however, under the leadership of a man they respected and trusted, they had played a considerable role in the Indian wars. Their contribution to the construction of the railroad was significant, and they had won the ultimate praise of every commander under whom they served.

The colorful Pawnees, eager for action, and the restless and capable Frank North, appealed to many of the officers who welcomed a break from the ordinary. The North brothers were always ready for a hunt, a horse race, or an Indian fight, and they and their scouts lent some adventure to an essentially monotonous task. The critics of the scouts were chiefly men such as Lt. Eugene F. Ware, whose sense of racial superiority allowed no Indian, friendly or hostile, to be capable of any worthwhile service, or officers such as Carr, who initially found it hard to adjust to their Indian ways. Colonel Augur, perhaps, best recognized the strengths and limitations of the Pawnees. A dispatch which he sent to Grenville Dodge at the climax of their service of guarding the railroad can serve as their valedictory, "North and his Pawnee Scouts have done well. Let them know that I think so."[50]

Notes

[1] Waldo Rudolph Wedel, *An Introduction to Pawnee Archeology,* Bureau of American Ethnology, Smithsonian Institution, Bulletin 112 (Washington: Government Printing Office, 1936), 7–25.

[2] Alfred Sorenson, "A Quarter of a Century on the Frontier, or The Adventures of Major Frank North, the 'White Chief of the Pawnees'," Frank Joshua North Collection, MS448, Nebraska State Historical Society Archives, Lincoln, the story of North's life as told by himself and written by Alfred Sorenson, circa 1880. The standard source of information on the scouts is George Bird Grinnell, *Two Great Scouts and Their Pawnee Battalion* (Cleveland: The Arthur H. Clark Company, 1928). Grinnell's account is based largely upon the Sorenson manuscript and the recollections of Luther H. North. Robert Bruce, *The Fighting Norths and Pawnee Scouts: Narratives and Reminiscences of Military Service on the Old Frontier* (New York: Privately printed, 1932) is also a valuable source, compiled largely from the letters of Luther North. An extensive collection of Luther North letters and two diaries of Frank North, 1869 and 1876–77, are in the archives of the Nebraska State Historical Society. The records, reports, and correspondence of the War Department are, of course, a prime source of information on the Pawnee Scouts and contain evaluations unclouded by the passage of time.

[3] Benjamin F. Lushbaugh, Pawnee Indian agent, to William M. Albin, superintendent of Indian affairs, Sept. 30, 1864, *Report of the Commissioner of Indian Affairs for the Year 1864* (Washington: Government Printing Office, 1865), 383.

[4] Eugene F. Ware, *The Indian War of 1864* (New York: St. Martin's Press, 1960), 158–59, states that an earlier company of Pawnees under North accompanied General Mitchell

west from Plum Creek in July 1864. He commented on the lack of discipline of the group. This is the only mention of a Pawnee company previous to the group raised in August under the direction of Curtis. It seems probable that Ware was mistaken in this recollection and had telescoped events with the passage of years.

[5] Nelson Cole (1833–99) was colonel of the Second Missouri Artillery. He served as a brigadier general of volunteers during the Civil War and again during the Spanish-American War. Samuel Walker (1822–93) was lieutenant colonel of the Sixteenth Kansas Cavalry. Francis B. Heitman, *Historical Register and Dictionary of the United States Army* 1 (Washington: Government Printing Office, 1903):997.

[6] *The War of the Rebellion: A Compilation of the Official Records of the Union and Confederate Armies,* ser. 1, vol. 48, pt. 2 (Washington: Government Printing Office, 1896), 1049, 1131. The order was rescinded by Brig. Gen. John Pope, department commander.

[7] Fred B. Rogers, *Soldiers of the Overland* (San Francisco: Grabhorn Press, 1938), 178.

[8] *Official Records,* ser. 1, vol. 48, pt. 2, 1217; George Bird Grinnell, *Two Great Scouts,* 90–94; E. H. Palmer, "History of the Powder River Indian Expedition of 1865," *Transactions and Reports of the Nebraska State Historical Society* 2 (Lincoln: State Journal Company, 1887):208.

[9] Sorenson, "Quarter Century," 91; *Official Records,* ser. 1, vol. 48, pt. 1, 366.

[10] George B. Grinnell, *The Fighting Cheyennes* (Norman: University of Oklahoma Press, 1956), 212–13; Colonel Cole's report, *Official Records,* ser. 1, vol. 48, pt. 1, 366–68.

[11] Grenville M. Dodge, Council Bluffs, to Lt. Gen. William T. Sherman, St. Louis, Jan. 14, 1867; Gen. Ulysses S. Grant, Washington, to Sherman, Jan. 26, 1867, Selected Documents, Letters Sent and Received, Department of the Platte, Records of the United States Army Commands, Record Group (RG) 98, National Archives, Washington, D.C. These microfilm copies are at the Nebraska State Historical Society. Unless otherwise indicated, correspondence, reports, and muster rolls hereinafter cited are from this source.

[12] Col. Christopher C. Augur, Omaha, to Lewis V. Bogy, commissioner of Indian affairs, Feb. 27, 1867; 1st Lt. Henry G. Litchfield, Omaha, to Frank North, Pawnee Agency, Feb. 28, 1867.

[13] Pawnee Battalion Muster Rolls.

[14] Capt. Lewis Merrill, Columbus, to Augur, Mar. 12, 16, 1867.

[15] Col. John Gibbon, Fort McPherson, to Augur, May 20, 1867.

[16] Dodge to Augur, May 25, 1867.

[17] Report of the Operation of the Department of the Platte, January 1, 1867, to September 30, 1867. Augur referred to the Black Hills of southeastern Wyoming west of Fort Laramie and not to the better known Black Hills of South Dakota.

[18] Augur to Frank North, Aug. 14, 1867.

[19] Maj. Richard I. Dodge, Plum Creek, to Augur, Aug. 19, 1867.

[20] Luther Hedden North, "Recollections of Captain L. H. North," Luther Hedden North Collection, MS449, Nebraska State Historical Society Archives, Lincoln.

[21] Augur to Frank North, Aug. 19, 1867.

[22] Report of the Operation of the Department of the Platte.

[23] Sherman to Augur, Sept. 30, 1867.

[24] Frank North, Fort Kearny, to Litchfield, Oct. 31, 1867; Litchfield to Augur, Oct. 31, 1867; Augur to Litchfield, Nov. 2, 1867; *Nebraska Herald* (Plattsmouth), Nov. 7, 1867.

[25] Sherman to Augur, Apr. 29, 1868; Augur to Frank North, Mar. 30, 1868; Webster Snyder, superintendent, Union Pacific Railroad, to Augur, Apr. 30, 1868.

[26] Maj. Gen. Philip H. Sheridan, Fort Leavenworth, to Litchfield, July 8, 1868.

[27] Litchfield, Fort McPherson, to Augur, Aug. 3, 1868.

[28] J. J. Aldrich, "Diary of a Twenty Days' Sport: Buffalo Hunting on the Plains with the Pawnee, Accompanied by Major North, U.S.A., and an Escort of Forty U.S. Pawnee Soldiers, Captain Morris and Matthews, and Four Private Gentlemen," *Omaha Weekly Herald,* Aug. 19, 26, Sept. 2, 1868. Five years later, without North's leadership, the tribe, while on a hunt in the same general locality, was terribly mauled by the Sioux and never fully recovered.

[29] Frank North, Wood River, to Maj. George D. Ruggles, Aug. 8, 1868.

[30] Report of Capt. Henry E. Noyes, Mar. 11, 1869.

[31] Luther North to Jacob C. North, Nov. 28, 1874, MS449.

[32] Col. Eugene A. Carr to Ruggles, June 17, 1869.

[33] Report of Operations, Republican River Expedition, June 30 to July 20, 1869.

[34] Frank North diary, Aug. 7–19, 1869. This North diary appears in Donald F. Danker, ed., "The Journal of an Indian Fighter: The 1869 Diary of Major Frank   J. North," *Nebraska History* 39 (1958):87–177.

[35] Frank North diary, Sept. 26, 1869.

[36] Report of Lt. Col. Thomas Duncan, Republican River Expedition, Aug. 18 to Oct. 7, 1869.

[37] Lt. William J. Volkmar to 2d Lt. William C. Forbush, acting assistant adjutant general, District of the Republican, Fort McPherson, Nov. 19, 1869, transmitting Carr's report, "Journal of the March of the Republican River Expedition," entry for Oct. 3, 1869.

[38] Report of Operations, Oct. 28, 1869.

[39] Frank North to Augur, Aug. 2, 1870; Report of Operations of the Department of Platte, Oct. 25, 1870. *Memorial Leaves, Inscribed to the Memory of Major Frank J. North* (Columbus, Nebr., 1885).

[40] *Memorial Leaves.*

[41] Sheridan to Sherman, Aug. 10, 1876, Letters Received, File 4163, "Sioux War Papers," Records of the Adjutant General's Office, RG 94, National Archives; hereinafter cited as "Sioux War Papers."

[42] Capt. William F. Drum to Frank North, Aug. 18, 1876, "Sioux War Papers."

[43] Frank North diary, Oct. 23, 1876.

[44] Memorandum regarding captured and surrendered ponies of the Sioux, Jan. 20, 1896, "Sioux War Papers."

[45] Gen. George Crook to Sherman, Jan. 8, 1877, "Sioux War Papers."

[46] Frank North recorded in his diary on November 24, 1876, that the discoverers of the village were Sioux. Other sources indicate that they were Shoshones.

[47] Luther North to Dr. Richard J. Tanner, Jan. 7, 1930, Richard J. Tanner Collection, MS1345, Nebraska State Historical Society Archives, Lincoln.

[48] Crook to Sherman, Jan. 8, 1877, "Sioux War Papers."

[49] *Ellis County Star* (Hays, Kans.), May 24, 1877, as quoted in a letter to the author from Robert W. Richmond, Kansas State Historical Society, Topeka, Sept. 15, 1960.

[50] Augur to Dodge, Aug. 18, 1867.

Chapter 4

The Battle of
Massacre Canyon

Paul D. Riley

Much has been written and filmed about the Indian wars in the trans-Missouri West, conjuring up the image of the United States Cavalry fighting and defeating some band or tribe of Indians. But there is another image of which the term "Indian wars" could and should remind us: Long before Europeans came to the Americas, long before Nebraska was settled, Indians were engaging in intertribal warfare. These wars, ranging from minor raids to out-and-out battles, continued in varying degrees almost to the turn of the century.

Two miles east of Trenton, Hitchcock County, in an attractive roadside park stands a towering granite shaft erected by the federal government in 1930 to commemorate the Battle of Massacre Canyon, which occurred on Tuesday morning, August 5, 1873. Half a mile west of the park, U.S. Highway 34 curves down into a canyon and crosses a tree-lined, spring-fed creek, which flows through the lower reaches of the canyon into the Republican River Valley. The battle took place two miles up this canyon, where the abrupt canyon walls are lower and the valley much narrower.

Today that stretch of canyon has no extraordinary quality to set it apart from any other canyon in southwest Nebraska, but on the afternoon of August 5, 1873, the view was far from ordinary. The first to view the battlefield that afternoon were Capt. Charles Meinhold and Company B, Third Cavalry, U.S. Army, accompanied by Acting Assistant Surgeon David Franklin Powell. The latter described the scene in a letter to the *Omaha Herald*:

> It was a horrible sight. Dead braves with bows still tightly grasped in dead and stiffened fingers; sucking infants pinned to their mothers' breasts with arrows; bowels protruding from openings made by fiendish knives; heads scalped with red blood glazed upon them—a stinking mass, many already fly-blown and scorched with heat.[1]

These were the Pawnee dead, resulting from a surprise attack by more than a thousand Sioux upon 350 Pawnee men, women, and children as they moved up the west bank of the canyon on their summer buffalo hunt. It was one of the largest intertribal battles in historic times, leaving approximately seventy Pawnees dead. It is considered to be the last major battle between two Indian tribes in the United States.

During the preceding twenty years the Pawnee, once Nebraska's most powerful and noted Indian tribe, had declined both in influence and numbers, the result of disease and warfare. From the Civil War onward they had allied themselves with the whites and had halfheartedly begun to learn the new ways. This included some of the warriors enlisting in the U.S. Army, serving under Maj. Frank Joshua North and gaining wide fame as the Pawnee Scouts. Their determined zeal in aiding the army in seeking out their traditional enemies, the Sioux and Cheyenne, did nothing to lessen old antagonisms.[2]

The Sioux settled into an uneasy truce with the army during the early 1870s, while they were still in the process of being settled on reservations, but their raids against the Pawnee reservation continued. After signing a treaty with the United States in 1857, the Pawnee had been settled upon a reservation which is present Nance County in east central Nebraska. The government promised them protection from their enemies, but members of the tribe continued to find themselves and their horse herds threatened by raiding bands of Brulé and Oglala Sioux. The Loup River flowed through the reservation to the Platte, and its three major forks served as a natural highway between the Pawnee and the Sioux living in northwestern Nebraska and the Dakotas. Women were killed in their cornfields, and horses were stolen, embittering the Pawnee tribe.[3]

A series of Quaker agents under President Ulysses S. Grant's Indian reform policies now administered the Pawnee, and they continually warned their wards that they must keep the peace. In the main they did, though parties of young men regularly slipped away on horse-stealing raids, often going as far south as Oklahoma. Pressures from the advance of white settlements around the reservation also created problems. Thieving whites decimated the Pawnee wood reservation, and homesteaders pastured their horses and cattle on remote sections of the Pawnee land. The dogmatic ethics of the determined Quakers only further confused and irritated the Pawnees, especially the young warriors. No aspect of Pawnee life was too minor to be ignored by the agents, who in turn credited the Pawnee chiefs with having more power than they actually had.[4]

In the spring of 1871 Quaker agent Jacob M. Troth announced that the federal government was proposing a peace treaty between the Pawnee and Spotted Tail's Brulé Sioux, their most frequent raiders. The Pawnee were not impressed. Too often in the past thetribe had been victimized both by treaties and the Sioux. Sky Chief (Te-la-wa-hut-lai-sharu) of the Republican or Kitkehahki band (later to die at Massacre Canyon) spoke of his doubts at a council with the agent on March 27, 1871:

> Spotted Tail may tell the truth. . . . [F]or our part we tell the truth when we say we don't go on the war path. . . . I want to make peace at Washington and see if Spotted Tail tells the truth.

Then, in an aside to the other chiefs, he added:

> Our great father at Washington thinks he can make us do just as he pleases. We have one man over us and he makes us do as he wants.[5]

Other chiefs joined in the discussion, all agreeing peace would be a fine thing but all doubting the trustworthiness of Spotted Tail and his ability to keep his own warriors in line. For this reason they insisted such a treaty be signed in Washington rather than at the Santee Sioux reservation as the government desired. They believed the Sioux would take more seriously a treaty signed with pomp in Washington rather than one signed locally. The possibility of such a treaty was discussed on several occasions, but it never developed beyond the talking stage.[6]

Indians and their agents seldom worked well together, but the religious beliefs of the Quakers seemed to create additional misunderstanding. Being men of reason, they could not understand why the Pawnee desired the old ways, when it was obvious—at least to the Quakers—that civilization offered the one bright future. Their extreme honesty and their pacifism were particularly confusing to the Pawnee, a people to whom horse stealing was a fine art and limited warfare was an everyday fact of life. Also, common to most missionaries, the Quakers were blind to the highly intellectual religion of this monotheistic people. In fact, the Pawnee belief in one god apparently made missionary efforts more difficult. At a council held June 8, 1872, Agent Troth confused the issue by saying:

> I thought this would be a good time to read and explain about God— You believe in the same God as we do. . . . I call on you to know how to meet and talk about God.

One by one the chiefs replied, speaking of their god, trying to reconcile him with the god of the Quakers. Sky Chief said:

> As soon as our children get old enough to understand, their father tells them of God.

Eagle Chief of the Pita-how-e-rat band said:

All persons in the tribe will tell you the same story about God. . . . [W]e tell our children about God. . . . [W]e still have things that God gave us and want to keep them. It is good to have a certain day to rest. You know better than we for you have writings and we have none so forget.

Petalesharo, the main chief of the Pawnee, then added a comment of his own:

We are done talking about God I suppose.

Sky Chief closed the discussion, leaving the agent with nothing to say:

Now we are done talking about God—we would like to hurry up the Annuity money or something else before we go on the Hunt.[7]

The Pawnee were a semisedentary people living in permanent earthlodge villages and planting crops of corn, beans, and squash. Nearly half the year, however, was spent on the buffalo range between the Platte and Smoky Hill rivers. The summer hunt began about the first of July after their crops were planted; they returned in time to harvest in late summer. The winter hunt began in early November and usually lasted until after the New Year. It was upon these hunts that the Pawnee depended for their meat supply, as little wild game and buffalo had been available near the reservation for many years. Councils between the Pawnee chiefs and their agent devoted much time to the upcoming buffalo hunt. Although the Pawnee were dependent upon the hunt, the Quaker agents deplored it, for the Pawnee were then virtually free from agency control and were free to live in the old way without interference. As the years passed and the buffalo diminished in number, due to mass slaughter by whites, the Pawnee had to travel farther and farther from the reservation, thus increasing the possibility of their having trouble with Sioux hunting in the same region.

For the summer hunt of 1872 Agent Troth hired John Burwell "Texas Jack" Omohundro of Fort McPherson to travel with the Pawnees as trail agent. The noted frontiersman was instructed to let the hunters do as they would, but in matters dealing with whites or other Indians he had the right to command. Prior to 1869 when Maj. Eugene Asa Carr's Republican River Expedition cleared the valley of hostiles, the Republican Valley and its watershed had been the domain of the Indians. Southern Cheyennes and Brulé Sioux were all but permanent residents there, while Pawnees, Omahas, and Otos visited there on seasonal hunts. After Carr's expedition Cheyennes seldom came so far north, while Spotted Tail and his Brulés were placed at Whetstone Agency in Dakota Territory and visited the valley irregularly in small bands. Only Whistler and his small band of Cut-off Oglalas lived permanently in the region, their main village being near Stockville, Frontier County, though most winters they moved at least part of their village to the Stinking Water Creek in Hayes and Chase counties. Professional hide hunters, mainly from Kansas, entered the region and slaughtered the buffalo by the thousands, while scattered frontier settlements in two years' time had spread up the valley from Webster County in 1870 to Red Willow County in 1872. The following year the frontier was moved another twenty-five miles west, and Hitchcock County was organized. Even on the buffalo range the Indians were being restricted.[8]

Even so, the summer hunt of 1872 was successful. The Pawnees left their reservation on Monday, July 8, accompanied by a party of Ponca Indians, and they were joined by Omohundro at Grand Island on Saturday, July 13. From there they crossed the divide to the Republican country, reporting to Capt. John D. Devin of the Fourteenth Infantry at Camp Red Willow, a temporary military post established to allay fears of the frontiersmen as well as to afford any necessary protection to the several surveying parties in the area. The Pawnees had been furnished with "4 white flags 3x4 ft. with a large P in the center," to identify them.[9]

Omohundro's letters and reports of the hunt have not been located, but on a part of the hunt the Pawnees were accompanied by Luther Hedden North and George Bird Grinnell, both of whom left written accounts. The young Grinnell, who was later to gain fame as an author, ethnologist, and conservationist, was on his second trip to the West, and he was much impressed with his first meeting with Pawnees and their traditional methods of hunting, though he realized the day of the buffalo would soon be at an end.[10]

In late August or early September the successful Pawnees and Poncas visited Camp Red Willow and the adjacent frontier settlement:

> We had 2,700 Pawnees and Ponca Indians here two or three days, and they killed 200 or 300 buffalo, drove off some cattle and stole two or three horses and tried to sell them, but the owners paid them something to help them hunt them up and bring them back. Poor things. They mean no harm, but it is so natural to steal that they can't help it, and the troops being here, they were afraid to be too barefaced about it.[11]

The author of the above, Washington Mallory Hinman, operated a sawmill at Red Willow and was a former resident of Lincoln County. Hinman was far more charitable toward the Indians than most frontiersmen, but then Hinman had lived on the frontier since the early 1850s and had had time to get to know and understand the Indians of the Plains.[12] Most frontiersmen, at least those writing letters to the state press, felt more in line with the opinions of J. F. Zediker of Franklin County, who wrote:

We find a very general dissatisfaction prevailing hereabouts, on the frequent passing through this region, of the reserve Indians. Three times within the past six months, the Otoe, Pawnee and Omaha tribes have passed through this section, and being out now, will soon pass through again. The last time they passed through they were more annoying than ever before, as they made it a point to travel more *slowly* and *beg* their living as they went. . . .

We are willing to pay our share of tax to build comfortable dwellings, to clothe and feed them, and to pay soldiers for guarding them. . . . But after we have done all thus, we cannot consent to have them passing through our peaceful domain several times a year, to beg and plunder, and to frighten our families. And to kill off, and drive out of this region, all the game which nature, and nature's God, has placed here for the benefit of the poor frontier settlers, who are trying to earn an honest livelihood by tilling the soil. . . .

This is not the voice of one man, but of the indignant multitude along the Republican Valley.

Our own private opinion is, that the Indian is as good as the white man, so long as he behaves himself. . . . We believe them no better than the white man, and he must earn his bread by the sweat of his brow.[13]

By early October the Pawnees were preparing to start on their winter hunt. Omohundro had served the Pawnees, or at least their agent, well and applied for a second appointment as trail agent. Troth was favorable, but, before the Pawnees departed, Omohundro had decided to join his best friend, William Frederick "Buffalo Bill" Cody upon the New York stage, taking the "Wild West" to the East. No trail agent was appointed, and the Pawnees, who were joined by some Otos, left for the Republican in the middle of November.[14]

While the Pawnees were hunting their way west along the Republican, Whistler and his Cut-off Oglalas were hunting on the Upper Republican, probably in Colorado, while their women and children were in camp on the Stinking Water. The winter was not overly severe, but sometime in late November or early December Whistler, accompanied by Fat Badger and Hand Smeller, started for Fort McPherson supposedly to ask for supplies. Somewhere along the way between the forks of the Republican and the mouth of Medicine Creek, they visited the hunting camp of two trappers or hunters. All versions agree that the Indians begged for food and were fed. They asked for more and were refused. Later one of the Indians tried to steal from the breadbox, and one of the hunters stamped the lid on his hand. Frightened at what had been done, the whites plotted together and suddenly turned and murdered the three Indians. They hid the bodies along a creek and then hurriedly left the region. Much speculation as to the identity of the murderers has appeared in print with several frontiersmen confessing the crime. The most likely candidates for this dishonor are Mortimer N. "Wild Bill" Kress, pioneer settler of Adams County and noted hunter and trapper on the Republican, and his partner, John C. "Jack" Ralston, an easterner. At least their contemporaries thought they were the killers, and so it appeared in the press at that time.[15]

Shortly after this, the Pawnees and Otos were camped at the forks of Beaver Creek, the present site of Atwood, Rawlins County, Kansas, about thirty miles south of the later Massacre Canyon battle site. One account says the Pawnee women and children had been left at or near the Red Willow Creek settlement, though no writer of that time or later makes mention of a Pawnee encampment in the area.[16]

The few minor mentions of the events at that campsite are contradictory, particularly those written by white informants. According to La-sharo-teri, described as the second chief of the Pitahauerat band of Pawnees, they had left their horses in camp and had had a buffalo surround on foot. While the camp was all but unguarded, the Sioux swept down and stole over a hundred of their horses. Either in pursuit or later while hunting, four Pawnee youths came across the Sioux and gave chase. They were apparently decoyed into a trap, and one Pawnee was killed. At about the same time John Story Briggs, trader to the Oto tribe, who was following the Indians with trade goods, was robbed by some Sioux of his horses and goods. The identity of the Sioux is not known, though they were probably Cut-off Oglalas, possibly joined with some Brulés. One account claims that Spotted Tail led the raid himself, though this is unlikely. The Pawnees were forced to cache their buffalo meat as well as their tents and other equipment and return to the reservation on foot, most of them arriving there in terrible condition. Some of the women earned food by tanning hides at the various trading posts scattered along the Republican.[17]

Reports in the press are very confused, not only as to the exact details of the raid, but they also succeed in combining it with the murder of

Whistler and his two men. At first it was reported Pawnees had killed them, then later that the real murderers had fixed evidence so the Sioux would blame the Pawnee. The raid by the Sioux (described as a battle) was supposedly in retaliation for the murders, though another account says the Sioux chief was killed in the battle itself. At any rate the raid was a serious defeat for the Pawnees. Not only did they lose their meat and robe supply, but they lost their horses, vital to the Pawnee economy as well as their most obvious sign of wealth and prestige. The encounter was a disaster to both the Pawnee economy and ego.[18]

While the Pawnees were on the winter hunt, Agent Troth had been replaced by William Burgess, another Quaker. Their poverty, referred to as unprecedented in the tribe, was a shock to him, and he spent much time aiding the tribe in an attempt to convince the Bureau of Indian Affairs of the necessity of delivering the Pawnee annuity goods earlier than usual.[19]

On July 2, 1873, Agent Burgess appointed John William Williamson as trail agent for the summer buffalo hunt. He was just twenty-three years old, having been born June 28, 1850, near Delavan, Walworth County, Wisconsin. At the age of twenty-one Williamson came to Nebraska, home-steading in Boone County. He soon moved permanently to the Pawnee Agency at Genoa, where he was employed as an agency farmer. In a de-tailed account of the buffalo hunt and battle, *The Battle of Massacre Canyon: The Unfortunate Ending of the Last Buffalo Hunt of the Pawnees*, Williamson wrote that he had been selected as trail agent in May, though as late as June 24 Burgess wrote that he had not yet selected anyone. According to Williamson, "I did not apply for the place and was surprised when one of the chiefs came to me and informed me that they had de-cided to request the government to appoint me to accompany them."[20]

Because of the unforeseen events of the hunt, Williamson's letter of instructions from Burgess throws important light on the hunt and the battle:

[Wednesday] 7 mo 2nd day [187]3

To John Williamson

Under the commission of Hon. Edw. P. Smith, Commissioner of Ind Affrs . . . I hereby appoint you to have the oversight of the Pawnee Indians on their Summer hunt. Your salary will be one hundred dol-lars per month for the time in actual service.

The Pawnees will leave the Reservation about the 3rd of July and proceed toward Grand Island, thence up the Platte valley to some point near Plum Creek [Lexington], thence southward to the waters of the Republican where they propose to hunt and continue near six weeks but may probably be absent about two months. While you are not [to] interfere with their regular or customary modes [of] conducting their hunting operation you are authorized to give them such counsel as the circumstances in your judgement shall dictate and to use all precaution to guard [against] any predatory raids or from any incursions by their enemies and give due notice if any should occur. You are to see that they do not [take] property, commit depredations on the settlers [or interfere] in any way with the rights of whites or others, to keep them together as much as practicable and aid them in maintaining friendly relations with all classes of Indian tribes or other people. You are to notify me by letter when you leave the Platte valley and every week thereafter give a little sketch of your operations and of their success, sending the same as often as you meet with an opportunity to reach the mails or by runners when necessity may require. You will also give me notice of the nearest P.O. address where letters may reach you. You will also notify me about the time they propose to return, the route they take and any other particulars that may seem important.[21]

That same day Burgess wrote the commander of the Department of the Platte at Omaha notifying him of the hunt and included a copy of Williamson's letter of instruction. He also gave permission for Lester Beach Platt, a young man from Baltimore, to accompany the hunt. Platt was a nephew of Lester B. Platt, who had served as Pawnee agent prior to the Quaker policy. The elder Platt had then become government trader to the Pawnee tribe, and for a time his wife continued to teach in the agency school.[22]

The 350 Pawnees left the reservation on Wednesday, July 3, and for a month they hunted on the Beaver and Prairie Dog creeks in southwestern Nebraska and northwestern Kansas. The Pawnees had great success, though 1873 was the last good year for large-scale hunting in the region. About August 2 the Pawnees turned north to the Republican to begin their slow return to the reservation, and on the night of August 4 they camped near the present site of Trenton in Hitchcock County. Here they were warned by a party of white buffalo hunters that a great number of Sioux were in the region. Thinking this was a scheme to get them out of the region, the Pawnees did not take the warning seriously.[23]

The hunters were telling the truth. Not only were the usual Cut-off Oglalas in the area, but the Brulé Sioux were present in force, with the total numbering over a thousand warriors. Never again would there be so many Indians in the Republican Valley. Spotted Tail and "a large number of Lodges" left the Fort Laramie region for the buffalo range in the middle of April without a trail agent. Pawnee Killer and his band of Cut-off Oglalas (not to be confused with the Whistler and Black Bear bands) with Antoine Janis as subagent arrived on the Republican early in the summer, camping on Blacktail Deer Creek (Arickaree Fork or the North Fork of the Republican).[24]

On Sunday night, July 6, Pawnee Killer's camp was raided by a party of Ute braves. They were able to steal ten horses and get away undetected. The Sioux assumed the horses had only strayed, and no search was made for them. The following night the Utes returned and stole fourteen horses. In the morning the Sioux began hunting their strayed horses and found a Ute moccasin and arrows. A short distance from camp, they found where the Utes had killed a colt. The Sioux camp was alerted, and one hundred warriors took off in pursuit. About twenty-five miles west of their own camp, the Sioux found the abandoned camp of the Utes, which had consisted of twenty-one lodges. According to one account:

> The pursuit was hotly pushed and thirty-nine horses died on the road from exhaustion. The advance of the Sioux, seven warriors, got up with the rear guard of the Utes, numbering eleven warriors, about 3 o'clock P.M.; fighting immediately ensued, resulting in the defeat of the Sioux, with the loss of one man and three horses killed, and six men wounded. Others of the Sioux arriving the Utes left. The exhaustion of their horses precluded further pursuit on the part of the Sioux. On their return to camp a strong disposition was manifested to make an expedition to the Ute country for revenge; from this, however, they were dissuaded by interpreter Antoine Janise.[25]

Shortly thereafter, perhaps as a cautionary measure, Pawnee Killer moved his camp to the Frenchman or Whiteman's Fork of the Republican in present Chase County. Toward the end of July, seven hundred Brulé Sioux under subagent Stephen F. Estes arrived in the same region and camped on Stinking Water Creek, a fork of the Frenchman.[26]

Estes and his Brulés had visited Sidney on their way to the buffalo range. On July 21 Estes visited the commandant of Sidney Barracks and requested rations for the Indians. On the following day Secretary of War William H. Belknap turned down the request on the grounds that the army would not be able to replace the rations even if reimbursed by the Bureau of Indian Affairs. Apparently Estes continued to press the issue, for on August 4 Belknap authorized the issuing of sugar and coffee to the Brulés, then thought to be camped at Julesburg, Colorado. The authorization came too late, however, for by this time the Brulés were far to the south on the Stinking Water. It is a possibility that this unfortunate delay served as an additional irritant in preparing the Brulés for a warlike stance, just as the Cut-offs were probably anxious to avenge their July defeat at the hands of the Ute raiders.[27]

On the morning of August 3 six Oglala warriors returned to the Cut-off camp and reported they had come across the Pawnees, about whose presence in the Republican country they apparently had no prior knowledge. According to Janis:

> Little Wound came to me and asked if I had any orders to keep him from going to fight them, I told him I had not. He said he had orders not to go to their reservation or among the whites to fight them but none in regard to this part of the country. I told him I would go with him and see the Pawnee but he said it would be of no use as the young men had determined to fight them. They say I stopped them from going to the Utes and they came and stole their horses and killed one of their men and they thought the same thing would occur if they did not strike the Pawnees first.[28]

The Oglalas then sent representatives to the Brulé camp inviting them to join in the attack. Estes tried to prevent their going but failed to do so, as he later wrote:

> I would respectfully state . . . that my failure to avert the attack and consequent massacre of the Pawnees so far as the Brulés were concerned was due in great measure to the ignorance and bad advice given by Sub-Agent Janis to the Indians under his charge. . . . [Janis left] "Little Wound" impressed with the idea that he had a perfect right to make war upon the Pawnees, if he so desired. Fortified with this belief several of the head-men from the "Cut Off" visited my camp and informed the [Brulés] of what Janis had told them, and invited them to join in the attack. As a natural result of Indian character the [Brulés] contended that they had as good right to make war upon the Pawnees as the "Cut Off." They could not understand why one band of Sioux should be prohibited from going to war and not another. As a consequence, although every effort was made by myself and interpreter to prevent a conflict, they proved useless.[29]

On August 3 the combined Sioux force, numbering over a thousand warriors, started down Frenchman's Fork toward its juncture with the Republican just east of Culbertson, a new trading post established the previous month. The first settlers had arrived in Hitchcock County in April, and there were now a dozen or so frontiersmen living along Blackwood Creek east and north of the trading post. One small party of Sioux raided the home of Galen E. Baldwin, stealing property and destroying goods while Mrs. Baldwin and the children (Mr. Baldwin was not home) watched from their hiding place in the creek bed. This is the only known time that any of the Hitchcock County frontiersmen were bothered by Indians.[30]

On that same evening, August 4, a fatal decision was being made at the Pawnee camp. Williamson later wrote:

> At 9 o'clock that evening three white men came into camp and reported to me that a large band of Sioux warriors were camped twenty five miles northwest, waiting for an opportunity to attack the Pawnees. . . . Previous to this white men had visited us and warned us to be on our guard against Sioux attacks, and I was a little skeptical as to the truth of the story. . . . But one of the men a young fellow about my age at the time, appeared to be so sincere in his efforts to impress upon me . . . that I took him to Sky Chief who was in command that day for a conference. Sky Chief said the men were liars; that they wanted to scare the Pawnees away from the hunting grounds so that white men could kill buffalo for hides. He told me I was a squaw and a coward. I took exception to his remarks and retorted: "I will go as far as you dare go. Don't forget that."[31]

At that point Williamson failed as trail agent. In a conflict between boyish egotism and his empowered duty, egotism won. His letters of instruction from Agent Burgess had been clear. If the possibility of trouble with other Indians arose, Williamson had the authority as well as the orders to use this authority to compel the Pawnees to do as he saw fit. Unfortunately the young greenhorn cared more about his own masculine image than he did his legal wards. The freedom of the hunt and the buffalo range after months of Quaker dictation caused Sky Chief to act rashly, and unfortunately Williamson did not have the maturity to withstand the chief's harangue.

The following morning, Tuesday, August 5, instead of moving east down the Republican Valley to probable safety, the Pawnee camp went downstream two miles and then turned northwest, following along the west bank of a canyon that cut almost entirely through the point of high divide which separated the Republican and Frenchman Valleys. The lower reaches of the canyon are steep, and the spring-fed creek is lined with cottonwood and ash. About three miles from its mouth the canyon has

low walls and finally blends into the divide. A short distance to the north
of this point is the head of another canyon which leads down into the
Frenchman Valley, and the Pawnees were apparently heading for this
route down from the divide.[32]

As they rode along, Sky Chief apologized to Williamson for his speech
of the previous night, but the chief was still so convinced of his own
wisdom that he did not send out scouts. Buffalo were sighted on the
divide, and the Pawnee men and their chief scattered to hunt, leaving
the women, children, and old men to continue their trek. A young warrior borrowed Williamson's gun and rode off to hunt, leaving him un-
armed. The Sioux killed several of the hunters first, and Sky Chief, caught
off guard, was one of the first to die. Shortly thereafter, according to
Williamson:

> I noticed a commotion at the head of the procession, which had
> suddenly stopped. I started to ride up where three of the chiefs
> were talking, when a boy of sixteen rode up and stopped me. Dis-
> mounting, he tied a strip of red flannel on the bridle of my horse,
> and after remounting told me that the Sioux were coming. What
> significance was attached to the red flannel on the bridle I was never
> able to learn.[33]

The women, children, and pack horses were hurriedly ordered into
the canyon, while the men regrouped and prepared to fight the Sioux.
Williamson conferred with Ter-ra-re-cox, a chief of the Skidi band, and
they agreed that the Pawnees should fall back down the canyon to the
trees, but Fighting Bear of the Kitkehahkis rashly demanded they make
their stand where they were, and in the end he won. Soon the main
element of the Sioux appeared, and, as the men rode out to meet them,
the Pawnee women began to chant the Pawnee war song. Williamson
advised Platt to get away down the canyon, which he did. When it became clear that the Pawnees were overwhelmingly outnumbered, it was
suggested that Williamson ride out and try to parlay with the Sioux. With
an interpreter he rode out a short way, but the Sioux ignored their white
flag and swept down upon them, firing as they came. The truce party
fled to the canyon, Williamson having his horse shot out from under him
just as he reached safety. The Sioux divided so that they controlled both
banks of the low canyon and were able to shoot down into the mass of
terrified Pawnees. Fighting Bear engaged in a duel of tomahawks with a
Sioux chief, and Williamson aided him by shooting and wounding the
Sioux.[34]

A retreat down the canyon was then ordered, and the packs of robes, meat, and equipment were cut from the horses. The withdrawal was a rout as the Sioux shot from both banks of the canyon into the fleeing Pawnees. Williamson joined in the flight, which left him with searing memories:

> I often have thought of a little Indian girl, who evidently had fallen from her mother's back, in our retreat down the canyon. She was sitting on the ground with her little arms raised as if pleading for some one to pick her up. As I passed I tried to pick her up but only succeeded in touching one of her hands. I couldn't return so she was left behind to suffer a horrible death.[35]

Royal Buck, founder of the little settlement at the mouth of Red Willow Creek thirty miles to the east, visited the canyon a few days later and in describing it was the first to use the name by which it is still known— Massacre Canyon:

> The first thing we met [at] the head of the canyon was the loading thrown off their pon[i]es, and this was done in a space of fifty yards, and over this space the ground was literally piled up with packed meat, robes, hides, tents, camp kettles, and in fact everything they carry on their hunting expeditions. . . . In one place is a pond hole two or three rods long, where, I should judge, near twenty bodies were lying in the most sickening state of decomposition. . . . In only one place is there any sign of resistance. This was about a mile and a half from the commencement of the retreat; here eight warriors took shelter behind a sort of bank or opening on one side of the canyon, and all of them are lying there in death, a squaw and pappoose with them.[36]

As the Pawnees reached the Republican Valley, the Sioux turned back up the canyon to the spoils of battle. The squaws who fell behind were raped, the bodies were mutilated, and some of them were burned on piles of camp robes. Why the Sioux withdrew after killing so few is not known. Williamson wrote that they were scared off by the arrival of the cavalry, but military reports show that Capt. Charles Meinhold and his small command were camped at the mouth of Blackwood Creek a dozen miles downstream and knew nothing of the battle until the Pawnee survivors arrived there. It is possible the Sioux had heard rumors of the military presence; perhaps in their excitement they simply quit, or perhaps it was their desire for the Pawnee goods and prisoners. Whatever the reason the Sioux ceased to follow the Pawnees and returned to their camps on Frenchman and Stinking Water creeks.[37]

Captain Meinhold and his command had left Fort McPherson in the Platte Valley on July 30 for a routine tour of the Republican country. This was done to keep track of the Indians, pacify the frontiersmen, and if needed protect the numerous surveying parties. In spite of Whistler's murder 1873 had been quiet on the frontier, and the army had not stationed troops in the valley that summer as it had the three previous years. Though the settlers at Culbertson, two miles west of Meinhold's camp, heard the sounds of the battle ten miles to the west, the military camp was apparently too far away. The first Meinhold knew of the battle was when Williamson, Fighting Bear, and two other chiefs crossed over from the south bank of the Republican and came into camp. At about the same time the first of the retreating Pawnees came into sight. The chiefs asked for military protection and to be allowed to join the army in finding the Sioux. Instead Meinhold told the Pawnees to continue down the Republican at least as far as Red Willow, while he would visit the canyon that afternoon.[38]

Meinhold's command rode to the battlefield and found two survivors, a wounded woman with a badly injured baby in a pool of water. Dr. Powell placed them in a more comfortable spot while the rest of the canyon was toured. When they returned, the woman was gone, and it appeared she had killed the child, which had fresh wounds on the head. A frontiersman from Red Willow County, William S. Fitch, who ran a small trading post on the Driftwood south of present McCook, also visited the canyon that afternoon with an eastern tourist. They found a wounded woman, probably the same one Dr. Powell had seen, and they took her by wagon back to Indianola, just east of the Red Willow settlement, where she died. The army counted sixty-three dead—thirteen men and fifty women and children. A census was later taken at the Pawnee reservation by Agent Burgess, and he concluded that the slain included twenty men, thirty-nine women and ten children, along with twelve wounded and several children still missing after eleven prisoners had been returned.[39]

Two Pawnee chiefs had remained in Meinhold's camp while he toured the canyon. Upon his return Meinhold (as he later reported)

> told the Pawnee chiefs to bring back about twenty men, and as many pack animals as they choose, to carry off the large amount of dried meat, camp equipage, furs, etc., abandoned by them in their flight, and that I would hold the Sioux in check, should they renew their attack.
>
> The Chiefs agreed to be back at sunrise next morning. I waited

until ten o'clock a.m. but the Pawnees not returning, I resumed my march.[40]

Meinhold in his report says the command then marched twenty miles up the Frenchman where they camped for the night, which should have brought them almost to the mouth of the Stinking Water. Lt. Joseph Lawson, a few enlisted men, and the guide, Leon Pallardie, were sent out to scout for the Sioux parties. The results of the scout were negative, as Meinhold reported:

> After the massacre the Sioux ran off at full speed, due west [north], in the direction of Alkali Station, not even stopping at night, as I ascertained afterwards. . . . I thoroughly scouted the country up the Stinkingwater, thence to the heads of Blackwood and Red Willow, without finding any signs of Indians.[41]

Dr. Powell's account is only slightly different:

> From this point Lieut. Lawson with a small party scouted along the stream as far as Stinking Water, where Pallarday, the guide found signs showing that a war party had recently passed northward towards Ogalalla. Captain Meinhold's scout visited places during this trip over which troops have never before passed.[42]

Leon Francois Pallardie was an old frontiersman, having come west with the American Fur Company as early as 1849, and he had served as guide and scout for the army at Fort McPherson since 1865, also working as an independent Indian trader. Probably no other person knew the Upper Republican country so well as he, and he had lived among Cut-off Oglalas and Brulés for many years. His inability to locate or follow a thousand warriors on horseback or to locate their villages (since it is likely the Brulé village was within ten miles of the army camp) is amazing. One can only conclude that Pallardie (if not Meinhold) had no interest in locating the Sioux. The command consisted of the two officers, one guide, and forty-nine enlisted men. Even allowing for Pawnee exaggeration, Meinhold and Pallardie knew they were following a huge war party. With the Sioux in an excited state of mind, it might have been foolhardy for the small company of soldiers to attempt to visit their villages. It would appear that Pallardie, and perhaps Meinhold, recognized the wisdom of the old cliche, "Discretion is the better part of valor."[43]

While the army toured the Frenchman and Stinking Water valleys, the Brulés were in their camp on the latter, and Stephen Estes gathered what information he could before writing his report for the Brulé agent at the reservation in Dakota Territory. He collected the prisoners the Brulés had taken—two girls, a woman, and a boy. He also reported that one Brulé had been killed and two or three mortally wounded. He expected Janis and the Cut-off Oglalas to join his camp within two days, after which he would take the prisoners to North Platte where they could be returned to the Pawnee reservation. Janis also wrote a report telling of his inability to control the Oglalas. His Indians had taken seven prisoners—three women and four girls aged two to ten years. He reported no Oglalas killed, but two were wounded. From other evidence, however, it seems likely that six Sioux were either killed or died of their wounds.[44]

Instead of waiting for the Oglalas Estes moved the Brulés to the Oglala camp on the Frenchman "about twelve miles above the timber." He collected the prisoners, and on August 8 he and Janis started for the Platte Valley. The Oglalas had been less eager to give up their prisoners than had the Brulés. Just before leaving, four Oglalas from the Red Cloud Agency came into the camp with the information that Utes had been seen on Chief Creek, a tributary of the Republican in the very western part of Dundy County. A raid was suggested, but Estes successfully interfered, saying that, if they went, he wanted nothing to do with them and that he would return to the reservation. The Cut-off bands of Pawnee Killer and Two Strikes were determined to go anyway, though there is no record whether or not they went. Estes, Janis, and the prisoners camped on the prairie the evening of their departure. In the morning they were amazed to find the Brulés in the hills around them, apparently frightened at the possible desertion of their subagent. Estes remained behind to gather the Brulés together while Janis went on with the prisoners. This took Estes several days, and, once done, he and the Brulés headed back to their reservation in Dakota, arriving there on August 27.[45]

The Pawnees, meanwhile, had been making their way back to their reservation. They had reached the settlement at Red Willow the afternoon of the battle. Their arrival created great consternation, as is shown in the reminiscences of a young widow, Sarah Wildman Leach:

> My only real experience with the Indians, however, occurred in 1873. I was working for Mrs. John Byfield near the mouth of the Willow. The Byfields had a store there. It was supper time and Mrs. Byfield told me to go into the cellar and freeze some ice cream while she prepared the rest of the meal. Soon she came running down [into the] cellar with my frightened children clinging to her hands. The children were crying "They'll kill us, they'll kill us," and Mrs. Byfield told me the place was surrounded by Indians. We did not know what to do, but I finally opened the door and looked out. I saw coming

toward me a white man, which greatly reassured me.[46]

As the Pawnees had lost all their supplies, Williamson purchased flour and sugar from Byfield to sustain them on the long journey back to the reservation. The chanting and wailing of the mourning Pawnees was an experience the Red Willow settlers never forgot. The Pawnees continued on downstream to Arapahoe, where they turned north and crossed back over the divide, as they had come the month before. They reached the Platte Valley at Plum Creek, where they received medical assistance from Dr. William M. Bancroft, after which they were put on trains and sent to Silver Creek, the railroad station nearest the reservation.[47]

On August 25 Agent Burgess sent Samuel C. Longshore, a teacher at the reservation, back to Massacre Canyon with authorization to bring back what goods he could find belonging to the Pawnees. Royal Buck reported that Longshore collected about six tons of robes, meat, and camp equipage. A great amount of goods had been taken by the frontiersmen of Red Willow and Hitchcock counties, some of which Longshore was able to retrieve. No doubt the battle was a boon to the frontiersmen of Hitchcock County who had arrived only that spring and had had but a poor farming season. Though only a few people lived there, the county was formally organized on August 30 in spite of reported fears of continued Indian problems. About the same time as Longshore's visit Agent Burgess also sent Williamson back to the battlefield to bury the dead, most of whom were laid along the canyon bank with dirt pushed off to cover them.[48]

For several months Burgess had correspondence with those trying to be paid for what years later in reminiscences they passed off as acts of humanitarianism. Antoine Janis tried to collect money for feeding the Pawnee prisoners. Dr. J. S. Shaw, a Red Willow frontiersmen, tried to collect for the burial of the Pawnee woman at Indianola. Dr. Bancroft of Plum Creek submitted a bill of sixty dollars for his work, but Agent Burgess cut it down to twelve "on account of the meager services [rendered] and he consented under protest when I paid the bill." John Byfield was paid $35.65 for the flour and sugar that Williamson had purchased at his trading post.[49]

The Pawnee made no more tribal buffalo hunts in Nebraska, and by 1876 all of the tribe had left for the Indian Territory, allowing their lands to be sold to the government and then opened to settlement as a part of the public domain. It has been said that the battle at Massacre Canyon played an important role in the Pawnee decision to leave Nebraska, but there is no documentation to support this claim. In fact, in councils with their agent the battle was barely mentioned. John

Williamson retained the friendship of the Pawnee and moved with them to the Indian Territory for several months before returning to Genoa, where he lived until his death on March 12, 1927, a highly respected frontiersman and Indian authority.[50]

On the fiftieth anniversary of the battle in 1923, the citizens of Trenton held the first Massacre Canyon Pow-Wow with Sioux survivors in attendance. The celebration was held annually (except for the World War II years) until the late 1950s. One of the more noted powwows was that of 1925, when both the Sioux and Pawnee survivors attended, and for the first time members of the two tribes smoked a pipe of peace. The Trenton people worked diligently to get the site of the battle appropriately marked, first through the state legislature and then through Congress. U.S. Representative Ashton C. Shallenberger succeeded in getting $7,500 appropriated for the marker, one of the few occasions when Congress passed a funding bill for the marking of what can be termed a *local* historical site. The thirty-five-foot-tall monument of Minnesota pink granite weighing ninety-one tons was dedicated September 26, 1930. It was placed on a point of land jutting out over the Republican Valley and overlooking the mouth of Massacre Canyon. Due to highway relocation, the monument was moved to a new site along U.S. Highway 34 in the late 1950s, where it is a popular spot for tourists.[51]

It is ironic that the major Nebraska monument to its once most powerful tribe, as well as its most powerful Indian ally, is a monument not to their grandeur but to one of their most noted defeats. Unfortunately it is an apt memorial to an Indian policy that only suffered the Indian ally, while tending to over-placate the Indian hostile. The Indians suffered many wrongs at the hands of the whites, but it should be remembered there was death, pillage, and rapine upon the Great Plains long before the arrival of the whites.

Notes

[1] David Franklin Powell letter, Aug. 17, 1873, *Omaha Daily Herald*, Aug. 21, 1873, as cited in Paul D. Riley, "Dr. David Franklin Powell and Fort McPherson," *Nebraska History* 51 (Summer 1970):163.

[2] George E. Hyde, *Pawnee Indians* (Denver: The University of Denver Press, 1951), 213–35.

[3] Ibid.

[4] "Pawnee Agency Council Minutes," Indian Archives Division, Oklahoma Historical Society, Oklahoma City, photostatic copy in Nebraska State Historical Society Archives, Lincoln, hereinafter cited as "Council Minutes." The council minutes are for October

1870 through July 1875 and usually include a complete transcription of the dialogue between the Pawnee chiefs and their agent. The minutes provide the most detailed and valuable information available on the Pawnee tribe.

[5] "Council Minutes," Mar. 27, 1871.

[6] Ibid., Mar. 27, 28, 1871.

[7] Ibid., June 8, 1872.

[8] Paul D. Riley, ed., "The Red Willow County Letters of Royal Buck, 1872–1873," *Nebraska History* 47 (Dec. 1966):371–73,392.

[9] Jacob M. Troth to Brig. Gen. Edward O. C. Ord, July 11, 1872; Troth to John B. Omohundro and Baptist Bayhylle, July 25, 1872, "Pawnee Agency Letterbook," Indian Archives Division, Oklahoma Historical Society, photostatic copy in Nebraska State Historical Society Archives, hereinafter cited as "Letterbook."

[10] Donald F. Danker, ed., *Man of the Plains: Recollections of Luther North, 1856–1882* (Lincoln: University of Nebraska Press, 1961), 170–74; John F. Reiger, ed., *The Passing of the Great West: Selected Papers of George Bird Grinnell* (New York: Winchester Press, 1972), 58–72. In the latter Grinnell tells of North and himself being attacked by Sioux on the open prairie south of Red Willow on their way back from the buffalo hunt. North does not mention such an encounter nor do any of the several letters available by Republican Valley frontiersmen; military reports from the region are equally silent as to Indian depredations in the region.

[11] W. M. Hinman letter, Sept. 1872, *Omaha Weekly Herald*, Sept. 18, 1872.

[12] *Compendium of History, Reminiscence and Biography of Western Nebraska* (Chicago: Alden Publishing Company, 1909), 772–73.

[13] J. F. Zediker letter, Dec. 16, 1872, *Daily State Journal* (Lincoln), Dec. 23, 1872.

[14] Troth to Barclay White, Nov. 9, 1872, "Letterbook."

[15] Joseph G. Rosa, *They Called Him Wild Bill: The Life and Adventures of James Butler Hickok* (Norman: University of Oklahoma Press, 1964), 143–54; Riley, "Royal Buck," 381–84; *Lowell Register,* Feb.6, 1873, as cited in the *Omaha Daily Herald,* Feb. 19, 1873.

[16] F. M. Lockard, *The History of the Early Settlement of Norton County, Kansas* (Norton: Champion Press, [1894]), 4, 5, 81; *Omaha Daily Herald,* Jan. 15, 1873.

[17] "Council Minutes," Jan. 13 and 24, 1873; William Burgess to White, Jan. 21, 1873, "Letterbook."

[18] *Omaha Daily Herald,* Jan. 12, 15, 17, 1873; "Corn Dodger," Jan. 27, 1873, *Omaha Republican,* Feb. 7, 1873.

[19] Burgess to White, Feb. 20, 1873, "Letterbook."

[20] *Genoa Leader–Times,* Mar. 18, 1927; J. W. Williamson, *The Battle of Massacre Canyon: The Unfortunate Ending of the Last Buffalo Hunt of the Pawnees* (Trenton, Nebr.: *Republican Leader,* 1922), 1; Burgess to White, June 24, 1873, "Letterbook."

[21] Burgess to Williamson, July 2, 1873, "Letterbook."

[22] Ibid.; Williamson, *Massacre Canyon,* 7.

[23] Williamson, *Massacre Canyon,* 2–7.

[24] D. R. Risley to Ord, Apr. 12, 1873; George A. Woodward to the assistant adjutant

general, Department of the Platte, July 25, 1873, Letters Received, Whetstone Agency, Records of the Bureau of Indian Affairs, Record Group 75, National Archives, Washington, D.C.; hereinafter cited as "Whetstone Agency Letters."

[25] George A. Woodward to asst. adj. gen., July 25, 1873, "Whetstone Agency Letters."

[26] Ibid.

[27] W. F. Barnard to the secretary of interior, July 22, 1873; William H. Belknap to the secretary of interior, Aug. 4, 1873, "Whetstone Agency Letters."

[28] Antoine Janis to J. W. Daniels, Aug. 5, 1873, "Indian Office Documents on Sioux–Pawnee Battle," *Nebraska History* 16 (July 1935):155, hereinafter cited as "Indian Office Documents."

[29] Stephen F. Estes to E. A. Howard, Aug. 28, 1873, "Indian Office Documents," 153.

[30] Galen E. Baldwin, *The West in Early Days* (n.p., n.d.); a typescript can be found in the Nebraska State Historical Society Library, Lincoln.

[31] Williamson, *Massacre Canyon*, 7.

[32] Ibid.

[33] Ibid., 8.

[34] Ibid., 8, 9.

[35] Ibid., 9, 10.

[36] Riley, "Royal Buck," 390, 391.

[37] Williamson, *Massacre Canyon*, 10; Capt. Charles Meinhold to 1st Lt. John B. Johnson, post adjutant, Fort McPherson, Aug. 17, 1873, National Archives, photostatic copy of report in possession of author [The research papers of the late Paul Riley are housed at the Nebraska State Historical Society, where the copy of this report should be found.–Ed.].

[38] Ibid.

[39] Ibid.; William S. Fitch, "Massacre Canyon," *Indianola Reporter*, July 30, 1925; Burgess to White, Sept. 13, 1873, "Letterbook."

[40] Meinhold to Johnson, Aug. 17, 1873.

[41] Ibid.

[42] Riley, "Dr. Powell," 163.

[43] Ibid., 169 n.13.

[44] Estes to Howard, Aug. 6, 1873; Janis to Daniels, Aug. 5, 1873, "Indian Office Documents," 150, 151, 155.

[45] Estes to Howard, Aug. 28, 1873, "Indian Office Documents," 152, 153.

[46] Sarah Wildman Leach Black, "Memoirs of Pioneer Days in Southwest Nebraska," *Maywood Eagle–Reporter*, July 13, 1929.

[47] Black, "Memoirs"; William M. Bancroft, "Plum Creek (Lexington) Nebraska," Nebraska Society of the Daughters of the American Revolution, *Collection of Nebraska Pioneer Reminiscences* (Cedar Rapids, Ia.: Torch Press, 1916), 59, 60; Burgess to White, Oct. 14, 1873, "Letterbook."

[48] Riley, "Royal Buck," 393; Williamson, *Massacre Canyon*, 13.

[49] Burgess to Janis, Sept. 25, 1873; Burgess to John Byfield, Sept. 27, 1873; Burgess to White, Oct. 14, 1873; Burgess to Byfield, Dec. 24, 1873; Burgess to J. S. Shaw and Louis B. Korns, Jan. 19, 1874, "Letterbook."

[50] *Genoa Leader–Times,* Mar. 18, 1927; "Council Minutes," 1873–74 passim.

[51] Asahel L. Taylor, "Building the Massacre Canyon Monument," *Nebraska History* 16 (July 1935):171–77; *Souvenir Edition: 25th Anniversary of the Founding of Massacre Canyon Pow-Wow* (Trenton, Nebr.: Trenton Register, 1948), 20–23.

Part 3

Red Cloud Agency
in the Spotlight

Although small bands of raiders occasionally roamed the Platte and Republican country through the early 1870s, the Indian threat to the burgeoning railroad settlements had ended. The attention shifted northward to the Black Hills and the Great Sioux Reservation, the lands guaranteed to the Sioux in the Fort Laramie Treaty of 1868.

Before the treaty, Lakota warriors and their Cheyenne and Arapaho allies had closed the Bozeman Trail, ridded themselves of the hated soldier forts that guarded it, and brought the U.S. government to the peace table. Red Cloud, the Oglala patriot–warrior, had transformed himself from a wildly successful war leader to a nationally recognized political figure. His every word and deed, whether in Washington before the president or at the agency bearing his name, captured the attention of the reading public. When the Red Cloud Agency relocated from the North Platte River near Fort Laramie to the White River in northwest Nebraska, attention followed to that locale. The government representatives stationed at this lonely outpost of civil authority soon became mired in controversy and threatened with danger. The agent to Red Cloud's Oglalas inevitably demanded military protection, and the army obliged in 1874.

Charles W. Allen rendered an eyewitness account of "the flagpole incident," a noted Red Cloud Agency episode in 1874 whose sparks nearly set off a powder keg. His reminiscence, "Red Cloud and the U.S. Flag," appeared in the October–December 1940 issue of *Nebraska History* (21:293–304). Allen wrote an immensely valuable first-person account of the Ghost Dance troubles on Pine Ridge Reservation and the 1890 Wounded Knee Massacre, a copy of which the Nebraska State Historical Society holds. His sketch of the earlier flagpole incident appeared as an early chapter in this autobiography. The excerpt in *Nebraska History* remains one of the few surviving accounts.

Harry H. Anderson, noted Plains Indian wars authority, examined "The War Club of Sitting Bull the Oglala," in *NH* 42 (Mar. 1961):55–62. The scholarly studies of material culture and vintage photography have long garnered attention by students of the Indian wars and of the frontier military, and Anderson neatly combines both in this early article. His study, which relied heavily on first person accounts, also illuminates much about the affairs of Red Cloud Agency during this fitful time.

Chapter 5

Red Cloud and the U.S. Flag

Charles W. Allen

Editor's note: Among the many frontier friends of the editor of this magazine was and is Maj. Charles W. Allen of Martin, South Dakota. His life is
one of the most picturesque of all the men on the Nebraska frontier.
Leaving home while yet a boy, he found his way to the Great Plains and
the Rocky Mountain region. He became in turn a mule driver on freighting trains, soldier in a frontier regiment, homesteader, manager of a
blacksmith shop, editor of frontier newspapers, postmaster at Pine Ridge
Agency, cattleman, poet, and historian.

In recent years Major Allen has written the story of his life. From the
manuscript of this story, with his permission, the editor has chosen one
of the most dramatic narratives of all the true stories of the Indian frontier. It is the story of the raising of the United States flag at the Red
Cloud Indian Agency in October 1874; the resistance of Red Cloud and
other Indians to raising the flag; the conflict between the United States
and the Sioux Indians over the event; the conflict between rival groups
of the Indians themselves; the near precipitation of a battle which inevitably would have ended in the complete destruction of all the white men
at the Red Cloud Agency and at Fort Robinson three miles away; and the
final outcome of the controversy, with the flag of the United States flying at the top of a tall pole above both white men and Indians at Red
Cloud Agency.—Addison E. Sheldon.

Allen's Account

My wife and I lived on our little homestead, where I cut hay and gar-
dened between freighting trips. I was so engaged when one balmy autumn morning I met an old friend known as "Big Bat." This was Baptiste
Pourier, post guide and interpreter, who importuned me to accompany
him to Fort [Camp] Robinson and the Red Cloud Agency, as he had been
ordered to deliver despatches there by ten o'clock the next day. Never
having been over that section, I was glad to accede to his wish. . . .

Red Cloud Agency

Soon we were again among the trees where the embryo river in the form of a rippling brook wound its serpentine course through the falling leaves that were stirred from their branches by the cool October breeze. Within a mile or two of the mouth of this picturesque canyon, where the little valleys begin to broaden and the little stream with its numerous springs gradually deepened into the White River, the road left its banks and rose to the top of a hill at the edge of an extensive valley surrounded by irregular pine ridges. In front of us on either side of the road a large Arapaho village met our gaze. A little farther on near the mouth of Soldier Creek lay Fort Robinson, and up this branch still farther to the north was a large Cheyenne village. In plain view to the east was a cluster of buildings, and from the front of one rose a crude miniature tower with portico attachments, which through the haze of morning were suggestive of some ancient feudal castle. This was the Red Cloud Agency, and round about it up the rivulets that came out of the hills camps of family groups of lodges were scattered in every direction. However, Red Cloud's main camp of thousands a little farther east was obscured by a low chain of grass-covered hills.

All this panorama lay before me as we dismounted and I stood holding our horses while Big Bat delivered his despatches to the commander at the post. When he rejoined me, I learned that he was given the remainder of the day and the next to rest before returning to Fort Laramie. So we cantered merrily down toward the agency, and after visiting for awhile I amused myself by looking it over. . . . I found that uppermost in the minds of its residents was the controversy between Chief Red Cloud and Dr. [J. J.] Saville, the Indian agent, over the erection of a flagstaff.

It seems that the Indians, being entirely ignorant of the general significance of this simple patriotic ceremony of raising the flag over all public institutions, felt that it was only an emblem of their natural enemy—not of the soldiers themselves but of the army in action—and that in some way the placing of the flag over the agency would make soldiers of them.

Red Cloud and many—but not all—of his headmen joined in the opposition to the raising of the flag. It is said that Red Cloud in emphatic tones told the agent that it should not be done, that the soldiers already had the flag floating over their fort, and they should be satisfied with that.

The agent, being right and knowing it, told Red Cloud with equal emphasis that the flag would be raised. It was reported that the chief and agent had had several quarrels over it, when one day the agency teams pulled into the yard with a fine tall pole and deposited it in the court under the angry glances of many eyes, but no actual opposition arose, and the men went on about their business.

Whether these controversies were conducted by the agent in a calm, prudent, and conciliatory manner is not now known, but current rumor had it that both he and the chief were hotheaded. One thing is certain: if the agent permitted temper to usurp the place of cool reasoning, he and many others soon had ample reason to regret it.

The last Oglala agency to be named for Chief Red Cloud was situated in a picturesque bend of White River a mile or two above the present site of the city of Crawford, Nebraska. It stood on fairly level ground and was built in the form of a square, with its principal face to the south, but it also faced the east and the west, with the inner space at the rear of the buildings forming a sort of court. To the north were located the wood and hay yards, with the barn and large barnyards on the crest of the hill that leads down to the river. All of the long ricks of dry pitch-pine cordwood, the long, tall stacks of hay—in fact, everything save the three entrances of the main building—were surrounded by a tall fence of native pine lumber furnished by the sawmill on the river bank below the hill. On each side of the main buildings, across the space of an average town square but not at very regular angles, were numerous log residences and the traders' stores.

A word about Fort Robinson, which I had visited previous and observed with some care. It comprised all the buildings considered necessary to the customary military post of the frontier but larger than were required for the few companies of cavalry then occupying it. These buildings, like those of the agency, were of rough lumber sawed from the nearby pines, with here and there one of sawed or peeled logs. Near all the living quarters, mess houses, and the bakery were ricks of fine, dry pine wood. Hundreds of cords of it were ricked at right angles on the east and north fronts of the main buildings, serving as temporary fence and windbreak. In the yards near the spacious barn were long, tall ricks containing hundreds of tons of hay.

I had noticed these details naturally without any particular motive as one is apt to do on entering an interesting place for the first time, but this picture in a different setting and with very different possibilities came vividly to my mind less than twenty-four hours later.

Having spent the afternoon and evening in visiting and looking over the agency, I returned to the cabins for the night and awakened next morning to a day of strange entertainment.

There seemed nothing unusual about the early morning of October

27 [23], 1874. The same clear sunshine tempered the soft, balmy breezes that characterized the late fall weather in this latitude. Yet everyone seemed to feel that strange events were pending. Rumors? Yes! The air was full of them. It seemed that everyone eagerly sought or more eagerly gave of them. On the western front the denizens of those vast spaces listened to and liked them. To them rumor was the spice in the lonely monotony of their lives, as radio is to the lonely lives today. They knew, of course, that rumor was always accompanied by the aggravating static of unreliability, but they also knew it to be self-analyzing and that sooner or later its component parts, its truth—if any—would stand revealed.

As visitors (mostly women) were continually coming and going from the Rocky Bear lodge that stood on a spring creek near the agency, rumors of the flag dispute grew thicker and darker. We remarked also that riders were beginning to scatter hither and yon, yet with an evident plan. Most of them were in warrior regalia, their steeds painted in varied colors and decked with feathers of gaudy hue on mane and tail. We soon discovered that each hill and prominent knoll was occupied by several warriors, sitting their mounts silently in the capacity of sentinels.

Our view from the depression by the spring branch was not extensive to the east and south, but to the north the short distance to the box elder trees skirting the river and the high stone hills beyond was unobstructed. It was also clear up the river to the post and the Cheyenne and Arapaho villages and the whole pine-encircled amphitheater in which they nestled. To the south and west, as far as the base of the timbered hills, only the outlines of a galaxy of small prairie hills were visible. We could see the lodges farthest south of the agency and the open spaces near them, and about each of these we saw bunches of ponies, all hobbled.

At the time I was not sufficiently versed in the customs of the Indians to realize the significance of this arrangement, and my companions, thinking perhaps that I knew as well as they, said nothing of the fact that these ponies were being held in readiness to be packed or hitched to travoys containing all the camp equipment, should occasion arise.

It was about nine o'clock when first a low, rumbling sound from the east reached our ears. As its source approached, it grew louder and clearer and was easily recognized as the thundering of horses' hoofs, and we realized that the threat of opposing the flag-raising was being carried out. We could also distinguish the sounds incident to the hurrying and scurrying of the people at the agency and adjacent lodges.

Presently Rocky Bear came slowly down the hill road, turned to the bend where his ponies were feeding, dismounted as he took off their hobbles, then drove them past us up to a small corral. When they were safely behind the bars and he had exchanged a few words in low tones with the old woman who had remained to watch the lodge, he rode past us again in stoical silence on his return trip to the agency.

The speed of the charge had slackened as the riders neared the lodges east of the agency buildings. The wild, rhythmic sound that for some time had mingled with the clatter of hammering hoofs now swelled into the ancient war song of the Sioux, pierced continually with shuddering yells of defiance.

Thus far we had judged the momentous proceedings by the sounds arising therefrom, but our understanding was afterward fully verified by the many recitals of those within the stockade—that inviting but dangerous trap that appeared to be the only shelter from the terror confronting them. It soon contained not only the agent and all of his employes, but every civilized person in the vicinity except ourselves and one or two others who were caught on the east side of the agency.

We were on the west side, which was no ill luck, however, for had the riot gotten from under control (which at all times it seemed on the point of doing), there was but one fate awaiting all—death, either swift or lingering, with the additional horror of cremation for those who would have faced their slayers inside the stockade or at the military post.

I learned from John Farnham, who was employed at the agency at that time, and from Big Bat and others that Louis Richards [Richard] and Joseph Bissonette, Jr., were then the official interpreters of the agency. They were intelligent mixed-bloods of the Sioux, of middle age, and with standing and influence among their people. Others of the same class were equally efficient as interpreters, among them being Louis Shangrau and William Garnett, who, with the two first mentioned, were of the Oglala, Red Cloud's band of Sioux.

There were other interpreters from the Spotted Tail and Missouri River bands who chanced to be present on this occasion: Louis Bordeaux, John Brugier [Bruguier], and Louis Robideaux. Bordeaux was official interpreter at the Spotted Tail Agency and was noted for his fluent command of both the English and the Sioux Indian languages. There were several others whose names I failed to learn, but all were of mixed blood. No white interpreter was used that day. It required men of the tribe who were loyal to both sides to be effective, and only through the untiring efforts of these men was catastrophe averted.

Under the direction of the agent and the guidance of the experienced men about him in a room just behind the platform of the portico from which they spoke, these interpreters, in relays of two, were kept busy constantly haranguing their excited and misguided brethren in the interest of peace.

All those on the agency hill could see the approaching mass of men, estimated to have been about fifteen hundred mounted warriors, increasing their speed gradually but methodically until within half a mile from the agency, where they began their charge. They slowed down as they came to the outer edge of the village, through which they scattered and reassembled on the open spaces about the buildings. There they came to a halt while Red Cloud, accompanied by several of his subchiefs, opened and passed through the double gates, then marched out to the center of the court where lay the pole that was to have served as flagstaff. Here, with axes that had been hidden under their blankets, they cut the pole into short lengths and then returned to disappear among their waiting comrades. Immediately John Farnham was despatched to the gate, to take the part of "Horatius at the Bridge."

During all of this time there was a roar of argument, voices raised in conflicting sentiments among the Indians assembled in front and earnest pleadings for peace from the interpreters on the balcony.

The advocates for and against the execution of a sentence of death and destruction continued hour after hour. Often they came to blows with whips or bows (wild Indians did not use their fists) on the heads and shoulders of their opponents, accompanied by assorted epithets, and the wild shrieks and yells of opposing forces were continuous. Yet the neverending stream of pacific oratory rolling out over the heads of the avengers was steadily producing the desired effect as the hours passed.

The women of the nearby lodges and camps, practically all of whom were for peace, contributed their share by following the usual Indian custom of preparing feasts for all, friend and stranger alike. Those not busy with the food mingled with the seething throng, collecting them in parties of three to five by coaxing them to "come and eat," and taking care that a goodly number of the most rabid agitators were included. Always the invitation was accepted, and, stalking sullenly or riding, they went in to the feast. Though they ate rapidly and returned at once to the strife, it was with temper more pliable and demeanor more sane, try as they would to conceal it.

This was true also of the massed cordon of those on foot completely surrounding the stockade. They had enlarged knotholes and cut other openings through the high board fence with their butcher knives, giving them a clear view of everything within. They carried tufts of dry grass under their blankets and were ready at the signal to hurl firebrands onto the ricks of wood and stacks of hay in the yards.

It was nearly eleven o'clock, and we were moving about our restricted space in the cabin yards when there came riding coolly and quietly down the road from the agency a young man who was recognized at once as Michael Dunn, the boss of the beef herd a few miles south. It seems that he was at the agent's office and was caught with the others. He was acting in the capacity of courier to the post to which service he had volunteered. We divined the purpose of the trip and admired his unconcerned attitude and even gait—the surest warrant of safety. The Indian outlooks [lookouts] on the hills paid little attention to his movements.

It was not long after he entered the post until we saw a file of cavalrymen move out and take the road toward us. As the detail passed, we counted some twenty-five or thirty men, with Mike Dunn riding in front beside an officer whom my companions recognized as Lieutenant [Emmet] Crawford [of the Third Cavalry].

This passing of soldiers toward the stockade was the most ominous incident we had yet observed. My companions, who understood Indians, felt positive that their appearance would be like a lighted match to the magazine and that their smaller number was an invitation. For a short time it seemed that their prophecy was to be fulfilled, for when the detail first appeared on the scene we could hear pandemonium break loose in wild yells and the resumption of noisy strife. Then there was a rush for the soldiers which the peace party frustrated, and this led to another and more personal mix-up in which the usual taunting language was heard, together with vigorous whipping over the head with quirts and switches. It was said that one of the warriors laid hold of Lieutenant Crawford's bridle rein, but the lieutenant reached down and caught him by the shoulder, whirling him from the path as he kept steadily on to the gates that were quickly opened by John Farnham and as quickly closed after the detail had filed through.

It was natural and fitting that when the little city of Crawford sprang up at this historic point, it should be named for the man who heroically executed his orders that day in the face of a situation that presaged certain death. It was for this and other meritorious conduct during the years that followed that this gallant officer received the promotions rapidly accorded him.

The friends of Red Cloud claimed that he had overplayed his hand and lost control of the day, as his only object was to prevent the flag-raising. It was said that he and his advisors had remained inactive in a nearby lodge during the whole disturbance. Be that as it may, another staff was soon secured, and the flag went up without opposition.

I have never learned of a reasonable excuse for sending for those soldiers. Under the circumstances they could not have rendered any saving service. They were a dangerous aggravation to the Indians at first, but a different idea soon prevailed among them. They did not even try to follow the soldiers through the gate. Why should they? If the threatened storm had broken, they would have been just so many more mice in the trap. The troop was well equipped with arms. Yes, but so were we all. Arms, when outnumbered a hundred to one, might just as well have been toothpicks.

However, so far as the question of safety was concerned, the little detail might as well be there as at their home post, of which we had a complete view. The verdure between us, which for years had been ravaged by fire and by the later onslaught of camps and herds, was not dense, and from the beginning of the disturbance to its end we could see that all the prairie ground lying between the post and the base of the pine-covered hills to the west and north was black with Cheyenne and Arapaho warriors. Sitting silently on their mounts, they virtually surrounded the post on all sides save the east, which faced the agency. The significance of this arrangement was plain, as they were waiting for the first puff of smoke to go up over the stockade as a signal for the onslaught, and they would have duplicated at the post whatever occurred at the agency. This means that within ten minutes after such a signal, the weakly garrisoned post would have been a seething inferno, with Death stalking on every side over its parade grounds and through all of its byways. The tinder of its pine structure and other inflammable material would have furnished a flaming sepulcher for those who remained in the post, and those who fled would have met death at the hands of the cordon of Indians who awaited their appearance.

As the afternoon wore away, the portents of peace became more apparent. The watchers on the hills were constantly but quietly retiring from their positions, and the babble of voices was subsiding. About half past two o'clock the troop of cavalry marched back to the post. Groups of Indian riders were seen frequently moving toward the east, and the women were returning to their lodges. Then Rocky Bear came riding past, and, seeing a more serene face as he lowered the bars and turned his ponies out to graze, we knew that the nightmare of uncertainty was ended.

From that moment until bedtime we were in constant conversation with those who had witnessed the whole proceeding. It was then we learned that before the boss herder, Michael Dunn, had volunteered to take a despatch to the post, the agent had sent a loyal Indian, named Speeder, on the same mission, but his own people had intercepted him and beaten him so badly that he lived only a short time.

The following morning Big Bat and I started on our return trip, leisurely. About midnight we camped in the hills twenty-five miles north of Fort Laramie and rested in our saddleblankets until the gray dawn, then proceeded to the post and home.

Chapter 6

The War Club of
Sitting Bull the Oglala

Harry H. Anderson

One of the more noteworthy items in the Nelson A. Miles Collection of
Indian artifacts belonging to the Museum of the American Indian in
New York City is a lever action Henry repeating rifle bearing the inscription "Sitting Bull from the President for Bravery and Friendship." The
Sitting Bull to whom this rifle was given was a headman of the Oglala
Sioux and as much a friend to the white man as his more widely known
namesake, the Hunkpapa Sitting Bull, was an enemy.[1] On October 23,
1874, in the so-called "flagpole affair" at old Red Cloud Agency near
Fort Robinson, the Oglala Sitting Bull performed one of the significant
acts of "bravery and friendship" for which he was awarded the engraved
repeater by President Ulysses S. Grant. And interestingly enough, this
reward, in the form of one unusual weapon, was a recognition of services
rendered with another very distinctive instrument of combat—Sitting
Bull's famous three-bladed war club.

Eyewitness accounts of the flagpole affair, one of the several wild riots
that took place at Red Cloud Agency in 1873 and 1874, include descriptions of the Sitting Bull war club. This incident had its beginnings in an
attempt by the Red Cloud agent, Dr. J. J. Saville, to set up a flagpole
inside the agency stockade. A considerable force of northern Indians,
the nonagency hunting bands who had come to winter on free government beef, entered the stockade to destroy the pine trunk that was to fly
the national standard. Agent Saville's attempts to prevent the northern
warriors from chopping the pole to pieces proved fruitless, and he sent
an appeal for assistance to nearby Fort Robinson.

In his haste the excited Saville neglected to emphasize to the military
authorities either the violent attitude displayed by the Indians or the
large number of warriors involved in the demonstration. Only a single
troop of cavalry was sent to Saville's aid. Before this detachment could
reach the agency, it was surrounded by a huge crowd of angry Sioux,

who shouted insults at the soldiers and did everything possible to pro-
voke them into firing and precipitating an engagement. A fight was nar-
rowly averted by the intervention of the agency Sioux. These Oglalas,
permanent residents at Red Cloud Agency, beat back the northern Indians with war clubs, whips, and gun butts and opened a path for the
soldiers to reach the stockade.[2]

Among the leaders of the agency Indians was Sitting Bull, a headman
of the Oglala Kiyuksa band. Billy Garnett, Sioux mixed-blood and long
time interpreter at Pine Ridge Agency, was present at the time and some
years later gave the following description of the incident:

> Just then the Minor Sitting Bull appeared on the scene with his
> three knives on a sweeping handle. He was knocking men and horses
> right and left with the power of a giant and commanding the Indi-
> ans to scatter and depart from the agency.[3]

All accounts of the dispersal of the northern Indians place emphasis
on the strength and personal courage displayed by Sitting Bull. Yet considerable credit for his effectiveness must be given to the weapon he
used. Two other old residents of Pine Ridge Reservation who were at the
Red Cloud stockade during the flagpole affair confirm Garnett's description of the war club. According to Richard Stirk, Sitting Bull "had a big
knife a long handle about three feet long with 3 blades in it." Ben Tibbitts
also referred to the weapon as "a long knife—3 or 4 blades in a long
handle."[4]

The summer following the flagpole affair, in June 1875, Sitting Bull
was a member of a large delegation of Oglalas and other Sioux who were
summoned to Washington for conferences regarding the proposed relin-
quishment of the Black Hills by the Indians. While in the capital, in
recognition of his support of Agent Saville and as an example to the
other Sioux leaders, Sitting Bull was presented with the engraved rifle
by the president.[5]

Barely a year and a half later Sitting Bull was killed, and ironically it
was this weapon that placed him in the situation that resulted in his
death. In the fall of 1876, when a government commission came to Red
Cloud Agency with the treaty taking the Powder River and Black Hills
country from the Sioux, Sitting Bull rebelled at the pretension of the
commissioners that this agreement would be beneficial to the Indians.
He angrily broke up one meeting with the government representatives
by driving the Sioux chiefs out of the council room with the same three-
bladed knife he had used during the flagpole affair. A short time previ-

ous to this the engraved rifle had been loaned to a friend going to the hostile Sioux camp of Crazy Horse, and now Sitting Bull, disgusted with the situation at the agency, set out for the northern country to get back his rifle.[6]

When Sitting Bull reached the Crazy Horse village, then located on the lower Yellowstone between the mouths of the Tongue and Powder rivers, he found considerable sentiment in the camp for ending the current hostilities with the whites, the so-called Sioux War of 1876. Sitting Bull agreed to lead a delegation into the military cantonment at the mouth of Tongue River to see what terms the army was prepared to offer. As the peace party approached the post, they were met by a number of their hereditary enemies, the Crows, who were then serving as scouts for the army. After a preliminary exhibition of friendship the Crows treacherously fired upon the Sioux, murdering Sitting Bull and four others in the advance party.[7]

Col. Nelson A. Miles was commanding officer at the Tongue River post, and he acquired Sitting Bull's engraved rifle after the killing. The rifle was part of the Miles Collection given to the Museum of the American Indian by the Miles family in 1929.

The other part of the Oglala Sitting Bull's distinctive armament, the three-bladed war club, attracted the interest of the present writer several years ago after the examination of a collection of photographs taken at Fort Laramie in 1868. Two of these Fort Laramie views depict a group of white men and Indians, including one warrior identified as "Packs the Drum."[8] In several contemporary accounts Packs the Drum, or Drumpacker, is recorded as an alias of Sitting Bull the Oglala.[9] These two pictures, therefore, provided views of Sitting Bull at a much earlier age than had previously been available.

The photographs, however, are even more significant because they show Sitting Bull holding a war club of particular construction—a handle at the end of which were fixed two knife blades. At first it appeared that this was the celebrated war club used by Sitting Bull at the time of the flagpole affair, but upon careful examination, important inconsistencies were noted. First, the weapon in the photos appeared to be only a little over two feet in length, while Garnett, Stirk, and Tibbitts all had the distinct impression that it was longer, Stirk saying about three feet. More important, these descriptions all mentioned three blades. The club in the photos showed only two. Since the Indian in the photos had been identified as Drumpacker or Sitting Bull and he was holding a war club of this unusual type, it seemed that perhaps the recollections of Judge Ricker's informants were at fault.

A chance inquiry to the Museum of the American Indian where the Sitting Bull rifle is displayed brought the surprising reply that the Miles Collection did, in fact, contain a war club in the form of knife blades fixed in a wooden handle. A photo that followed vindicated the memories of Garnett, Stirk, and Tibbitts, for the weapon was exactly as they described it, a long sweeping handle into the end of which were fixed at ninety degree angles, three very wicked looking Green River blades.[10] This was the Sitting Bull war club that had been used in the flagpole affair. It had come into the possession of Colonel Miles in December 1876, but apparently its uniqueness had not been fully appreciated because of the even more unusual nature of the other Sitting Bull weapon, the engraved repeating rifle.

The war club was fashioned from a piece of board varying from $5/8$ to $3/4$ inches in thickness. Its overall length is forty inches. The width at the handle grip is $1 1/4$ inches and $1 3/4$ inches at the upper end. Three six-inch Green River blades are inserted into the heavier end. Attached to the handle are three grizzly bear claws and a rawhide trailer onto which are sewed a number of brass trade bells.

As for the war club in the Fort Laramie photographs, it clearly was an earlier version of the weapon used with devastating effect by Sitting Bull to establish his reputation as a leader among the Oglala warriors. An approximate estimate of the size of this 1868 model can be obtained from a careful examination of the photographs.[11] It takes little imagination to appreciate why this and the improved pattern of 1874 were so effective in the hands of as courageous a warrior as Sitting Bull.

In view of his strong friendship for the white man it seems more than unfortunate that Sitting Bull's accomplishments have not been properly appreciated, particularly in view of the notoriety afforded the less peaceably inclined of his fellow tribesmen such as Red Cloud, Crazy Horse, and the Hunkpapa Sitting Bull. Yet, small consolation though it may be, more is known about the personal weapons of Sitting Bull the Oglala, his engraved rifle and now his three-bladed war club, than of those belonging to any other notable personality among the Indians of the Great Plains.

Notes

[1] This contrast is emphasized in Mari Sandoz, "There Were *Two* Sitting Bulls," *Blue Book Magazine* 90 (Nov. 1949):58–64. This article may be found also in *Hostiles and Friendlies: Selected Short Writings of Mari Sandoz* (Lincoln: University of Nebraska Press, 1959).

[2] For a more complete account of this incident and the other difficulties caused by the northern Indians at Red Cloud Agency from 1871 to 1875, see George E. Hyde, *Red Cloud's Folk: A History of the Oglala Sioux Indians* (Norman: University of Oklahoma Press, 1937), 197–229, and Roger T. Grange, "Fort Robinson, Outpost on the Plains," *Nebraska History* 39 (Sept. 1959):193–208.

[3] Interview by Eli S. Ricker with Billy Garnett at Cane Creek, S.Dak., Jan. 10, 1907, tablet 2, Eli S. Ricker Collection, MS8, Nebraska State Historical Society Archives, Lincoln.

[4] Interviews by Ricker with Richard Stirk at his home north of White River in South Dakota, Nov. 10, 1906, and with Ben Tibbetts at his home north of White River and eighteen miles above Interior, S.Dak., Nov. 12, 1906, tablet 8, Ricker Collection.

[5] *New York Tribune*, June 7, 1875.

[6] Garnett interview. Sitting Bull's actions at the Black Hills councils were the subject of a report by Col. Ranald S. Mackenzie, commanding officer at Fort Robinson, to his superiors, Generals George Crook and Philip H. Sheridan. See George W. Manypenny, *Our Indian Wards* (Cincinnati: Robert Clarke & Co., 1880), 355, 356. Manypenny, who was a member of the treaty commission, denies Sitting Bull performed any acts of a violent nature or that he broke up the council. However, Billy Garnett, an interpreter at the council, gives much the same account of the incident in his interview as does Colonel Mackenzie's report. Garnett also is the source for the statement that Sitting Bull left the agency to get back his rifle. The *New York Sun*, Apr. 21, 1877, contained a letter from Red Cloud Agency that reported Sitting Bull had been sent to the Crazy Horse camp by General Crook in an attempt to get the hostiles to surrender. "Peace-talkers" were sent out by the army both before and after Sitting Bull's departure, but in view of the charges by Colonel Mackenzie, it is highly unlikely that Sitting Bull served in such a capacity.

[7] *Army and Navy Journal*, Feb. 3, 1877.

[8] Mrs. Margaret Blaker, archivist of the Bureau of American Ethnology, Smithsonian Institution, Washington, D.C., kindly supplied copies of the two photos in question. They first appeared in Merrill J. Mattes, "The Sutler's Store at Fort Laramie," *Annals of Wyoming* 18 (July 1946):134,135, and later in Martin F. Schmitt and Dee Brown, *Fighting Indians of the West* (New York: Charles Scribner's Sons, 1948), 36. The originals are in the William Selby Harney Collection of the Missouri Historical Society, St. Louis. The identifications were secured by Walter Mason Camp from elderly informants, both white and Indian, on the Sioux reservations in 1918.

[9] The Garnett interview states that Sitting Bull "also had the name Drum Carrier." White Bull, a nephew of the Hunkpapa Sitting Bull, told Stanley Vestal that the Indian called Young Sitting Bull who was killed at the Tongue River post (later Fort Keogh) was also known as "Drumpacker." Stanley Vestal, *New Sources of Indian History, 1850–1891: The Ghost Dance, The Prairie Sioux, A Miscellany* (Norman: University of Oklahoma Press, 1934), 182. Finally, in the testimony taken during the investigation of affairs at Red Cloud Agency under Agent Saville, there are references to the headmen at the agency, including "The One that Carried the Drum" (so called by the trader Jules Ecoffey). *Report of the Special Commission Appointed to Investigate the Affairs of the Red Cloud Indian Agency, July, 1875* (Washington: Government Printing Office, 1875), 216.

[10] Frederick J. Dockstader, director of the Museum of the American Indian, New York, N.Y., to the author, Feb. 13, 1959. I am indebted to Mr. Dockstader for per-mitting me to examine the war club during a visit to the museum in March 1960 [Since the original publication, this institution is now a part of the Smithsonian Institution's National Museum of the American Indian.–Ed.].

[11] The 1868 club was made from a cut-down gunstock. This was the most common type of knife–club weapon used by the American Indians.

The walled enclosure of Red
Cloud Agency, where the
government agent attempted
to fly the American flag.
Courtesy NSHS (J82-80).

Agent J. J. Saville, whose
imprudent actions helped
precipitate the "flagpole
incident." Courtesy NSHS
(F711.5-4).

Charles W. Allen, eyewitness to the Red Cloud Agency
"flagpole incident." Courtesy NSHS (P853).

Rocky Bear, an Oglala Lakota leader at Red Cloud Agency.
Courtesy NSHS (s856.9-5).

This portrait, taken in an Omaha studio, featured three noted Lakota personalities: Red Cloud (*standing, right*); Sitting Bull, the Oglala (*seated, left*); and
Spotted Tail (*seated, right*). Courtesy NSHS (M613-8a).

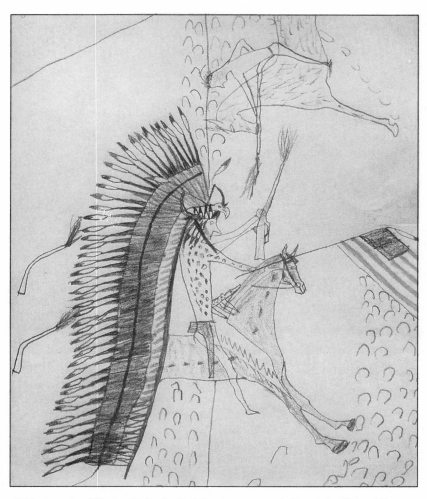

Self-portrait of Sitting Bull, the Oglala. An esteemed ally of the United States, Sitting Bull held a rifle in one hand and an American flag in the other, his three-bladed club rested at his side. Courtesy Thaw Collection, Fenimore House Museum, Cooperstown, New York (т366).
Photo credit: John Bigelow Taylor, NYC.

Sitting Bull (*third from left*), the
Oglala warrior with the famous war
club, was photographed at Fort
Laramie holding an earlier version of
his fearsome weapon. Courtesy NSHS
(R539:II-4).

Gen. Nelson A. Miles, sporting his
Civil War Medal of Honor, acquired
Sitting Bull's club and rifle after the
latter's death at the hands of Crow
Indians. Courtesy NSHS (P853).

(*Above*) The cords of wood along the post trader's store at Camp Robinson served as de facto breastworks. Courtesy NSHS (R659-4571).

(*Left*) Pvt. James B. Frew, formerly of the Fifth U.S. Cavalry, as a civilian. Courtesy NSHS (FI98).

(*Opposite*) Gen. George Crook led Frew and his comrades during the infamous "Horsemeat March." Courtesy NSHS (P853).

Soldiers resorted to killing their exhausted mounts for food during Crook's 1876 debacle. Courtesy NSHS (M883:19-7).

William Garnett, mixed-blood interpreter (*seated, center*), participated in the surround of Red Cloud's village. Also pictured are Red Cloud Agency notables: (*standing, left to right*) He Dog, Little Wound, American Horse, Little Big Man, Young Man Afraid of His Horse, and Sword; (*seated, left to right*) Yellow Bear, Jose Merivale, Leon Pallardie, and Three Bears. Courtesy NSHS (J82-78).

Judge Eli S. Ricker interviewed William Garnett and dozens of other soldiers, Indians, and frontiersmen of the Old West. Courtesy NSHS (R539:1-2).

(*Opposite above*) Lt. John G. Bourke, one of the officers who fought Crazy Horse in 1876, anxiously awaited his 1877 arrival at Red Cloud Agency and Camp Robinson. Courtesy NSHS (B774-2).

(*Opposite below*) Camp Robinson bordered Sioux country but sat in the center of the Sioux war storm. Courtesy NSHS (R659-4570).

(*Above*) Arapaho leaders whose people lived at Red Cloud Agency during the Sioux War of 1876–77. Dr. Valentine T. McGillycuddy (*standing, second from the left*) attended to Crazy Horse during his last hours. Courtesy NSHS (1392:15-3).

Chips, the friend who prepared Crazy Horse's protective medicine, and his wife, 1907. Courtesy NSHS (R539:25-2).

White Calf told Eleanor Hinman of his recollections of Crazy Horse. Courtesy
Sandoz Collection, University Archives Special Collections,
University of Nebraska–Lincoln (PC0727 1392:14-11).

Little Bighorn battlefield, site of Crazy
Horse's greatest military triumph. He lost
his life, though, in western Nebraska.
Photograph by Solomon D. Butcher, 1909.
Courtesy NSHS (C987-15).

Lt. John B. Babcock received the Medal
of Honor for his actions at the 1869
Skirmish of Spring Creek, Phelps County,
Nebraska. Courtesy the National Archives
(III-SC-93590).

Medal of Honor recipient Sgt. Patrick J.
Leonard, Company C, Second U.S.
Cavalry. Courtesy NSHS.

Three soldiers from this post, Fort
Hartsuff (1874–81), received the Medal
of Honor for actions in Nebraska.
Courtesy NSHS (H335-58).

An artist's fanciful depiction of Buffalo Bill Cody's 1872 exploit at South Loup Fork. Courtesy NSHS (1387).

Lt. Babcock remained on horseback during his 1869 "deed of valor." Courtesy NSHS (596).

Part 4

Sioux War Saga

Before full-scale war erupted between the U.S. Army and the Sioux and their allies in 1876, the nation's attention understandably may have been diverted from the northern plains. The United States was poised for a look to its past by celebrating its centennial and a look to its future by nominating a new slate of presidential candidates. The defeat of Lt. Col. George A. Custer's command abruptly refocused the public's attention to the here and now.

Many of the notables who carried out and eventually ended this war—George Crook, Ranald Mackenzie, Red Cloud, and Spotted Tail—made northwest Nebraska their headquarters at times. Camps Robinson and Sheridan and the Red Cloud and Spotted Tail agencies, in the eye of the storm although located hundreds of miles away from the Little Bighorn, saw the war's end in 1877 with Crazy Horse's May surrender and September death. Each of the following four chapters, in turn, reveals the Sioux wars as very much a Nebraska story.

It should come as no surprise that the historical literature on the Sioux wars is voluminous and rich, even without including the events along the Little Bighorn. Poorly represented, though, are accounts by the enlisted man, which makes Paul L. Hedren's article of considerable significance. "Campaigning with the Fifth U.S. Cavalry: Private James B. Frew's Diary and Letters from the Great Sioux War of 1876," *NH* 65 (Winter 1984):443–66, gave a young cavalryman's perspective—poor punctuation, misspellings, and all—of "campaigning with Crook." The scholarly annotation by prominent Sioux wars historian Hedren added considerably to our understanding of Frew's military career and the events he described, especially the skirmish in Nebraska at Warbonnet Creek and the battle of Slim Buttes in Dakota Territory.

Such annotation is lacking for Eli S. Ricker's "The Surround of Red Cloud and Red Leaf: Interview of William Garnett," *NH* 15 (Oct.–Dec., 1934):288–91. Ricker interviewed Billy Garnett on the Pine Ridge Reservation, South Dakota, on January 10, 1907. The interview and a biographical sketch of Garnett appear on tablets 1, 2, 8, and 22 of the Ricker Collection, held by the Nebraska State Historical Society. Although few of the Ricker interviews have been published, the collection has been available for decades to scholars, who have found gems in its rough, hand-written pages. Red Cloud's embarrassment at the hands of Mackenzie and the Pawnee Scouts, as witnessed by mixed-blood interpreter Garnett, is one of many Sioux wars events whose details Ricker thankfully preserved.

For "War and Peace: The Anxious Wait for Crazy Horse," *NH* 54 (Winter 1973):521–44, the late Oliver Knight won the James L. Sellers Memorial Award for the best article to appear that year in the magazine. His well-written analysis of the Indian "peace-talkers" showed that politics played as important a role in settling the Great Sioux War as did military campaigns.

No history of the Sioux wars can be told without examining the actions of Crazy Horse for the years 1876–77. His death at Camp Robinson marked the end of the Sioux wars and the end of the period covered by these *Nebraska History* articles. Through her interviews of Crazy Horse's contemporaries, Eleanor Hinman attempted to get at the whole man, his entire life and career. The result was "Oglala Sources on the Life of Crazy Horse: Interviews Given to Eleanor H. Hinman," ed. Paul D. Riley, *NH* 57 (Spring 1976):1–51. Her 1930s fieldwork preserved on paper the oral traditions of several Oglala elders, all of whom contributed greatly to our knowledge of this enigmatic leader. Long out of print, "Oglala Sources" provides many of the still limited biographical details recorded for Crazy Horse, perhaps the single most important collection of such first-person data.

Chapter 7

Campaigning with the Fifth U.S. Cavalry: Private James B. Frew's Diary and Letters from the Great Sioux War of 1876

Paul L. Hedren

Introduction

Literary materials on the Great Sioux War of 1876–77 are plentiful, at least on most aspects of the extended campaign. One topic only lightly treated, however, is the regular army enlisted man who fought in the war. Military historians have been faced with the problem that officers alone filed official reports of campaigns and battles. Officers more frequently kept journals, had wider personal correspondence, and in subsequent years were more inclined to write their reminiscences. Generalities about the line soldier who fought the campaign are usually gleaned from the army's own sparse records, and *his* war is less well known. Few were literarily inclined; some men, in fact, could barely write their names. Recent discovery, then, of a diary and letters written during the campaign of 1876 by an enlisted soldier of the Fifth U.S. Cavalry is an important addition to the literature of the war. It is a rare look at events as seen from the ranks.

Author of these unique documents was James Barcus Frew, a somewhat literate young Missourian who joined the army, was then exposed to one of the harshest Indian campaigns in the history of the American West, and ultimately pressed for and received an early release from his enlistment. Exactly what prompted Frew to enlist is unclear. A letter from his father, George W. Frew, and other records indicate that he was born in a farm family on January 9, 1856. Don Rickey, Jr., in his chronicle of enlisted life, *Forty Miles a Day on Beans and Hay*, comments on the harsh realities of nineteenth-century rural life and how farm youth were often lured to the army by the romance of the West or the glitter of gilt buttons and blue uniforms.[1] As well, however, Frew had military ante-cedents: a great-grandfather, grandfather, and father had served respec-tively in the Revolutionary War, War of 1812, and Civil War. Perhaps young Frew was driven to enlist by a familial patriotic calling, particu-larly since the United States was just embarking upon a well-publicized campaign against the Plains Indians.

Regardless of his motives, twenty-year-old Frew enlisted for five years at an army recruiting station at Cincinnati, Ohio, on May 25, 1876. When the recruiter asked whether he was twenty-one, the army's legal age for enlistment without parental consent, Frew said that he was, and his lie was readily believed. His vital statistics recorded that day were: occupa-tion, harness maker; eyes, blue; hair, brown; complexion, ruddy; height, five feet six inches.[2]

More is learned about Frew in the letters written to his family and in his diary kept for three and one-half months during the 1876 Sioux cam-paign. These primary documents, drawn up as they were on scraps of paper, are presented exactly as written. Punctuation and capitalization are lacking, and spelling is often phonetic. Evident as the letters proceed is Frew's change of attitude about his experiences, from that of exuber-ance and optimism to expressions of the harshness about field service and combat, and finally to his bitterness and desire to get out of the army.

James Frew's saga begins with a letter from his father George. James apparently had written his family that he had joined the army. Their astonishment is obvious:

St. James Mo[3]
June 76

Well son we received your written from Cincinati saying you had enlisted and was to say the least surprised—but it may be not so bad after all if you live to get through with it—the principal danger is from sickness of which you must gard against by every possible means—now son let me give you some advice—the rules in the armey are as you probably know *very* strict and obediance to ever order required to the *letter*—now to insure good treatment and respect is to obey promptly your commanding officer—it is not the place I would desire to see you in but as you have enlisted carry it out like a man—

my Father and grandfather were soldiers and Honerable ones in the wars of 76 and 12 and sence you have undertaken it go through with it like a man and don't bring dishonor on the old Scotch name of Frew

one word more by the way of advice   dont *never* let a drop of whiskey enter your mouth for that is the bane of a soldiers life—that is the great objection I had to your enlisting   the mass of the armey is made up of recless men—now I beleve   if you pursue a strait forward course get in the good will of your officers through good behaveyer with your good looks and learning you will be advanced and many a favor shown you that you wold not get otherwise—again save your money   send it home and i will put it in Bank or to some good man at Intrust so that when you get Home you will have something to go on—one word in regard to the Armey and I have done—watch the Sutler   as a general rule thay are land sharks   bye nothing you can do without—as you are in the Armey make it pay and come out like a man—you will have money plenty to bye you a improved farm   then get you a wife and settle down for life—it was allways my hope that I wold have my children about me but prehaps it is all for the best—all i can say is do your best and God Bless you and keep you from harm—do not keep me in suspence but write every two weeks   give me the name of your captain and col it might be if they belonge to any of the orders i do i could get you some favors   it would not Hurt any thing shure   now i will tell you about the Farm   i rented the new ground to Rose   it is in corn your farm is in Hungarian   he gives me one half of the corn in the shock and half the grass cut on the ground—the Hill side i have in sorgum and potatoes   i have oats in the far end under the Bluff and in the orched all looks well   my corn in the bottom looks well i have a good fence all on my side of the crick—i have all the ground back of the bluff in corn or rather Rose has   i give it to him the first year to clear it up   my grape vines is very nice—i set out 25 more apple trees this spring   all doing well   every thing on the place looks well but your dog he has been sick for a week but is geting better—the gun is all right   old Black had a fine calf and gives all the milk we want—cherry does well to will calv this fall so we will have a winter cow   times is very Hard   no money to be had, thair will be a large Harvest of oats and wheat—thay moved the Round House to Dixon[4] and St. James is dead   we cannot sell any thing in the town—Job Smith and Hobert has failed thair stores locked up   some other merchents expected to fail   well son I must quit—*dont* fail to write often—

i remane Dear Son yours truly
Geo W Frew

James Frew's own letters begin one month following his enlistment. He was quickly moved from Cincinnati to the cavalry recruit depot at Jefferson Barracks, south of St. Louis. There, customarily, new recruits were provided with their first uniforms and an introduction to the army routine. This lasted only until there existed sufficient recruits to justify transporting them to duty assignments. Frew in the early summer was caught up in the large-scale troop movements during the ensuing campaign, for he notes how his leaving St. Louis was sudden and unexpected.

Frew mentions "his" company. It is uncertain just when he learned he was to be assigned to the Fifth Cavalry, but clearly he knew it at Fort Leavenworth, Kansas, his next stop west of St. Louis, and it was earlier ordained that he go to the cavalry when the army shipped him to Jefferson Barracks. Specifically, he was headed to Company D, commanded by Capt. Samuel S. Sumner. Until early June 1876, Company D had been stationed at Fort Hays, Kansas, also the home, Frew notes, of regimental headquarters, staff, and band. In early June eight companies of the Fifth, including Company D, were called to the northern Plains as part of the army's mobilization against the Sioux and their allies, the Northern Cheyenne. Frew spent another eight days following the traces of his company before finally joining it in Wyoming.

The Letters and Diary

Fort Levenworth Kas
June 23rd/76

Dear pearents   I arived here yesterday all right and I take the opertunity to drop you a few lines   my leaving St. Louis was very sudden and unexpected   I expected to stay three or four months

I had barly time to go and see Nellie before I started

I felt like Jumping off at Franklin[5] as I came along—you sayed in your letter to Nellie that you wrote me a long letter   I did not get it have only had one since I come to St Louis

I do not know how long I will remain here and I dont care   this is a good place   it is on top of a mountain overlookin the Mo river   it is cool and pleasant and plenty to eat   this is an infantry post   no cavalry here at all but our company is in Black Hills now and I dont know whether we will be sent to it or to fort hays (Headquarters) there is only two of us

in regard to the pay cavelry and infy both get the same $13 per mon for the first year 14 for next 15 for next and 16 for the last two $18 for 2nd Enlistment   I enlisted for five years   thay take no men for three years now   not since 1861   my wages will be $15 from the beginning and all I have to do will be to take care of my horse carbine and saber and mend halters and things[6]   I dont have any fatigue duty or picket duty to do except as corperal of the guard

did you get all of my things   two coats and vests pants shoes shirts and ties   I dont care what you do with them but keep my collar button   it is sollad gold   you say John is going to Sedalia   I think it is a good move   it is the most beautiful country that I ever saw from Jefferson city to Sedalia and on to Kansas City   you can see nothing but pariria as far as you can see and it is good too   the crops look well   it is 30 miles to Kas city from here   50 to topeka

I had four pictures taken at Cincinnati   I gave Sarah one and mort and Emma one and told Sallie to send the other to you   if you have written any letters to me at St Louis they will be forwarded to my company   I will get them when I get there

the reason I did not keep my shirts is it would cost me extra for washing

tell John he had better go over on the other road near Sedalia   I think he could do well   if he could get in a military post he could do well   they pay $75 and $100 per month but it is hard to get in unless he searve one enlistment[7]

you need not answer this letter for I may go from here at any time   I will write to you as often as possible   don't worry about me for I am as well off as if I was at home   tell grandma to take good care of her self and not let the ticks eat her up   and father dont take it so hard about me leaving   it is the best i could do   dont work to hard I wish I could be there to help you but it is out of the question   this is all for this time so good by

love to all   Jim
Company D 5th C

this is the Hotest day I ever felt   I dread the traveling Evening.
R*cd* orders and transportation to go to fort Russell[8] tomorrow at 10
ocl*k*   they give us comutition money for 6 days   it will take 6 days
to go there   we go to denver co*l* take the Kas Pacific R.R. and go to
Russel up on the platt   will write as soon as i get there—Russell is
in Y.T.[9]   both the cavelry and *inf.* ar armed with Nedle guns[10]

Jim Frew's trip west passed without unnecessary delay. As he recounted,
he traveled the Kansas Pacific Railroad from Fort Leavenworth to Denver, Colorado, and then north to Cheyenne, Wyoming. With a short pause
at Fort D. A. Russell, near town but not at all close to the Platte River as
he suggests, Frew joined an escort for Lt. Col. Wesley Merritt, Ninth U.S.
Cavalry, who, in anticipation of his promotion to colonel, Fifth Cavalry,
was enroute to his new regiment. Especially charming in the next letter
is the mix of geographical naiveté, general misinformation, and soldier
bias shown by one who had been in the army for only a month and who
had not yet even joined his regiment. And it is remarkable how quickly
recruit Frew understood a common soldier complaint about their government simultaneously feeding and fighting the Indians. He refers, of
course, to the Interior and later War Department responsibility, through
assigned Indian agencies, to care for the same Sioux and Cheyennes that
the army was warring against in the nation's centennial year.

Fort Laramie June 27th 76

Dear Pearients   I arived here at 4 this evening all right   we left
Levenworth the 23rd   went to Chyenne then to *ft.* Russell   then
on to here as escort for our *Col.*   we came in an ambulance from
Russell did not see any indians   Now I must tell you about the
country   the country from levenworth to aboline 125 miles is
beautiful parara all in cultivation   I saw wheat fealds as far as I
could see back and 3 or 4 miles long   the farmares have the best of
machinery   then from aboline all the way here is a vast dessert
plain   all sand hardly any grass   have not seen a tree since i left
Levenworth   denver is right at the foot of the rocky mountains the
tops ar covered with snow   it is very cool here   the wind off the
mountains is cool

I saw lots of Buffelow and antelopes as I came along   we past through the south range of Black Hills[11]   coming here there is lots of partys going to the Black Hills in spite of the indians   my company is on there way to Join the expedition   they are near custer city now about 100 miles from here[12]   we will leave here in the morning with an escort to Join them   the col will go with us they want every man they can get   gen crook had 2 engagements he got whiped lost 7 killed and 15 wounded about 40 men killed alltogether in the 2 and about the same number of sioux killed[13] there is talk of calling volentears

before it will be settled the sioux muster 13000 braves and are well armed—as we came along we would pass a team of goods for the indians   then a team of goods for soldiers one department feeding them and the other fighting them   I expect gen Sheridan[14] will relieve Crook and take command himself   our Col is a perfect gentelman   he was gen in the volentiers servase   his name is Merritt

I do not know when I can write again   it may be two or three months befor I can send word again but I will write as soon as possible   there is nothing but stage lines between here and Cheyenne (pronounced) shian

we stoped for dinner at topeka Kas but I did not see anything of tiptons   every thing is dear here   whiskey 25 cts per drink concequently most every body is temperate   well I must quit and go to bed for I will have a long ride tomorrow   this is all for this time   you need not answer this   I will write as soon as I can dont worry about me   yours J.B. Frew Com. D. 5th C

28th   the order is for every man to be ready for the road at 12/00 we have an escort   a hole company goes with us

I must go and get ready   yours as usual   Jim

The "hole company" accompanying Merritt, Frew, and others to the camp of the Fifth Cavalry was Company K, Second U.S. Cavalry, commanded by Capt. James Egan and stationed at Fort Laramie. Egan's "grayhorse troop," as they were commonly known, was a workhorse outfit for southeastern Wyoming during the summer.

Frew commenced his diary July 1, the date he notes when he joined his Company D on Sage Creek, sixty miles north of Fort Laramie. Penned on bits and scraps of paper, his diary entries were typically brief. Sometimes days were skipped when little, in his observation, happened. But brief or not, these entries are an insightful record of day-to-day campaigning with the Fifth Cavalry, providing word pictures of the barest elements of existence—water "thick as cream with alkali," or beef "worth its weight in gold"—commentary usually missing from the official narratives of this or any campaign.

Frew provided essential clues, too, to the Fifth Cavalry's clash with Northern Cheyennes at Warbonnet Creek, Nebraska, on July 17. In this brief dawn encounter the Fifth turned back several hundred heretofore peaceful agency Indians who were enroute to various northern camps in the Powder River country. Actually only one Indian was killed, a subchief named Yellow Hair, but Frew corroborates other testimony that William F. "Buffalo Bill" Cody downed the Cheyenne. Later, other soldiers claimed that they had slain Yellow Hair, when Cody not only did but also took the chieftain's scalp, proclaiming it as the first for Custer. Frew, incidentally, is curiously quiet about the demise of Custer, even though the Fifth Cavalry had learned on July 6 of his death at the Little Bighorn River in Montana.

July 1 Joined my *co* at Sage Creek   very cold Rain
     marched to Cheyenne River
  2 G *co* started out to scout for indians seen by coady
  3 more indians in site   two more *cos* gon out   D *co* on
     picket   fine weather
  4 wagons left for sage creek   co went to scout around another way
     marched 60 miles   very Bad water   water thick as cream with
     alkali
  5 found rifle pitt and two men killed and Horses[15]
  6 marched to sage creek   no breakfast
 11 still in camp on sage creek   drew Beef   first since we
     came on scout   worth its weight in gold
 12 en rout for Laramie   camp on Running water[16]
 13 camped on RaweHide creek   cool with rain
 14 orders to go to Red Cloud   marched 18 miles
     camped on Rawhide   fished in the creek   caught a few
 15 ordered to sage creek again   marched 33 miles to
     Running water   very hungry   no supper

16 arrived at Sage creek   rested for an hour   marched on to
   indian creek   45 miles   nothing to eat till late at night
17 indians reported by the pickets   the command ordered
   to secreet in the ravines   But two couriers arriveng
   from agency being in danger coady fired on them Killing the
   chief Yellow Hand   the rest tried to rescue him but we charged
   on them killing six   followed them into the agency 40 miles[17]
18 started for laramie   10 miles
19 camped on runing water   25 miles
20 Raw Hide   28 miles   met recruits going to agency to
   companys stationed there   Rashons Run short today
21 marched to laramie   very hungry   nothing to eat for 36 hours
   Co C arived from scouting   they captured 14 ponys packed for the
   warpath
22 rest and preparing to start for crooks comd[18]   bathed in the platt
23 camped on Bulls Bend of the platt   35 miles   caught a fine mess
   of fish
24 camp unnown   27 miles   Gen carr and Dr Killed some sage
   hens[19]
25 camp at ft fetterman   22 miles   three men deserted taking there
   Horses and equipments[20]
26 made 12 miles marching slow to let other cos cach up
27 camp at Welton springs   very pore water
28 made 22 miles   co F and C cam up with us
29 camped on N fork of powder River   25 miles
30 camp on powder River at old fort Reno[21]   28 miles   found 3
   wagons there   the oners had been Jumped by indians and
   abandonded everything
31 camp on old womans creek   30 miles   Killed Buffalo

Aug 1 stoped to cook coffee at a beautiful mountain stream
   took up the march at 5 p.m.   35 miles   camped on deer creek
   saw a fine lake
2 camp on goose creek   35 miles   passed fort Phill Karney on
   crow creek   saw a monument put up for those killed there
   90 in nomber[22]
3 camp on tongue River   Joined crook
4 layed over preparing to start for sitting Bull

The arrival of Colonel Merritt's ten companies of Fifth Cavalry at
George Crook's camp on August 3 bolstered the general's forces to nearly

2,200 effectives. After stripping this command of excess baggage that could retard its advance, on August 5 Crook resumed operations. The Sioux and Cheyennes, who had checked Crook at Rosebud Creek on June 17 and had annihilated the Seventh Cavalry only eight days later at the Little Bighorn, did not remain idle during that same period, but had broken up their large camp, and in small bands were seeking haven in the obscure reaches of the vast Yellowstone River drainage.

As Frew recounts in the continuation of his diary and in a letter home, the next several weeks were marked by few highlights. On August 10 Crook's Big Horn and Yellowstone Expedition, as it was properly designated, joined the forces commanded by Brig. Gen. Alfred Howe Terry. Together these troops, including the surviving elements of the Seventh Cavalry, ambled eastward for three more weeks. Indian signs were few and old, and the troops, most of whom had now been in the field for three months or longer, were wearing out.

Aug 5 started for Sitting Bull with 500 mule packed   18 miles
      camp on tongue River
  6 camp on tongue river   20 miles   very Rough country
      crossed River 17 times
  7 camp on Rose Bud   27 miles   Beautiful country but Hilly
  8 changed camp 2 miles down RoseBud   started out at 1 p.m.
      made 18 miles down R.B.   very heavy indian trail   lik a road[23]
  9 camp on R.B.   20 miles   very cold   made a lodge to sleep in
 10 met Gen terrys command   went in camp on R.B.   18 miles
      got grain from Terry
 11 Both commands start on the trail   camp on tongue River
      12 miles   found the Bodys of 2 men scalped by indians[24]
      Lieut Eaton shot in Hand accident[25]
 12 camp on tongue R   10 miles   rain all day   every thing wet
 13 tongue R.   25 miles   rain all day   9 of the Horses giveout   left
      behind   1 mule give out   packed with Hard tack   we made a raid
      on it
 14 Branch of powder R   18 miles
 15 camped on powder R   16 miles   8 horses give out   country very
      Rough
 16 powder R   22 miles   Rain   Boys very hungry   Being ishued 2
      days Rashons and eating them in one day   after ariveing in camp
      a fawn Run through the ranks causing lots of fun

17 arrived at Yellowstone   2 Boats here with supplys for us   sent a
letter Home

Montanna Ter
Yellow Stone River
Mouth of powder River Aug 19th 76

dear pearants and friends   I take the opertunity to write you a few
lines to let you know how I get along   this is the first time have had
a chance to write or I would have written sooner   did you get the
letter i wrote at Laramie   I Recd a letter from you at feterman July
25th but had no chance to answer it as we left there in an hour after
and went to crook   then we struck the trail and followed it ever
since   followed it 28 days with out laying over a day and still did
not catch them   it is a very large command numbering about 3400
and about 400 indians   every time they draw Rashons they have a
dance and make the night hideous with there yells (the indians)

we have layed over here two days. there is a steam Boat here with
supplys   I Just got this letter paper from the sutler   have not time
to write much   we move camp in an hour to go 4 miles up to get
more grass for the stock   the horses did not get any grain for 20
days   a greate many give out and was left behind   and three of
the infantry men give out   two of them died and one rather than
be left behind blew out his Brains[26]   I bought some cheese and
crackers and onions today—this is a very cold climate   I nearly
froze the 9th of Aug   had to walk lead our horses it was so cold   I
think we will start back to Kas soon   it will take a mon or more to
go back   this is all   good by   address as follows and I will
get it

James B. Frew Co D 5th Cav
via. Fort Laramie Wyo Ter

23 still in camp on Yellowstone   had a general drownd out last night
24 marched up powder R   18 miles   3 of the boys who were sick
went down on the Boat to fort Lincoln[27]
25 camped on powder R   15 miles

August 26 was a pivotal day for Crook's army. It marked the day in
which the Big Horn and Yellowstone Expedition cut loose from Terry's

command and also the beginning of one of the most harrowing experiences ever to befall United States troops, the Starvation March. Crook's moves were calculated. Although he could have marched directly east to Fort Abraham Lincoln, near Bismarck, and there resupply, he elected on September 5 to turn toward the Black Hills, following a relatively fresh Indian trail. When the command turned south, Crook ordered his troops on half rations. At that rate enough food remained to last four days; the Black Hills lay, at best, six or seven days away.[28]

As the Bighorn and Yellowstone Expedition trudged southward, conditions worsened. Torrential fall rains buffeted the command daily, thoroughly soaking the troops and transforming the vast prairie land into a quagmire. Each step by horse and man alike was an ordeal. Adding further discomfort to the plight of these hapless men was the barren land. The route was entirely devoid of wood, and the tufts of grass collected were often too wet to burn. The horses and mules suffered greatly. Grain rations were long since exhausted, and the grass was insufficient to prevent starvation. At first worn-out animals were simply abandoned, but on September 5 Crook ordered that they should be shot. That decree was quickly reversed, however, because it proved enormously demoralizing to the soldiers, and it was also realized that these pitiful animals were a food source that could ultimately ward off the total collapse of the command.[29] Although Frew first records in his diary the killing of horses for food on September 11, other accounts suggest that this was actually begun about September 5.[30]

Conditions had grown so critical that on September 7 Crook ordered Capt. Anson Mills, Third Cavalry, to advance to the Black Hills with 150 handpicked men riding the most serviceable horses and bring out as much food as could be purchased in the mining communities. Enroute, these cavalrymen chanced upon a sizeable Sioux village nestled in the Slim Buttes, a pine-dotted escarpment in northwestern South Dakota. Mills sent a courier back to Crook asking that he advance as quickly as possible, and in the breaking light of September 9 his cavalrymen attacked the camp. The fight at Slim Buttes proved an enormous success and the first major victory for United States troops in the long 1876 campaign. Moreover, the village contained winter provisions that fed Crook's troops for several days as they resumed their march to the Hills.[31]

The worst of the Starvation March, however, came after the fight at Slim Buttes. One of the Fifth Cavalry officers, 1st Lt. Charles King, remembered it:

Tuesday, the 12th of September, 1876—a day long to be remembered in the annals of the officers and men of the Bighorn and Yellowstone expedition; a day that can never be thoroughly described, even could bear description; a day when scores of our horses dropped exhausted on the trail—when starving men toiled piteously along through thick clinging mud, or flung themselves, weeping and worn out, upon the broad, flooded prairie. Happily, we got out of the Bad Lands before noon; but one and all were weak with hunger, and as we dragged through boggy stream-bed, men would sink hopelessly in the mire and never try to rise of themselves; travois mules would plunge frantically in bog and quicksand, and pitch the wounded screaming from their litters. I hate to recall it. Duties kept me with the rear-guard, picking up and driving in stragglers. It was seven A. M. when we marched from Owl Creek. It was after midnight when Kellogg's rearmost files reached the bivouac along the Crow. The night was pitchy dark, the rain was pitiless; half our horses were gone, many of the men were scattered over the cheerless prairie far behind.[32]

The ordeal ended on September 13 when provisions reached the expedition. For the next month the troops recuperated in the wondrous Black Hills, marching from grassy meadow to grassy meadow only as required for the horses and mules.

[Aug] 26 left powder River   Started SE for deadwood   mad 20
      miles   had to walk most of the way and lead our horses
    29 Boys crazy for tobaco   smoking coffee grounds   offer 8 to 10
      dollars for a plug   Boys discouraged   not knoing where they
      are going
    30 camp on Bever creek   Boys all complaining of sickness
    31 camp on foster mountains   12 miles   a fine grazing country

Sept 1 moved camp 7 miles for grass   over 300 of the Boys sick
      hardly able to ride myself   [not] fealing very well
    2 camp on bever creek   18 miles   Boys smoking coffee grounds
      & grass
    3 camp unknown   23 miles   water scarce
    4 camp on Little Mo R.   25 miles   100 miles from Ft Lincoln
      I gathered some Buffalo Berries   stewed them   the Hills all
      around are like sinders   all melted and run together

5 camp on Head waters of heart River   30 miles   down to Half
rashons
6 camped at a Big pond   no wood to Build a fire   lost a great
many Horses
7 camp = 40 miles   rain and cold   Boys in a desperate condition
Killing the played out Horses   no wood yet
8 camp in a range of hills   moved at least 30 miles   Boys feeling
very week for want of something to eat   15 Horses give out
today   mine nearly gone
9 came on indian village at Slim Butes   routed them at 4 in the
morning   some took refuge in a ravine close by and took us
till noon to get them out   they Killed three men before they
would come out   then we started to Build a fire to smoke
them out and The[y] came out covered from head to foot
with mud from diging to conseal themselves   american Horse
the chief Had his guts hanging out[33]   he died soon after
they came back with reinforcements at about 2 oclock
charged us from all sides but we drove them back   Kept up
a steady fire till dark[34]
10 camp 15 miles   I had to walk   my horse was killed yesterday
feal very Bad   nothing to eat but a piece of dried meat taken
from Indians   about 5000 pounds of it
11 camp 27 miles   plenty wood and water   Killed 25 or 30 ponys
to eat   the old sore Backed Horses are at a discount since we
got the indian ponys to eat[35]   in the absence of salt I opened a
cartrige   put the powder in my soup
12 marched 40 miles   mud very deep   I give out twice on the
road   Laid down got up went on   got in camp about 1 ock next
morning   lost about 300 horses   Killed over 30 ponys to eat
laid over till noon   waiting for the men to come in camp that
give out
13 Broke camp at noon   made 5 miles   camp on Belfuch River[36]
and got Beef and flour   Such a time cooking   Boys cooked till
near midnight
14 layed over   took all day   a sutler from crook city[37] came with
a wagon   we went through him like wolfs
15 camp on white wood[38]   7 miles   Boys in better spirits but
still weak
16 layed over to rest our selfs and the few horses that are left
general crook started for Laramie[39]   double rashons isued to
us   fresh Beef and flour

17   layed over   cooked all day   Baked Bread
18   camp on centennial park   12 miles   1¹/₂ miles from crook city   carried water to cook with from a mining sluce about a mile   saw them washing gold
19   camp on Box Elder   28 miles   found a company of 3rd Art[40] with supplys for us here   very cold and I was very tired and did not get any thing to eat till about 12 oclock that night   my rashons were in my Bundle of Blankets   some siticens were hired to haul our Bundles and did not get in till midnight
20   layed over   had Baked Beans for dinner
21   camp at rappid creek   15 miles
22   camp at spring creek   15 miles   took off my shirt and washed it   have had no change of clothing since august 4th
23   camp at custer city   met a train with supplys for us from laramie
24   layed over   Boys very dirty   I found some Rubys
25. 26. 27. 28. 29. 30. nothing worthy of note   only moveing camp for grass

Oct 1st–5th   our wagon train came in today   Boys in high glee   very cold weather   some snow   Burnes discharged by order his folks got him out[41]   we left custer city about the 10   some recruits and fresh horses joined us there   then we went on a 10 days scout on cheyenne river   from there to Red Cloud arived there about the 24th   started for sidney[42] next day arived at sidney *Oct* 31st

Oct 6th 76 Dacota T
Camp near Custer City

Dear pearants and friends   your wellcome letter is rec*d*   I got it Sept 29th dated Sept 18th   was glad to here from Home and friends again   we have been laying here since Sept 23

we dont know how long we will stay here but expect to go back to kansas soon for it is getting to be very cold up here   the day I Recd the letter was very cold and we were not fixed for it as all oure tents and a good many overcoats and Blankets were left in the wagon train at crooks camp on goose creek   when we started after the indians Aug 5th   we took our rashons on pack mules 500 of them and expected to ovetake them at Rose Bud creek and come back to the wagons in a few days but they went down RoseBud and sliped out between us and Terrys command   then we all followed the trail to the yellow stone and the trails splitt up and we started with 15 days rashons to go back to wagons   got about half way and crook took a notion to go across the country to deadwood   we traveled a day or two and layed over alternetly so he could prosspect untill our rashons were nearly gone   then we had to make forced marches from 25 to 45 miles a day and no grain for the horses and then marched within 18 miles of *ft* Lincoln on ¼ rashons but would not stop and had about 300 miles to go to deadwood[43]

it rained all the time   had 26 days rain and after we crossed the little M*o* River it came down to 2 hardtack a day   then nine days we had nothing but horsemeat two days we had no wood to make a fire and could not cook it   they only killed the sore backed and played out Horses   a detail came behind the command everyday an drove the abandoned Horses in to camp and Killed and ishued them to us on the 8th of Sept 150 men with the best Horses were sent on ahead to go to Deadwood to get rashons for us   it was about 200 miles and they accidently came upon the indian village   the scout Frank Gereard[44] came back and told us   we went and charged upon them at day Break the 9th   took them by surprise   captured over 300 ponys and run the Reds to the hills and 12 of them went in to a ravine near by   it was about 50 feet long and 20 wide 20 deep full of rocks and brush   we fired in to them for about two hours Killing five of them including american Horse there chief   then they gave themselves up   the dead ones were draged out striped and scalped two wounded squaws with papooses were let go   we lost five men killed and the scout White[45]   he was killed when he was going to shoot in the ravine   shot threw the Hart   all he sayed was Oh, Lord ive got it now Boys and rolled down the Bank

everything was quiett for a while   then about 3 oclk in the evening the picketts fired and were drove in and the indians charged upon us from every side   the Bulletts were flying al around us   our Horses were unsaddled so we were pushed out in line all round on foot   the firing was kept up till dark   then they retreated to the Hills   a few shots were fired during the night   there was about 5,000 pounds of dried meat in the village but a few of the 5th stole some of it and crook would not isue any to us[46]   gave it to the 3rd and 2nd cavelry and would not let us have any ponys eather and about 200 of the 5th were dismounted having eaten there Horses they were eaten up clean   even the Heart liver and lights and not a bit of salt

I made supe of mine put powder in for salt—about a thousand Buffalo Robe were Burned   the men were not aloued to take them the Horses and men were to weak to carry them   we went on next day and the 12th marched 40 miles from day light till midnight and lost over 300 Horses   about 200 of the men did not get in till the next day   i got in about 1 oclk   I was walking my horse Killed the day of the fight and the mud was about ankle deep   a good many men died of over exertion that night as well as Horses   the command layed over next day to wait for them to all come in and a party mounted on ponys were sent on to crook city and the next day a heard of cattle and wagons with rashons came from there   the boys were nearly wild with joy   you ought to here them shout

I have walked since we left the indians village   about 250 miles north of here 100 miles from deadwood   there is a good deal of gold here but the men have to hold on to there scalp with one hand while they dig with the other hand   the object in Crook's keeping us here is he has a Brother in law here whoe is a sutler and he is keeping us here to be payed so as to spend our money withe him he will not give us enough clothing so as to make us buy from him he has laid in a big stock   the paymaster is coming in a day or two but he will get none of my money   I have never heard crooks name mentioned but with a curse   the men fired into his tent tried to kill him   he thought it was indians[47]   this is all for this time would like to see you all very much   write soon and tell me if John went to texas

there is a man in the company was discharged by order the other day   he was under age—he got no pay and will have a hard time to get home   lives in Boston and several others are expecting to be discharged   about half the men will deseart as soon as they are payed   3 have all ready gone took horses and arms[48]   as soon as we get back to Kas I wish you would see about it and get me out certify that I am under age   enlisted without your knoledge and am your only support in your old age   let me know if you will do it immediately but dont do any thing till i write and tell you when i get payed and draw a lot of clothing   i will send you money as soon as i get a chance   i am fat and Harty   have not had a sick day   my Beard is as long as Johns was when he came home from osage

Jim

The arrival October 31, 1876, of Frew's Company D, along with Company K, Fifth Cavalry, at Sidney Barracks, Nebraska, marked the end for these men of the Great Sioux War. It had been a long, arduous campaign, scored by the triumphs at Warbonnet Creek and Slim Buttes—the sole army successes up to that time—but remembered more widely for the suffering during the forced marches into the Black Hills. This ordeal broke the health of countless officers and enlisted men alike, and it broke the spirit of many others, including young Frew. The adventurous fervor which sparkled in his early letters was gone by war's end. Now his attention was riveted on a path of escape, an early out due to an underage enlistment. Had Frew been of age when he joined the army in Cincinnati, he certainly would have fulfilled his five-year obligation. But now he wanted absolution for a patriotic lie, and forgiveness in this case was a discharge from the wholly glamourless life of a soldier.

Nov 7th/76
Sidney Barracks Ne*b*

Dear father   I recd a letter from you the 4th and answered it the same day saying that I would send the affidafid to Col Merritt but I have since taken the advice of the company clerk one Chas Gilbert[49] from cincinnati and a particular friend of mine   he says the proper way to do it is for you to send in affadavid to the Sec*t* of war   enclosed you will find a letter written by him   you coppy it and have another paper made out as soon as you get this but dont send it off till I write again and tell you that I have got my pay

we expect to be payed soon

I am well and hearty   I weigh one hundred and sixtyeight pounds that is more than I ever weight before   hopeing this will find you all well I am yours as ever   answer soon

James B. Frew
Co. D. 5th Cavalry
Sidney Barracks Neb

Sunday Nov 27th/76
Dear Pearients

I recived your last letter dated Nov 10th the 12th   was glad to here from you   I did not answer it becaus I kept waiting for the paymaster to come   did you receive my letter with a letter written by Chas Gilbert in it   tell me in your next   the way to work this thing is to send an affadavit to the secretary of war and he will send an order for my discharge   that is the way a fellow was discharged out of the company two months ago   the paymaster came this evening and will pay us tomorrow   I wish you would attend to immediately on receiving this as I will get no pay untill the first of January for this mon and next   I get five months and 6 days pay this time   there will be a great many men desert as soon as thay are payed   I know of seven or eight that will go for sure and good many will go in the spring[50]   I am having easy times now   not much to do and pretty fair grub

monday evening   got payed off today   I got $69.95 fix that thing as soon as you get this

this is all for this time so good by   love to all

James B. Frew
Sidney Barracks, Neb

Sidney Barracks Neb
sunday morning   Dec 17th/76

Dear father   I just received your letter dated 15th   glad to here from you   it is very cold and winday this morning and Inspection is just over   in regeard to the money I will send it immediately the mail goes out from here at eight oclock this evening   I will write to John today   I wish you would attend to that thing as soon as possible   write senitor Thurman and maybe he will hurry it up what I am afraid of is that we may have to go out on the scout again

we will be sent out in the spring sure and I will never go on another scout   the report here is that Gen McKenzy[51] had another fight and we may be sent for but we do not believe the report   well this is all for this time so I will close   give my love to all and write soon Yours as ever

James B. Frew
Co. D. 5th *C*

P.S. Who is elected president[52]
monday   could not send this last night   they would not register it
on sunday   will go at eight oclock this evening

Sidney Barracks Ne*b*
Jan 30/77

Dear father & mother   your welcome letter is Rec*d*   I was very
glad to here from you but sorry that father is not well—I wrote a
postle card to you telling you not to send the order   my intentions
were to take you by surprise   I did not need the order at all   the
Sec of war sent one here to Sumner   it came here the same day
that your letter did (the 20th)

Sumner put off discharging me thinking that the P.master would be
here the next week and then I could get my pay but he did not come
he could not put it off any longer so he gave me my discharge sunday
28th   I am a citisen again but I will have to wait here till the P.M.
comes any how for I have not enough money to Bring me home and
I have $40.00/100 comeing to me in the company and cant get a
cent till they are payed   it is expected that he will be here this week
but it is uncertain when he will come—I will come home as soon as
I am payed

this is all for this time   I will send you a card when I leave here
hopeing to be with you all soon   I am as ever

Your affectinate son
James B. Frew

Afterword

Since provisions indeed existed for the release from the army of young
men who had enlisted before the age of consent and without parental
approval, the intercession of James's father, George, brought desired
results. Paragraph 3 of Special Order No. 10, dated Adjutant General's
Office, Headquarters of the Army, January 15, 1877, read:

By direction of the Secretary of War Saddler James B. Frew, Company "D", 5th Cavalry, now with his command, will be discharged [from] the service of the United States on receipt of this order at the place where he may be serving. This soldier is entitled to pay &c., only under Paragraph 1371, Revised U.S. Army Regulations of 1863. By Command of General Sherman.

This discharge was effective January 28, 1877, at Sidney Barracks.[53] In accordance with the above mentioned Paragraph 1371 of the Army Regulations, Frew did not receive a final statement, which was a certificate given to soldiers at the time of their discharge noting certain physical characteristics, and a balancing of financial accounts. Frew, however, did receive an official discharge paper bearing the signature of his company commander, Captain Sumner, and also Sumner's endorsement in the "character" block: "Very good, a sober reliable man and a good soldier."

Frew returned to Missouri after his discharge and soon settled in West Plains in the south-central section of the state. On April 28, 1878, he married Isa Dora Clevinger at West Plains. Their union brought five children: daughters Jennie and Nelle, and sons George, Charles, and James Bently.[54]

The Frews subsequently moved to Harrison, Arkansas, in 1888, and there he established Frew Saddlery, one of the largest firms of its type in the Ozark Mountain country. The company operated continuously for over forty years in Harrison. Each of Frew's sons took up their father's trade, and one of George's saddles captured a first prize award at the 1904 Louisiana Purchase Exposition in St. Louis. With the growing popularity and availability of automobiles after World War I, Frew entered that business. Although he sold the first cars in Harrison, he recalled for the benefit of a newspaperman that "his automobile business was ahead of the town, and the venture was not highly successful." Forced to close the auto dealership, he again fitted up a small leatherworking shop in his home and catered to select customers who had purchased Frew products over the years.[55]

In the late 1920s when Frew was in his seventies, he enjoyed the limelight as an aged veteran who vividly remembered Indian fighting days. A controversy was brewing over the publication of *The Making of Buffalo Bill, A Study in Heroics* by Richard J. Walsh in collaboration with Milton S. Salsbury. This debunking biography cast Cody in faint light, and, as he could scarcely defend himself from the grave, other friends and associates stepped forward in his defense. Of special concern to Cody's Old Army associates was Walsh's reexamination of the fight at Warbonnet Creek, where he questioned Cody's singular exploit and ridiculed the embellishments given it in later published accounts, on the stage, and in the "Wild West" shows. All along, other soldiers and frontiersmen, undoubtedly in the best tradition of telling interrogators what they wanted to hear, related that they, in truth, had killed Yellow Hair, not Cody. The best evidence, however, was conclusive. Cody did kill the Indian, not in a manly hand-to-hand fight but with a shot through the heart at medium range.[56] Frew could hardly miss the national newspaper attention given these stories, and certainly he found the occasion to tell his own eyewitness version. Newspapermen picked up on Frew's straightforward account. He saw the killing, all right, but had all along dismissed the wild "duel" stories as circus ballyhoo. "If the embellishments would help the erstwhile scout to boost his shows, he certainly did not want to put a damper on it," he reported.[57]

Frew's final years seem to have been fairly stable. An Indian wars veteran's pension was approved by the Bureau of Pensions in 1927. In the mid-1930s, however, he was admitted to the veterans' hospital in North Little Rock, Arkansas, and he died there on August 16, 1939, aged eighty-three. James Frew's life was long and surely a satisfying one, and to his lasting credit the diary and letters he so carefully penned in the adventure of his youth survive today for historians and all others who might be interested in these important days of '76.

Notes

Karl Henry of Goleta, California, grandson of James Frew, allowed the editor access to the original diary and letters. Henry subsequently donated these documents to Nebraska State Historical Society, Lincoln, where they are catalogued in the archives as the James Barcus Frew Collection, MS4229.

[1] Don Rickey, Jr., *Forty Miles a Day on Beans and Hay: The Enlisted Soldier Fighting the Indian Wars* (Norman: University of Oklahoma Press, 1963), 22.

[2] *Registers of Enlistment in the United States Army, 1798–1914.* National Archives Microfilm Publications, Microcopy No. 233, Washington, D.C., 1956.

[3] St. James is in south-central Missouri midway between St. Louis and Springfield.

[4] Dixon is about twenty-five miles west of St. James. Both towns were on the same rail line.

[5] Franklin, a Missouri town, is located between St. Louis and Kansas City on the Missouri River.

[6] Frew was confused about the awarding of longevity pay. The scale was $13 per month for first and second years; $14, third year; $15, fourth year; and $16, fifth year. Frew's monthly wage of $15 reflected $2 extra as a saddler, a company-designated position. Company-duty men were commonly excused from routine fatigues. Rickey, *Forty Miles*, 109–10, 127.

[7] Pay at such phenomenal rates could only have been gained for quartermaster contract work such as the cutting of cordwood or forage.

[8] Fort D. A. Russell was located three miles northwest of Cheyenne, Wyoming.

[9] *Sic*. W. T. for Wyoming Territory.

[10] A needle gun was a common reference to the Springfield breech-loading rifles and carbines used by the army. These weapons had a long firing pin resembling a needle.

[11] This range today is known as the Laramie Mountains.

[12] Actually Company D and the rest of the Fifth Cavalry was camped on the Cheyenne River, about 110 miles north of Fort Laramie. Custer City was another forty miles beyond. Paul L. Hedren, *First Scalp for Custer: The Skirmish at Warbonnet Creek, Nebraska, July 17, 1876* (Glendale, Calif.: The Arthur H. Clark Company, 1980), 47; W. S. Stanton, *Tables of Distances and Itineraries of Routes Between the Military Posts in, and Certain Points Contiguous to, the Department of the Platte* (Omaha: Headquarters Department of the Platte, 1877), 28, 30.

[13] Col. Joseph J. Reynolds, Third Cavalry, with Crook nearby, led troops at Powder River, March 17, 1876. The soldiers, indeed, were defeated. General Crook personally led a refitted and enlarged army against Sioux and Cheyennes at Rosebud Creek, June 17, a battle that ended in a draw. The official tally of casualties at Powder River was four soldiers killed and six wounded; at Rosebud Creek nine soldiers killed, twenty-one wounded, with a report of eleven Indians killed. Adjutant General's Office, *Chronological List of Actions, &c, with Indians from January 15, 1837 to January, 1891* (Fort Collins: The Old Army Press, 1979), 61.

[14] Lt. Gen. Philip H. Sheridan, commander of the Division of the Missouri, Chicago.

[15] These men are thought to be Black Hills-bound miners, who were slain by Indians. Hedren, *First Scalp*, 50.

[16] Enroute to Fort Laramie; camped on the Niobrara River.

[17] The clash on Warbonnet Creek is told in Hedren, *First Scalp*.

[18] Merritt was under orders to join General Crook's command in northern Wyoming. The backtracking recounted by Frew (July 15–21) was merely an unplanned interlude, which coincidentally resulted in the army's first battlefield success in 1876.

[19] References are to Lt. Col. Eugene A. Carr, Fifth Cavalry, and Acting Assistant Surgeon Junius L. Powell.

[20] The deserters were Charles E. Bassett, Charles Gerhardt, and Alexander Harker, all privates in Frew's Company D, Fifth Cavalry. Muster Rolls, Company D, Fifth U.S. Cavalry, July–Aug., 1876. Adjutant General's Office, Record Group (RG) 94. National Archives, Washington, D.C.

[21] Fort Reno was located ninety-one miles north of Fort Fetterman on the old Bozeman Trail. It was one of three posts built in 1865 to protect that route, only to be abandoned in 1868 in compliance with terms ending the Red Cloud War.

[22] As with Fort Reno, Fort Phil Kearny guarded the Bozeman Trail from 1865 to 1868. The monument observed by Frew memorialized the dead of the Fetterman fight of December 21, 1866. Today this stone and grave are protected in the cemetery at Little Bighorn Battlefield National Monument, Crow Agency, Montana.

[23] This trail was indeed broad—8,000 to 10,000 Indians—but, according to officers in a position to judge, was two or more weeks old. Charles King, *Campaigning with Crook and Stories of Army Life* (New York: Harper & Brothers, 1890), 74.

[24] Others report finding only one body, presumed to be a white miner killed as much as a year earlier. Ibid., 84; John F. Finerty, *War-Path and Bivouac, or The Conquest of the Sioux* (Norman: University of Oklahoma Press, 1961), 165.

[25] Second Lt. George O. Eaton, Company A, Fifth Cavalry, lost a portion of his right index finger by the accidental discharge of his pistol as he attempted to check a night stampede of the horses belonging to his company. King, *Campaigning With Crook*, 83; George F. Price, *Across the Continent with the Fifth Cavalry* (New York: Antiquarian Press Ltd., 1959), 542.

[26] Newspaperman John Finerty recorded how some of the newly enlisted infantrymen were desperate, with "feet bleeding and legs swollen from the continuous tramp." Finerty, *War-Path and Bivouac,* 167.

[27] The steamer *Far West* evacuated to Bismarck those officers and men deemed by the surgeons to be too ill to continue the campaign. The three "boys" were Sgt. John Morgan, Farrier Edward Martin, and Pvt. John Remy, all of Frew's Company D. Muster Rolls, July–Aug., 1876, RG 94.

[28] Jerome A. Greene, *Slim Buttes, 1876: An Episode of the Great Sioux War* (Norman: University of Oklahoma Press, 1982), 11, 39

[29] Ibid., 41–42.

[30] Ibid., 42.

[31] The entire saga of Slim Buttes is chronicled by Greene, *Slim Buttes.*

[32] King, *Campaigning with Crook*, 138–39.

[33] American Horse, a Minneconjou Lakota subchief, was the headman in the village struck by Mills's detachment. He was prominent in the ravine fight mentioned by Frew, and, when those in concealment finally surrendered, American Horse was found fatally wounded. Crook's surgeons attended to him through the evening of September 9, but he died about midnight. Greene, *Slim Buttes,* 49, 80, 90.

[34] Other accounts suggest that the Indian counterattack came about 4:15 P.M. Frew fails to mention the wounding of a D Company comrade, August Dorn, in this afternoon fight. Ibid, 81–83.

[35] In addition to the dried meat captured by the troops, they also collected the Sioux pony herd. According to all accounts these grass-fed mounts had flesh that was decidedly tastier than cavalry horses or pack mules.

[36] Belle Fourche River.

[37] Crook City was located in the far northern Black Hills, northeast of Deadwood.

[38] Whitewood Creek flows northward from the Black Hills to the Belle Fourche River.

[39] Lieutenant General Sheridan had ordered Crook to Fort Laramie, not Laramie, to plan the continuation of the campaign.

[40] The escort with this supply train was actually from the Fourth. U.S. Artillery. The Third Artillery did not participate in the campaign of 1876.

[41] Pvt. Charles M. Burns, Company D, Fifth Cavalry, was indeed discharged per Special Order 155, Adjutant General's Office, at camp near Custer City, on October 5, 1876. Muster Roll, Sept.–Oct., 1876, RG 94. Interesting is Frew's statement: "His folks got him out." This surely was not his first introduction to an alternative manner of discharge, yet it played strongly in coming actions.

[42] Sidney Barracks, Nebraska, was to be the new garrison home for Company D.

[43] Frew has the route of march and distances traveled incorrect. Crook's army never countermarched. And they certainly never closed to within eighteen miles of Fort Abraham Lincoln, or they would have gone in. Frew, simply, was not privy to higher echelon decisions and reacted only to the supposition, gossip, and rumors circulating within the ranks.

[44] Frank Grouard, Crook's head scout.

[45] Charles (Jonathan) White, known more commonly by his nickname, "Buffalo Chips."

[46] Frew here is contradicted by the record and his own diary entry of September 10. The entire command shared the captured Indian provisions.

[47] Again, Frew knows little of the larger story although indeed there was scant good will toward Crook after the privation of the Starvation March. The troops remained in the Black Hills to recuperate. Clothing, food, and other comforts were ushered forth as quickly as taxed quartermaster and contract teams could bear them. The allegation that Crook had a brother-in-law functioning as a sutler is interesting but not substantiated.

[48] The soldier discharged by order for being underage was Burns, discussed in note 41. The muster rolls of Company D, Fifth Cavalry, show no deserters in the Black Hills, so the three "all ready gone" must have been from other companies.

[49] Pvt. Charles M. Gilbert was not recognized on the Company D muster roll as a company clerk, although he may have held a comparable duty in an unofficial capacity. Too, he may have been a "barracks" or "latrine lawyer," one who was always ready with advice, good and bad.

[50] Frew was correct this time, for the D Company muster rolls of November–December, 1876, and January–February, 1877, show a host of desertions from   the unit.

[51] Col. Ranald S. Mackenzie, Fourth Cavalry, commanded troops in a major victory over Northern Cheyennes, November 25, 1876, on the Red Fork of the Powder River, Wyoming.

[52] The year 1876 was an election year. Democrat Samuel J. Tilden captured the popular vote from Republican Rutherford B. Hayes. Hayes, however, was declared the victor on March 2, 1877, when disputed electoral vote counts were settled. Dee Brown, *The Year of the Century: 1876* (New York: Charles Scribner's Sons, 1966), 290, 337.

[53] Muster rolls, Jan.–Febr., 1877, RG 94.

[54] James B. Frew Pension File, National Archives, Washington, D.C. Genealogical data supplied to the author by Karl Henry, Frew's grandson, Nov. 27, 1983.

[55] Undated newspaper article, "Arkansas Man, an Eyewitness, Refutes Thrilling Tale of Buffalo Bill's Knife Duel," by Ralph A. Hull, James Barcus Frew Collection.

[56] Richard J. Walsh in collaboration with Milton S. Salsbury, *The Making of Buffalo*

Bill, A Study in Heroics (Indianapolis: Bobbs–Merrill Company, 1928), chap. 15; Don Russell, "A Very Personal Introduction," in Hedren, *First Scalp*, 16–17; Don Russell, *The Lives and Legends of Buffalo Bill* (Norman: University of Oklahoma Press, 1960), chap. 17.

[57] "Arkansas Man."

Chapter 8

The Surround of
Red Cloud and Red Leaf:
Interview of William Garnett

Eli S. Ricker

Mr. Garnett says that Red Cloud and Red Leaf were camped on Chadron Creek, four or five miles above the Price and Jenks Ranch (or Half Diamond E), that Red Leaf was about a mile above Red Cloud.

It was just at the close of the campaign of 1876, and the evils growing out of the loose manner in which the Indians were managed, which allowed them to go and come at will and to wander off to remote places from the agency, had been productive of great hardship to the country; and while the memory of this experience was fresh, the commanding officer at Fort Robinson, General [Ranald S.] Mackenzie, decided to bring the Indians near the agency so that their movements might be more easily watched. Red Cloud and Red Leaf were nearly thirty miles from the fort, and it was resolved to bring them in. The interpreter, William Garnett, was sent for and given orders to go to the camps of these chiefs and tell them to move up to the agency, and that, if they did not comply, their rations would be taken away, and, if they did not move in after that, that they would be brought in by force. They returned no satisfactory answer.

Garnett was sent to Red Cloud solely as he [Red Cloud] was recognized as the head chief; so he went to this chief's lodge, where he found Red Cloud and Red Dog, the latter generally doing the speaking for the former. Red Dog responded by saying that the troops might have the buildings of the Red Cloud Agency; that they had the Bissonnette house where they were (pointing just across the creek) to put their rations in; to tell General Mackenzie to send their rations down to them and the beef cattle; to tell this to the general and advised the interpreter to come along to assist in the making of the issue.

Ration day came, but they got no rations, and still they were obstinate and remained away. The same messenger was again called, and this time his instructions left no doubt that, after trying the persuasion of hunger,

General Mackenzie was preparing to make good the promise he had delivered to the chiefs, that he would use force if necessary to bring their camps to the agency.

The young man was started off about nightfall on the [–] day of October 1876 for the (Henry) Clifford ranch and stage station on the Sidney and Black Hills route. He was informed that General Mackenzie would move that night at a stated hour, 7 o'clock, with four companies of the Fourth Cavalry and four companies of the Fifth Cavalry, all in charge of Major [George A.] Gordon of the Fifth Cavalry, in the direction of the Indian camps on the Camp Sheridan trail next [to] the Pine Ridge. He was given despatches for the officer that he was informed he would meet at Clifford's on the Niobrara River.

He arrived there towards midnight, delivered his messages to Major Frank North, and after taking a fresh horse he led off at the head of forty-one Pawnee Scouts under the command of Luther H. North and moved rapidly north into the White River Valley to join General Mackenzie, whom he was either to intercept or overtake. Having passed Crow Butte and reached Ash Creek, he was hailed by an Indian in the distance toward the hills on the right, inquiring who he was. He answered back that he had some soldiers that he was taking down to Red Cloud's camp and that he (the Indian) should go to his own camp and not follow him. The Indian shouted back that soldiers had just gone along and were only a little way ahead. The guide knew that he must be close upon Mackenzie. He had been particular to advise his interlocutor not to come near the Pawnee Scouts, as a bitter enmity existed between them and the Sioux, and sight of each other was all the provocation needed to bring on a fierce clash of arms. This man belonged to Little Wound's band, which was in camp up the creek toward the hills. After a few miles travel the Pawnee advance came upon Mackenzie's rear guard, which was seized with a flurry, supposing that a heavy force of Indians were at their backs, and they dashed up to the main body announcing their belief to be the fact; but their excitement was quieted when the guide, who had sped in among them in the darkness, asked for the commanding officers and let it be known who he was.

Prior to this movement a one-armed man named Clark had been doing duty for General Mackenzie as an emissary in the Red Cloud and Red Leaf camps and mapping in his brain the routes to be followed when the troops should be led into positions before daylight to surround the Indians. When within four miles of the Chadron Creek, General Mackenzie divided his force equally and also divided the Pawnees equally and taking one body himself he moved on Red Cloud's camp, and Major Gordon taking the other and being guided by Clark was to surround Red Leaf; but by some error of Clark he led Gordon's command to Red Cloud's and surrounded the camp when General Mackenzie arrived as day was breaking. The general ordered Gordon to advance on Red Leaf's village, and he invested Red Cloud's. The sun was just peeping over the hills east of Chadron Creek when Major Gordon's approach on the upper village was announced by a boy who was seen at the top of a high hill just west of the camp, who cried out that the creek was full of soldiers coming up. A charge into the village was ordered, and the troopers rushed forward, William Garnett, the interpreter, outstripping the others and dashing in ahead to talk to the Indians and calm their fears, which he did with safety as they all knew him; and he hurriedly counseled them not to fire on the soldiers, telling them if they did not start a fight that they would not be harmed.

Major Gordon demanded to know where Red Leaf was, and it was found that he was not there but was somewhere near the agency with two or three lodges. Then the interpreter pointed out Quick Bear, who was approaching, as the chief next in rank to Red Leaf, and, though he denied that he was a chief, Garnett contradicted him to his face, having been in council with him and knowing well the truth of what he affirmed; whereupon Major Gordon leveled his revolver at him and told him that he wanted his arms and horses, and the Indian instantly promised to surrender them. Just at this moment an Indian standing close to the chief aimed at Major Gordon with a six-shooter, but the quick interference of Garnett and Quick Bear averted the danger. The Indians' arms were gathered in haste. The horses belonging to the Indians were brought into the camp, and their owners were permitted to use them in packing and moving.

The method was not so orderly down at the other camp, the Pawnees being allowed to take the horses of the captives about as they pleased, and some of them outfitted themselves with the best they could find. (The Pawnees were ordered when the troops became occupied with the Indians that they were to stampede the horses at the camps in the usual fashion. Ricker note.) About a mile and a half on the way the two commands came together. The Indian men and women marched separately in the column, all mounted. When Ash Creek was reached, the women were permitted to camp for the night while the men were taken on to the fort twelve miles farther. The column was met here by a convoy of provisions which had been sent for after the capture.

After the Indians with their effects were arrived at the fort and their lodges were put up, their baggage was searched for ammunition, and a considerable quantity was obtained. The same day their lodges were torn down and set up again, this time down at the agency. The following day a council was held in the agency stockade. This was a commission sent out by [the] government to take the Indian chiefs down to the Indian Territory to see the country so they might decide whether they would move down there or whether they would move over to the Missouri and have their agencies there. Spotted Tail and Red Cloud and Young Man Afraid [of His Horse] and others went down. These did not like the territory so the trip never amounted to anything, and next year (1877) the Sioux were taken to the Missouri, and the Cheyennes were moved to the Indian Territory. In a day or two after the council Garnett, Big Bat [Baptiste Pourier] and Frank Gruard [Grouard] were sent to the Spotted Tail Agency to get Indians for scouts. This was the beginning of the enlistments of Indian scouts, and it was [Brig. Gen. George] Crook's scheme and undertaking.

Chapter 9

War or Peace:
The Anxious Wait for Crazy Horse

Oliver Knight

In the early afternoon of a bright Sunday in May 1877 a sullen Oglala riding a white horse led a peace-chanting cavalcade into the environs of Camp Robinson, Nebraska, there to surrender their arms, give up their ponies, and forfeit forever the sweet freedom of the grasslands. Until Crazy Horse actually came into sight, however, there had been four months of anxious waiting, because his decision—more than that of any other man—would determine whether there was to be peace or continued warfare on the northern Plains.

Crazy Horse's surrender was an epochal moment in the history of the West. With the other large tribal groups having surrendered or found sanctuary north of the border, it removed from the field the last war leader whose "Hoka, hey!" could have been a magnet for the wild young men at the agencies. There would be scattered, small-scale fighting in the West after he capitulated—between then and the bleak winter days when Hotchkiss guns would drum the last death-song at Wounded Knee. But military leaders and others recognized his submission as signaling the end of massive Indian resistance on the North American continent.[1]

Irony stripes their recognition of the moment, for military leaders had become aware of Crazy Horse's stature only in the few months preceding his surrender. Throughout the fighting of 1876, Sitting Bull had personified the northern Indians, "Crazy Horse" being just the name of another Indian.[2] Gradually, however, Brig. Gen. George Crook, commander of the Department of the Platte, had become aware of Crazy Horse's position and charisma. Perhaps the vector was Frank Grouard, the controversial plainsman of disputed ancestry—probably black and Indian—who had been Crook's only reliable guide through the then-unknown Sioux country during the summer of 1876. Grouard had lived in the camps of both Sitting Bull and Crazy Horse and in time betrayed both. By 1877 Crook and his staff knew Crazy Horse was their key opponent. Speaking for Crook, 1st Lt. Walter S. Schuyler, one of his aides, would say later in the spring, "The chief fighting man is Crazy Horse, as a chief. . . . Sitting Bull is looked upon more as a council chief."[3]

One of the holdouts who had sought to preserve the Sioux way and Sioux lands, Crazy Horse was an extraordinary man by the standards of any culture. Unlike most Indians he possessed the genius of command. More, he was wrapped in a mystique that drew young warriors to his lance with eagerness and confidence, a mystique compounded of a selfless concern for his people, courage in battle beyond the call of Plains culture, and an almost secretive modesty. In the big camp on the Little Bighorn the Oglalas had made Crazy Horse a new kind of chief, a leader of warriors and wise father of his people.[4]

The son of an Oglala father and Brulé mother—the sister of Chief Spotted Tail of the Brulé—Crazy Horse was only in his mid-thirties when he stopped Crook at the Rosebud and eight days later led the warriors who wiped out Custer's immediate command, fanatically shouting to his warriors that it was a good day to die. After the thoroughly satisfactory fight with Custer on what they called Greasy Grass Creek, the Indians had "put the war back in the bag" for that summer, thinking the soldiers would have sense enough to do the same. Dismantling their huge collection of villages, the Sioux and Cheyennes had then broken into smaller groups, some scattering to favorite hunting grounds and some going to the Bighorns to cut new lodge poles.

But the soldiers surprised the Indians by not going back to their forts. The army had been given control of all Sioux agencies. These included the Red Cloud (Oglala) and Spotted Tail (Brulé) agencies, within forty-five miles of each other in northwestern Nebraska, policed by Camp Robinson and Camp Sheridan, respectively. Crook had deposed Red Cloud as chief of the Oglala in October 1876 and installed Spotted Tail as chief of all Indians at both agencies. The exchange had no effect on the Oglala governing structure. Guided by five hundred Sioux scouts, who enlisted at regular army pay, Crook had then sent Col. Ranald S. Mackenzie against Dull Knife's major Cheyenne village on a branch of the Powder River in late November. Mackenzie had sacked the village, driving the Cheyennes into the winter snows as paupers. Simultaneously, Col. Nelson A. Miles, operating in Brig. Gen. Alfred Terry's Department of Dakota, had remained in the Yellowstone country through the winter, fighting Sitting Bull in October and Crazy Horse in January and wearing down but routing neither.

Generals William T. Sherman and Philip H. Sheridan wanted Crook to strike again, but Crook persuaded Sheridan that the hostiles probably could be induced to surrender. Using Sioux as he had learned to use other Indians in the Pacific Northwest and Arizona, Crook sent spies into the hostile camps who came back with reports that the hostiles were willing to at least talk about surrender.[5] They were low on ammunition, game was scarce, and the soldiers seemed to be everywhere. From his scouts Crook knew what he could realistically expect.

On the basis of that intelligence, Maj. Julius W. Mason, commanding Camp Robinson, sent thirty Sioux under Sword, a minor Oglala war leader, to the hostiles on January 16, 1877.[6] Sword brought back information that showed the "backbone of the opposition had lost its former strength and that, if pushed vigorously in the spring, the enemy would gladly enough surrender."[7] From them and other Indians, Crook's officers learned that the hostiles would accept Spotted Tail as a negotiator.[8]

With that, Crook left Cheyenne, where he had been attending the court-martial of Col. Joseph J. Reynolds, and arrived at Red Cloud Agency on January 29, accompanied by one of his aides, Lieutenant Schuyler, Maj. Thaddeus H. Stanton, departmental paymaster, and Robert E. Strahorn, a *Chicago Tribune* correspondent who remained in the field with Crook's forces from March 1876 until May 1877.[9] He also called in another aide from departmental headquarters in Omaha, 1st Lt. John G. Bourke, a slender man of thirty, heavily mustached, eight years out of West Point.[10]

The first order of business at Red Cloud Agency was to pay the Sioux and Cheyenne scouts. Their payday overjoyed the scouts, some of whom said they would now trust the government, "because it has at last carried out *one* promise with them."[11] It did not matter whether a man was paid the right amount so long as it was in one-dollar bills or smaller currency. With their new-found wealth the Indians bought whatever caught their fancy at the trader's. One warrior groomed himself in a lady's kid gloves and another in a lady's straw hat. Crook let that go on for a time and then quietly passed the word to the headmen that money was to be spent carefully.[12]

What the army would not tolerate at the agency were the "harpies and vultures." Payday attracted "gamblers, whores and horse-thieves," whom Capt. Daniel W. Burke, post commander, arrested and confined in the guardhouse, keeping it full until he was ready to escort the lot to the boundary of the agency.[13]

On February 7 Crook, accompanied by key officers, 1st Lt. William P. Clark, chief of scouts at both agencies, Stanton, Capt. George M. Randall, who had been his chief of scouts the previous summer, and Strahorn, moved the short distance to Camp Sheridan to begin dickering with Spotted Tail.

Spotted Tail, designated by some as "probably the greatest Sioux chief of his period," was a hard bargainer with a strong and supple mind. For nearly twenty years he had been a peace advocate but never an Indian "Uncle Tom." Resourceful in negotiation, he had dealt with presidents, cabinet officers, and generals, often getting the better of the bargain for his people. His agency was where it was because he had simply refused to accept a move to the Missouri River dictated by the Indian Bureau.[14]

Now he was telling Crook what he wanted before he would travel hundreds of miles through snow to talk with his Oglala nephew, Crazy Horse, and the other hostiles. Spotted Tail insisted that Crook personally state liberal surrender terms, permit him to take a large body of warriors—a small escort would not have commanded respect in a warriors' camp; besides many men could carry more presents—and supply him with ammunition, food, and supplies. As his most important point, he wanted Crook's assurance that the general would help get the hostiles an agency of their own and in their own country.[15]

In three days of negotiation Crook agreed to those terms but laid down the government's fundamental requirement for the surrender of arms, ponies, and ammunition. However, Crook also promised amnesty for acts of the past.[16]

Having struck the bargain, Spotted Tail left about February 10 with approximately two hundred warriors and two interpreters who could send back written messages if necessary, Jose (Joe) Merivale, a Mexican-American from New Mexico, and F. C. Boucher. He promised to send immediate word by courier to Deadwood, Cantonment Reno, or Camp Sheridan, depending on where he found Crazy Horse's camp.

To receive the couriers Crook sent Randall to Cantonment Reno (later Fort McKinney, Wyoming) and three companies of cavalry to the Black Hills under Capt. Peter D. Vroom; the cavalry would also protect the citizens of the Hills against Indian raiders. Crook and his staff then left for the more commodious Fort Laramie on February 11.[17]

Thus, in a V-shaped ring around the south of Crazy Horse's country, three eyewitnesses took station and left records through which one can sense the milieu and detect the tangled web of human relationships that enwrapped the surrender of Crazy Horse. Strahorn went to Cantonment Reno with Randall. In the Black Hills the *Chicago Times* had L. F. Whitbeck. At Fort Laramie Bourke added to the diary that is a rich—and under-used—depository of social observation.[18] The Black Hills proved to be the liveliest area. Second Lt. Joseph F. Cummings—less than a year out of West Point—conducted a five-day campaign (February 21–26) in which his company destroyed a village of ten lodges—the Indians got away—and recovered 624 head of stolen livestock.[19]

If a green shavetail could do that much, the frontiersmen expected miracles from the older and more experienced Vroom, who arrived later. But Vroom disappointed them in not taking the field. Actually, his orders placed him in a tenuous position. His written orders directed him to protect citizens and property in Deadwood, but oral orders restrained him from offensive operations while Spotted Tail was in the field. His inactivity caused civilians to come into camp almost daily, in groups of from three to a dozen, complaining to him and threatening to go higher. But Whitbeck noted sarcastically that those "first-class lingerers and nuisances" all had ranches that would be ideal for a military post, and, just by chance, also had hay, beef, or something else for sale to the army.[20] Otherwise, camp life, graced by one woman, was tranquil. She was Mrs. Valentine T. McGillycuddy, wife of the surgeon. "When the troops are on the march she rides her handsome bay at the head of the column," a writer from the *Chicago Times* observed.[21]

The civilian tension showed in a dispatch from a citizen signing himself "Deadwood," who said, "We are all looking anxiously to see what may come of Spotted Tail's mission."[22] At the same time, though, Whitbeck reported that there had been "considerable talk in Deadwood and vicinity" about attacking Spotted Tail if he came there. Although inclined to dismiss the talk as "chaff," he said Vroom was under orders to escort the Indians safely through Deadwood, "and should any riotous conduct manifest itself among the citizens, they and not the troops will be the sufferers."[23]

By contrast Randall and Strahorn found life dreary when they reached Cantonment Reno on February 19. However, there was a sense of expectancy. A writer signing himself "Wyoming"—probably an officer, many of whom moonlighted as free-lance correspondents—said: "Events are transpiring that will in the course of a month lead to a renewal of hostilities or result in the establishment of peace. . . . We are awaiting the issue with considerable anxiety, as probably the fate of this cantonment depends upon the result." Strahorn likewise reported that the men were "at the very top-notch of anxiety to have the matter decided."[24]

Actually, any kind of change would have been welcomed just to crack the boredom. Commanded by Capt. Edwin Pollock, the 150 infantrymen, in a post composed of thirty log and mud huts, had a "don't care and slip-shod" attitude. The monotony of their routine was varied only by a mail rider once or twice a month and an occasional supply train. They whiled away their snowbound hours reading month-old newspapers and playing chess or whist. The loneliness can only be imagined for the one woman there, the wife of Capt. Samuel P. Ferris.[25]

Time dragged just as heavily for fifty or so hunters, trappers, and miners who lived in dugouts in the banks of the Powder River until the weather—and the Indian question—would permit them to enter the Bighorns. All the civilians were broke, but some were making a little money by building a bridge across the Powder for the post trader, who took it upon himself to build it when the army did not provide for it.[26]

The general mood of the troops at Reno can be sensed by "Wyoming's" morose remark: "This unvaried monotony month after month, becoming worse and worse until it verges into utter stagnation, is that which more than anything else . . . tries men's souls and we sincerely trust that soon Crazy Horse will appear or that orders from Gen. Crook will give us relief."[27]

At Fort Laramie life was pleasant and lazy for Bourke. After breakfast he and other staff officers listened to the band, inspected the stables, and then took care of any correspondence that had arrived the evening before. After lunch they read what they could find in the company libraries, including Macaulay, Prescott, Burke, and Thackeray. "Living on the frontier," Bourke said, "an Army officer's chances of literary treasures are so slight that he must cheerfully embrace whatever opportunities come within his reach without waiting for a selection."[28]

In common with many other army officers from the colonial period on, Bourke disliked "borderers" of any stripe, especially those he found at three "ranches" within three miles of the fort—Cooney's, Ecoffey's, and Wright's—which were combination gin mills and whorehouses. "In all my experience, I have never seen a lower, more beastly set of people of both sexes." Earlier he had written that the Black Hills, like all new communities, had become "a resort for the vilest and most unprincipled outlaws" and horsethieves who preyed on agency Indians. Later he would record that Vroom had been relieved of eighteen mules by the Black Hills citizens whom he had been sent to protect.[29]

Suddenly, the suspense was broken on April 4 when a courier from 1st Lt. Jesse M. Lee, agent at Spotted Tail Agency, arrived at Fort Laramie. He reported that Spotted Tail had succeeded and was then on the Belle Fourche with 1,600 Indians. On the same date Vroom telegraphed the same news brought in by Merivale. Crook did not react until the next day; Whitbeck from the Black Hills said Crook had been off on a fishing trip when the news arrived (maybe a telegraph operator gossiped). Calling in Randall and Vroom, Crook centered his people at Camp Robinson, which also was headquarters for Mackenzie's District of the Black Hills, where he arrived with his staff on April 11.[30]

In the interim Spotted Tail had indeed helped to end the war, but there was more to Spotted Tail's mission than met the eye. En route he had persuaded about a thousand Sans Arcs and Minneconjous as well as smaller bands, to surrender. He then sent a runner to Crazy Horse's camp on Otter Creek.[31]

As it happened, the Oglalas and Cheyennes in Crazy Horse's camp were just then on the verge of surrendering to Miles, who was trying hard to become Caesar of the Great North. From his Tongue River Cantonment, Miles had established contact with Crazy Horse's people, sharply divided into war and peace factions, through his interpreter, John (Big Leggins) Bruguier, and some Cheyenne captives. Reassured by the captives, the Oglalas and Cheyennes had accepted Miles's demand for "unconditional surrender." With criers having gone through the villages to announce that the war was over, the band had marched two days until Spotted Tail's runner intercepted them on Otter Creek. They halted there until Spotted Tail could tell them more.[32]

There then ensued a literal tug-of-war between Spotted Tail and Miles, a ravenous glory-hunter who ached to have the Oglalas and Cheyennes surrender to him, notwithstanding his overly frequent protestations (three times in one short report) that he did not care whether they surrendered at the Tongue or at the agencies.[33]

Having heard Spotted Tail's blandishments, sixteen chiefs led a delegation to Miles on March 18 to see whether he would modify his terms. Having almost had his quarry, Miles was plainly angry at being frustrated by Spotted Tail. His commander, General Terry, later shared that indignation, referring to Spotted Tail's mission as an "untoward interference with Colonel Miles' plans."[34]

In both private and official letters Miles said Spotted Tail had brought ammunition to the hostiles and promised them more at the agencies but quickly disavowed any implication that Crook had sanctioned it. Actually, Crook's officer might have looked the other way when the warriors had packed their ponies because Spotted Tail had insisted on taking ammunition. Miles also accused Spotted Tail of offering "liberal terms," as though Crook had deliberately plotted to out-bargain him.[35]

In spite of his delusions and accusations Miles undoubtedly was right in part, for evidence from two sources indicates that Spotted Tail played fast and loose with Crook's conditions. From the Black Hills, where Merivale had gone, Whitbeck wrote that Spotted Tail had told the hostiles they would have to give up only the arms captured in the Custer fight. Stronger evidence comes from Bourke. When the Minneconjous and Sans Arcs reached Spotted Tail Agency on April 14, he noted, "General Crook was very indignant with 'Spotted Tail' for endeavoring to save the Minneconju and Sans Arc from turning in their arms."[36] In view of Spotted Tail's record of gaining his point with other white men, it is not too much to conjecture that he gambled on Crook's compromising once the birds were in hand. It is also apparent that Spotted Tail told the Sioux they would have their own agency, making the most of Crook's promise to use his influence to that end.

On the other hand, there is evidence that Miles dealt under the table. Rabidly jealous of Crook—whom he accused of having been a failure in the Civil War and ever since—Miles frothed at the thought of Crook getting credit for "bagging" several thousand Indians when he felt he alone was responsible for their capitulation. As warriors came in from Crazy Horse's camp from time to time before the surrender, they told Clark that Miles had told them they would have to give up only their old ponies and their old guns. He could then report they had surrendered arms and ponies, while in reality they would keep their good ones. They said Miles also told them they would be treated badly if they surrendered to Crook.[37]

In the course of events Spotted Tail conferred with the hostiles in a general council on the Powder River but did not talk with Crazy Horse personally. Not wanting to talk peace with his uncle, Crazy Horse went off alone. In his absence his father assured Spotted Tail they would accept Crook's terms. Later some of them persuaded Crazy Horse to come along.[38]

Almost all the Sioux chose to go to the agencies, but the Cheyennes decided to let each headman take his band where he would.[39] It would appear only natural that most of the Indians, then numbering well over one thousand, would have chosen the agencies, knowing they would find food and supplies there. They had seen that Miles had nothing for them in his scrawny outpost of log huts, where even his horses and mules were going hungry. Moreover, there was Crook's amnesty against Miles's unconditional surrender (if the latter still obtained). Ultimately, only about three hundred Cheyennes surrendered to Miles. When he told them they could plant gardens to provide their own food, White Bull announced he would grow raisins because that was the best food the white man had.[40]

Not yet aware of what had transpired in the north, Crook arrived at Camp Robinson on April 11. He faced a situation in which the hostiles reputedly had agreed to surrender, yet the grass was beginning to green— the prelude to the war season. He had to know precisely what Crazy Horse intended to do.

To find out he authorized the Red Cloud mission, of obscure and somewhat contradictory origin. One version, oral testimony thirty years after the event, has it that Clark, as chief of scouts, bribed Red Cloud with the promise that he would use his influence with Crook to have Red Cloud reinstated as chief.[41] At the time, however, Bourke wrote that Crook had told Red Cloud that he was preparing to take the field immediately, to which Red Cloud responded by asking permission to go to Crazy Horse as a peace emissary. Crook replied he could go if he wished but not as Crook's representative. If he went, he was to tell Crazy Horse that "every day his surrender was deferred was one day closer to the moment" when troops would seek out and kill his warriors wherever found.[42] Schuyler reinforced the Bourke version soon afterwards, saying Crook had sent Red Cloud as an envoy to determine whether Crazy Horse wanted to surrender or fight it out. "Gen. Crook sent word to the Indians that he didn't care much, but he simply wanted to know what Crazy Horse intended to do."[43] The versions can be synchronized if one theorizes that Crook wanted Red Cloud to use his influence with the Oglalas and had Clark prime Red Cloud to ask permission, thus saving Crook from asking a favor of the man he had deposed as chief of the Oglala.

However it might have been arranged, Red Cloud was on his way almost overnight. With seventy warriors and a mixed-blood who could write messages for him, Red Cloud left on April 12 or 13, promising to send back periodic reports.[44]

Thus juggling several problems at once, Crook spent nineteen days at the agencies, simultaneously preparing to take the field against Crazy Horse if necessary and receiving the surrender of about two thousand Sioux and Cheyennes. Small groups had been straggling in during the preceding several weeks, including some Cheyennes under Little Wolf, who said his nearly naked and starving people had walked the entire distance from the Tongue to Red Cloud Agency, struggling through knee-deep snow between the Tongue and Belle Fourche.[45]

Having traveled the forty-five miles to Camp Sheridan on April 12, Crook received the first large contingent of former hostiles on April 14, the one thousand Minneconjous and Sans Arcs. After first obtaining permission about three hundred warriors swooped into Spotted Tail Agency, whooping and firing. About an hour later thirty headmen rode in line onto the parade ground of Camp Sheridan, wheeled to the left to face Crook, and surrendered in a handshaking ceremony. As their people ascended a hill to a campsite about a mile away, Bourke said they looked "for all the world like a swarm of black ants."[46]

Moving back to Camp Robinson, Crook received the surrender of about five hundred Cheyennes under Dull Knife and Standing Elk on April 21. Reduced to destitution by Mackenzie's attack in November, the Cheyennes lived in lodges covered with bits of canvas, hide, rags, and gunny sacks. Without utensils of any kind, the women carried water in skin bags. The regular arrival of smaller groups at both agencies made surrenders a matter of common occurrence, gradually swelling the total number of surrendered Indians.[47]

Crook conducted two conferences with the newcomers, a most important one with the Sioux at Spotted Tail Agency on April 15 and a perfunctory one with the Cheyennes at Red Cloud on April 22. Along with several pleas for justice and fair play, Spotted Tail made a strong bid for giving the Sans Arc and Minneconjou "a country they could call their own."[48]

In responding to Spotted Tail Crook said something about a reservation that could have been misconstrued all around. Both Bourke and a *Chicago Times* reporter used long quotations in recording both sides of the conferences, agreeing on essentials but differing in minor points of wording, except for one passage. Where Bourke quoted Crook as saying officials in Washington would "do anything in reason" if all the Indians came in, the *Chicago Times* man heard him say, "If I ask the great father to do anything for you, he will do it."[49] The *Times* quotation has more the ring of a council statement than Bourke's.

Two days after that statement appeared in Chicago, the headquarters of Sheridan's Military Division of the Missouri, one of Sheridan's aides, Maj. George A. Forsyth, arrived at Camp Robinson to talk about that reservation, for the Indian Bureau wanted to move the Sioux to the Missouri River. Implying that Crook had carried his point, Bourke wrote confidently that the reservation for the Sioux, Arapaho, and Northern Cheyenne would be in southeastern Montana. He defined an area bounded by the 104th meridian (two minutes east of the present eastern boundary of Montana), the 46th parallel, the Little Bighorn (the 46th parallel does not intersect the Little Bighorn, but he can be forgiven because the area had not been surveyed) and the Bighorn to the Yellowstone, the Yellowstone to the mouth of the Powder, and a line due east to the 104th meridian.[50]

However, Bourke was both overconfident and underinformed. On August 15, 1876, Congress stipulated that no more money would be appropriated for the Sioux until they ceded all lands west of the 103rd meridian.[51] In other words, Congress had already ordered the Sioux to quitclaim the Black Hills and their kingdom in Wyoming and Montana or starve. Unaware of that Bourke was agitated when a rumor reached Camp Robinson ten days later (April 30) that both Red Cloud and Spotted Tail agencies would be moved to the Missouri. "Now that these Indians have been allowed to surrender at this place and with the understanding that they were to live *here*, our Government has no right to violate the compact."[52] Both agencies were indeed moved to the present Rosebud and Pine Ridge reservations in present southwestern South Dakota after a brief stint near the Missouri River during the winter of 1877–78. The incident raises some questions about communications between Washington and the field in manipulating Indian negotiations; they are beyond the scope of this article but warrant a closer scrutiny than they have been given.

The large number of surrenders during the middle days of April, which ruled out a major campaign that summer, climaxed on April 27 when six Indian soldiers (that term was used more often than "scouts" at that time and place) brought a letter from Red Cloud—a semi-literate scrawl by his mixed-blood scrivener—saying definitely that Crazy Horse would arrive in eight or nine days.[53]

That was good enough for Crook. The Indians had done what he had asked. Now he would keep his word to them. Leaving Camp Robinson on April 28, he went to Chicago and Washington to do what he could about the reservation, unsuccessfully as it turned out. He took Schuyler with him but left Bourke as his eyes and ears at the agencies.

Throughout his stay Bourke studied the Plains Indian culture, foreshadowing the important contributions he would make to anthropology in future years. Visiting their lodges Bourke came to have a high appreciation of Indian family structure, their kindness to the aged and infirm, and the many gifts for the poor that were laid on the ground at dances and festive occasions. Using the white culture as a standard of comparison, he found that Spotted Tail and his ranking councillor, White Thunder, treated guests as courteously as did white hosts. In his lodge of "unexceptionable neatness" White Thunder "deported himself fully as well as the generality of white men," and Spotted Tail received Bourke's party "with urbanity, a virtue common to all Indians I have ever seen."[54]

Indian dances enthralled him and other observers, especially the first one they saw, an Omaha dance which the Sans Arcs and Minneconjous staged for Crook after the conference on April 15. Knowing that he was incapable of appreciating the symbolism of Indian dancing, Bourke simply described it as a dance in which the "masters of ceremonies"—painted in various patterns, most with a yellow imprint of a hand on the flanks and all wearing war bonnets that trailed to the ground—rode around the inside of the circle to announce the "next act." Performers, whose torsos were painted green, blue, yellow, red, black, and in various speckled, spotted, and striped patterns, came into the circle one by one to pantomime his or another's achievements, while a chorus chanted an account of the deed. Each costume was trimmed with sleigh bells, but one man was wrapped in sleigh bells from shoulder to ankle. Each performer wore a red or yellow headdress made of the hair from an elk's neck and ornamented by a single eagle feather. Bourke saw the dances as an "almost photographic picture" of acts of valor.[55]

At Camp Robinson they saw two other dances. Sioux women treated them to a slow-measured "squaw dance" in which the women stunned the onlookers with long dresses of antelope hide, beaded solidly as mail from waist to neck and with elaborate beading on sleeves and skirts. Borrowing red leggings and red blankets from the Sioux, the impoverished Cheyenne men staged a "spoon" dance in which seventy-five or eighty dancers took part. Into the circle a Cheyenne would ride and whisper to the drummers of a deed of prowess, bringing a deeper thud from the drums and loud whoops by the drummers. From time to time the dancers broke into two groups and would "yell and dance like fury."[56]

Through numerous conversations Bourke sought to learn of the tribes and their history. What is now fairly well established as anthropological and historical knowledge was just beginning, dimly, to enter the consciousness of whites interested enough to inquire. Spotted Tail said he did not know when the Sioux first got horses but knew they had come from the south. Fire Crow, a Cheyenne, claimed his people had been the first northern Indians to have horses.[57]

Bourke seems to have been more impressed by an Arapaho leader, Friday, than by any other. Friday, who had traveled through the Plains, told him that the Arapaho had still used dogs to haul travois when he was a boy and had first obtained horses from the Comanche. He also said an extensive intertribal trade centered at Bent's Fort on the Arkansas River ("Billy Bent's," he called it), where Sioux bows and arrows were obtained by Comanches in trading with Cheyennes and Arapahos who had, in turn, obtained them from Sioux at Fort Laramie.[58]

Bourke's recounting of Friday's stories leads to the surmise that Friday might have drawn the thirty-seven pages of unidentified pictographs in Bourke's diary (on leaves from old account books). The "writing" of such autobiographies—"brag skins," more humorous Indians called them—would appear to have been one of the means by which a number of earnest and sincere Indians sought to cement friendships with the whites. No Flesh, an eager but not so sincere Brulé, tried to ingratiate himself with Mrs. Anson Mills—and through her Captain Mills, commanding officer at Camp Sheridan—by drawing pictographs of his valorous history.[59]

At least one dog feast—"choked pup" to Bourke—was given in late April, which may have been the one Strahorn described in his autobiography.

At age ninety Strahorn garbled the time, place, and people, but he was too much a literalist to have cut this description from whole cloth:

When my turn came my dirty tin platter was served with the rear end of the backbone, with part of the poorly dressed tail attached (Strahorn obviously did not know that getting the tail marked him as one of the honored guests, in the ritual of the dog feast). After looking that large and disgusting offering of high hospitality over carefully to see whether I could detach as much as a mouthful without getting any of the hairy dog skin still liberally decorating it, I fairly sickened. . . . No worse insult could possibly be visited upon an Indian host than to refuse to eat liberally of such sacred offerings. . . . One fiendish glance was enough to induce the swallowing of anything. I can only add that I did my best and can taste that offensively strong, oily dog meat and glimpse its bloody, bristling backbone and tail hairs like a loathsome nightmare to this day.[60]

A most important part of life at Camps Robinson and Sheridan was the gathering of intelligence from the Indian camps. Building a force of Indian soldiers at both agencies, Clark, who became the authority on Indian sign language, maintained an elaborate spy network. Cheyenne soldiers spied on the Sioux constantly and vice versa, isolating troublemakers before they could make trouble.[61]

Indeed, the entire behavior of the Indians suggests that they may have adopted a new status symbol during the traumatic transition to a confined life. Proud and vain (in the most favorable connotations), the Plains Indian male had attained prestige as warrior, hunter, horse owner, or holy man. Now, it would appear, they sought that prestige through influence with the whites. The various accounts throughout the literature suggest that Indian leaders and would-be leaders sought to cultivate army officers for that purpose. "Some of these Indians become warmly attached to the officers, impart and receive confidences."[62]

Meanwhile, Red Cloud had asked for food for Crazy Horse's people. Lt. J. Wesley Rosenquest took ten wagons of food and one hundred cattle to Hat Creek, where he met the Indians on May 1, and became by repute the first white man to shake hands with Crazy Horse, who as a child had played with white boys around Fort Laramie. Nearly famished many of the Oglalas gorged themselves to the point of illness.[63]

As Crazy Horse neared, apprehension grew among the agency Indians, some of whom said they had heard he would not surrender his arms. That portended a crisis. Knowing that Crazy Horse was dangerous, Clark mobilized his Cheyenne soldiers just in case. Ever since the first few had surrendered, the Cheyennes had shown a marked hostility toward Crazy Horse. They had told officers that Crazy Horse had turned them away when they, in their rags after Mackenzie's attack, had sought succor in his camp. In later years the Cheyennes would tell that the Oglalas had shared what they had. The real reason they were so angry at Crazy Horse may have been that he had "soldiered" them when they had wanted to surrender voluntarily earlier in the winter; that is, he ordered his Oglala warriors to break the Cheyenne bows, take their guns and ponies, and beat them.[64]

On the morning of May 6, when it was known that Crazy Horse would arrive that day, Clark stationed a force of Cheyenne soldiers behind a bluff near the agency. They remained there throughout the day, await-ing the signal that would bring them into battle.[65]

With twenty Indian soldiers, Clark—known to the Indians as White Hat—rode out to meet Crazy Horse, accompanied by a *Chicago Times* reporter who had visited Crazy Horse's camp with another detail the day before. Five miles from the agency they met the Oglalas. In a valley be-tween two long, sloping bluffs, the two groups went through a handshak-ing ceremony, while Crazy Horse's 889 people blackened the surround-ing slopes. Letting He Dog do the talking, the scar-faced Crazy Horse remained silent. Saying he would surrender only to those in whom he had confidence, He Dog placed a war shirt and bonnet on White Hat. Clark then made the usual talk about everlasting peace and explained the procedure that would be followed in dismounting, disarming, and counting the people.

At that point Crazy Horse spoke his only words, "I have given all I have to Red Cloud."[66] Throughout the literature those words have been inter-preted consistently, as they were in the newspaper reports of the meeting, as meaning he had given all his personal possessions to Red Cloud. But the interpretation may be distortion. Since he most certainly held onto his Winchester and had characteristically worn a single feather rather than a war bonnet, he may have meant that he had yielded authority to Red Cloud. Red Cloud was a manipulative tribal politician, whereas it is easy to see Crazy Horse in Mari Sandoz's biography as a man of action who may have been inarticulate and unable to cope with political nuances.

That was the surrender. Contrary to some historical accounts, includ-ing Sheridan's annual report, Crazy Horse did *not* surrender to Crook personally; Crook was in Washington and would not meet Crazy Horse until May 25, 1877.[67]

With Clark, Rosenquest, and the Indian soldiers in the lead, the col-umn reached Red Cloud Agency about 2 P.M. There was none of the pomp, parade, firing, or whooping that had been part of some of the earlier surrenders (and which some authors have inserted in their accounts of this one). In five disciplined ranks, astride painted war ponies, the three hundred warriors wore their finest: war bonnets, blankets, ornaments of silver, brass, tin, and glass. Watching through field glasses from a distance, an officer exclaimed, "By God! This is a triumphal march, not a surrender!" From end to end of the two-mile-long column rang a solemn peace chant. Reaching their campsite in the White River bottoms, the Oglalas formed their lodges in a crescent about three-fourths of a mile from the agency.[68]

Thomas Moore, Crook's chief packer, took the ponies first, stopping the count at 1,700. Next came the guns, Clark allowing the Oglalas to surrender their weapons voluntarily, as they had requested. But when they relinquished only a token number, he announced firmly that he would search every tipi and take every weapon. To shield their humiliation the Oglala warriors asked that white men be withdrawn from the area. Dismissing all whites but two officers, Clark took his Indian soldiers on a search that lasted until 8 P.M. and netted 117 rifles and pistols, including two Winchesters that Crazy Horse gave up with neither objection nor assistance; he apparently had placed one Winchester on the ground in the first, token surrender of arms.[69]

Throughout, Crazy Horse, a sinewy man of about five feet, eleven inches, exuding command presence, remained silent and passive. He spoke to none of his conquerors until Frank Grouard and Bourke went to his lodge that evening.[70] On all sides the Anglo-Americans recognized that Crazy Horse's surrender meant that the big Indian wars had come to an end. For history it was an epochal moment. For the people concerned it was a sad collapse of a proud way of life. For the Lakotas—"The Men"—and the nation it remained for Bourke to write an apprehensive epilogue:

> If our Government will only observe *one-half* of its promises, the Indians will comply faithfully with their agreements, I am certain; the great danger of the future is not from the red man's want of faith so much as from the indifference of our Government to the plainest requirements of honor. Our own faith is worse than Punic; yet, we always prattle about Indian treachery.... If the Government will only keep its promises and treat these red men with justice, we shall have no more Indian wars.[71]

His premonition of dishonor was to prove well-founded.

Notes

[1] Gen. William T. Sherman and Lt. Gen. Philip H. Sheridan quoted at a Washington conference, *Chicago Times*, Apr. 27, 1877; U.S. Congress, *Report of the Secretary of War*, 45th Cong., 2d sess., 1877, H. Doc. 1, pt. 2, 1:85 (Serial 1794), hereinafter cited as *Report of the Secretary of War*; *Chicago Times*, May 7, 1877.

[2] This is abundantly clear in the dispatches of correspondents who covered the war and who undoubtedly reflected what army officers did not know about the enemy.

[3] Lt. Walter S. Schuyler, speaking for Brig. Gen. George Crook in a Chicago interview, *Chicago Tribune*, May 3, 1877. The reporter had sought an interview with Crook, but the general "referred the news-gatherer to his subordinate, as he did not desire to speak concerning matters in which he was personally concerned."

[4] Mari Sandoz, *Crazy Horse: The Strange Man of the Oglalas* (New York: Alfred A. Knopf, 1942).

[5] Crook in *Report of the Secretary of War*, 84. The workings of the spy system are described in the *Chicago Tribune*, May 3, 1877.

[6] Harry H. Anderson, "Indian Peace-Talkers and the Conclusion of the Sioux War of 1876," *Nebraska History* 44 (Sept. 1963):239–42; Diary of Lt. John Gregory Bourke, 127 vols., original in the Library of the United States Military Academy, vol. 19, 1825–26. Bourke's diary, of which the author used the microfilm publication, is immensely rich in details, but it was not a consistent day-by-day journal. The nature of the entries shows that he wrote what he could when he could. Both Anderson and Sandoz depict factionalism and family rivalries as a healthy counterweight to the historical stereotype of "the Sioux," or any other tribal group, as a monolithic people operating through unquestioned consensus.

[7] Bourke diary, 19:1825–26.

[8] Crook in *Report of the Secretary of War*, 84–85.

[9] Col. Joseph J. Reynolds and Capt. Alexander Moore were court-martialed and found guilty of misconduct in the attack on Crazy Horse's camp in March 1876. President Rutherford B. Hayes remitted the sentences.

[10] *Chicago Tribune*, Jan. 22, Jan. 31, 1877; Bourke diary, 19:1826.

[11] *Chicago Tribune*, Feb. 12, 1877.

[12] Ibid.; Bourke diary, 19:1829.

[13] Bourke diary, 19:1829.

[14] George E. Hyde, *Spotted Tail's Folk: A History of the Brulé Sioux* (Norman: University of Oklahoma Press, 1961), ix, xi, 111, 132, 200, 202n.

[15] Ibid., 240; Anderson, "Indian Peace-Talkers," 242–43.

[16] Bourke diary, 19:1835.

[17] Ibid.

[18] Robert E. Strahorn and L. F. Whitbeck will be quoted in the text when their dispatches were signed. Other newspaper writers were not identified by signature or initials at the end of their stories.

[19] General Orders No. 8, Headquarters, Department of the Platte, Mar. 14, 1877, copy of printed order in Bourke diary, 19:1842; *Chicago Times*, Mar. 15, 1877.

[20] *Chicago Times*, Mar. 31, 1877.

[21] Ibid.

[22] Ibid.

[23] Ibid.

[24] Ibid., Mar. 15, 1877; *Chicago Tribune*, Mar. 15, 1877.

[25] *Chicago Tribune*, Mar. 15, 1877.

[26] Ibid.

[27] *Chicago Times*, Mar. 15, 1877.

[28] Bourke diary, 19:1845, 1847–48.

[29] Ibid., 19:1839, 1848–49, 1857–58.

[30] Ibid., 19:1852, 1857–58; *Chicago Times*, Apr. 16, 1877.

[31] Anderson, "Indian Peace-Talkers," 246–48.

[32] Col. Nelson A. Miles to assistant adjutant general, Department of Dakota, Mar. 24, 1877, text released by Sheridan's headquarters, *Chicago Tribune*, Apr. 14, 1877, and other newspapers of same date. Part of Miles's report appears in *Report of the Secretary of War*, 496. Nelson A. Miles, *Personal Recollections and Observations of General Nelson A. Miles* (Chicago and New York: The Werner Company, 1896), 239.

[33] Virginia Weisel Johnson, *The Unregimented General: A Biography of Nelson A. Miles* (Boston: Houghton Mifflin, 1962), 153; Miles report, *Chicago Tribune*, Apr. 14, 1877; Miles to wife, Mar. 22, 24, Apr. 15, 1877, quoted in Johnson, *Unregimented General*, 163, 165, 169.

[34] Miles to wife, Mar. 22, 1877, in Johnson, *Unregimented General*, 163; *Report of the Secretary of War*, 496.

[35] Miles to wife, Mar. 17, 1877, in Johnson, *Unregimented General*, 162; Miles report, *Chicago Tribune*, Apr. 14, 1877.

[36] *Chicago Times*, Apr. 26, 1877; Bourke diary, 19:1868–69.

[37] Miles to wife, Mar. 15, 17, 1877, in Johnson, *Unregimented General*, 160–61; Miles to Sherman, date not given, quoted in Robert G. Athearn, *William Tecumseh Sherman and the Settlement of the West* (Norman: University of Oklahoma Press, 1956), 314; Bourke diary, 19:1886–88.

[38] Sandoz, *Crazy Horse*, 358; James C. Olson, *Red Cloud and the Sioux Problem* (Lincoln: University of Nebraska Press, 1965), 237.

[39] Anderson, "Indian Peace-Talkers," 249–50.

[40] Miles report, *Chicago Tribune*, Apr. 14, 1877; Miles, *Recollections*, 247.

[41] William Garnett interviews, from the Eli S. Ricker Collection, MS8, Nebraska State Historical Society Archives, Lincoln, quoted in Olson, *Red Cloud*, 238. If that offer was made, Crook did not go along with it, for Red Cloud seems to have gradually regained his place later in 1877 after the Indian Bureau resumed administration of the agencies.

[42] Bourke diary, 19:1885–86. In writing of events in the recent past, as in this synopsis

of Crook's conversation with Red Cloud, Bourke was not always precise about dates. It was under the entry of Apr. 27, 1877, recalling the conversation of "a week ago." Crook talked with Red Cloud either on April 11 or early on April 12.

[43] Schuyler, speaking for Crook in a Chicago interview, *Chicago Tribune*, May 3, 1877.

[44] Ibid., Apr. 14, 1877; *New York Tribune*, Apr. 28, 1877.

[45] *Chicago Tribune*, Mar. 12, 1877.

[46] Bourke diary, 19;1866–68; *Chicago Tribune*, Apr. 18, 1877.

[47] Bourke diary, 19:1905–8, 1917–18; *Chicago Tribune*, Apr. 23, 1877.

[48] *Chicago Times*, Apr. 18, 1877.

[49] Ibid., Apr. 18, 1877; Bourke diary, 19:1869–77.

[50] Bourke diary, 19:1901, 1904.

[51] Olson, *Red Cloud*, 224.

[52] Bourke diary, 19:1941.

[53] Ibid., 19:1918–19; *New York Tribune*, Apr. 28, 1877, gives the text of the note from Red Cloud.

[54] For an excellent appraisal of Bourke's work, see William Gardner Bell, "A Dedication to the Memory of John Gregory Bourke," *Arizona and the West* 13 (Winter 1971):319–22; Bourke diary, 19:1878.

[55] Bourke diary, 19:1872–82; *San Francisco Alta California*, Apr. 21, 1877, in Bourke diary, 19:1923, an account which Bourke would appear to have written; *Chicago Times*, Apr. 18, 1877; *Chicago Tribune*, Apr. 18, 1877.

[56] Bourke diary, 19:1934–35, and 20:1941–42; *New York Herald*, May 11, 1877, in Bourke diary, 20:1997–2004. Bourke may have written the *New York Herald* piece; it contains passages quite similar to corresponding passages in the diary. He pasted a copy in his diary and wrote his initials in the margin at the end of the story, as though he were imitating the newspaper style of the period in which terminal initials were a form of "by-line." If he did write it, the construction of the story would prove that he was artful at literary deception, concealing his identity well.

[57] Bourke diary, 20:1950–51.

[58] Ibid., 20:1963.

[59] Ibid., 18:1751–87; Anson Mills, *My Story* (Washington: Privately printed, 1918), 158, in which Mills's years are in error; Helen H. Blish, *A Pictographic History of the Oglala Sioux* (Lincoln: University of Nebraska Press, 1967), xx.

[60] Robert E. Strahorn, "Ninety Years of Boyhood," unpublished autobiography, Strahorn Memorial Library, College of Idaho, Caldwell.

[61] *Chicago Tribune*, May 3, 1877; *San Francisco Alta California*, Apr. 21, 1877, in Bourke diary, 19:1923; *Chicago Times*, Apr. 19, 1877.

[62] *New York Tribune*, Apr. 28, 1877.

[63] The officer's name appears as Lieutenant Rosecrans, erroneously, in some accounts. It appears as "Lt. Rosenquest" in both the *Chicago Tribune*, May 4, 1877, and *Chicago Times*, May 7, 1877, which is confirmed by Francis B. Heitman, *Historical Register and Dictionary of the United States Army* 1 (Washington: Government Printing Office,

1903):846; W. P. Clark, *The Indian Sign Language* (Philadelphia: L. R. Hamersly & Co., 1885), 422.

[64] Bourke diary, 19:1853, 1854, 1862; *Chicago Tribune*, May 3, 1877; George Bird Grinnell, *The Fighting Cheyennes* (Norman: University of Oklahoma Press, 1956), 382; Hyde, *Spotted Tail's Folk*, 238.

[65] Bourke diary, 20:1988; *Chicago Tribune*, May 8, 1877.

[66] *Chicago Times*, May 7, 1877.

[67] *Report of the Secretary of War*, 55.

[68] *Chicago Times*, May 7, 1877; *New York Tribune*, May 7, 1877; *Chicago Tribune*, May 8, 1877; Bourke diary, 20:1984–94; Sandoz, *Crazy Horse*, 361.

[69] *Chicago Times*, May 7, 1877; *Chicago Tribune*, May 8, 1877; Bourke diary, 20:1987.

[70] *New York Tribune*, May 7, 1877; *Chicago Times*, May 7, 1877; Bourke diary, 20:1984–94.

[71] Bourke diary, 20:1938, 1994.

Chapter 10

Oglala Sources on the
Life of Crazy Horse:
Interviews Given to Eleanor H. Hinman

Paul D. Riley

Editor's Introduction

In June 1930 Eleanor Hinman, a stenographer at the University of Ne-
braska, drove to the Pine Ridge and Rosebud Sioux reservations in South
Dakota. She was accompanied by Mari Sandoz, and they traveled in a
Model T Ford coupe. The two women—Miss Hinman was thirty, and Miss
Sandoz was thirty-six—were members of Quill, a literary club for women.
Miss Hinman had become interested in the life of Crazy Horse, the great
Oglala warrior, and the purpose of her trip was to interview Indians who
had known him. It is not known why Miss Hinman invited Mari Sandoz,
who at this time had written nothing about the Indians.

Their work at the reservation was aided by Helen H. Blish, a Lincoln
friend who had interviewed elderly Sioux for her graduate thesis. As
Miss Blish had done, they hired John Colhoff, official interpreter for the
Pine Ridge Agency. After their work was concluded, they visited the
Black Hills and the Custer battlefield.

On October 9, 1930, Miss Hinman sent a copy of her interviews to Dr.
Addison E. Sheldon of the Nebraska State Historical Society:

> Here at long last is the record of our interviews on Crazy Horse. I
> put them into your hands to do what you think best with. By way of
> keeping faith with our friends up on the reservation, I want their
> stories to go on record in their own words somewhere so that any
> student of Indian or frontier history who digs deeply enough into
> the materials may find them. The interviews are of very unequal
> value, but I think you may find some of them of interest in connec-
> tion with some of your own studies. Thanking you for your assis-
> tance and encouragement, I am, Sincerely yours, Eleanor Hinman.

The interviews are published as they were presented to the Society by Miss Hinman; her footnotes and introduction are not changed. Much research has been published on the subject in the intervening years, but it does not seriously change any of her work. It is not known why Miss Hinman decided to discontinue her biography of Crazy Horse, but she turned her other materials and the interviews over to Miss Sandoz, who published *Crazy Horse, the Strange Man of the Oglalas,* in 1942. The author's dedication reads: "To Eleanor Hinman, who spent many faithful months on a biography of Crazy Horse and then graciously volunteered to relinquish her prior claim to me."

Eleanor Hinman was born in Lincoln on December 9, 1899, to Edgar Lenderson and Alice Julia (Hamlin) Hinman. Her father was a member of the philosophy department at the University of Nebraska. After attending the Lincoln schools, she entered the university and was graduated in 1920. As a feature writer for the *Lincoln Daily Star,* one of her finest articles was an interview with Willa Cather in November 1921. Miss Cather gave few interviews during her long career as a novelist, and the one with Miss Hinman is yet today basic to any Cather scholar. After holding various positions in Lincoln, Miss Hinman retired to San Francisco [and died in 1982].

Information regarding the history of the interviews was provided by Dr. Helen Stauffer, Kearney (Nebraska) State College [University of Nebraska–Kearney] English professor, who is writing a biography of Mari Sandoz [published as *Mari Sandoz, Story Catcher of the Plains*, University of Nebraska Press, 1982].

Interviewer's Introduction

The young Oglala war leader Crazy Horse (Tasunke-Witko) was the soul of the Indian defense of the Black Hills in 1876, of which Sitting Bull was the voice. This was recognized by Lt. Gen. Philip H. Sheridan in his report to the secretary of war for 1876. More recently, the military gifts and the patriotic motives of Crazy Horse have been enthusiastically acknowledged by white historians, notable among them P. E. Byrne, John Neihardt, and Grace Hebard.[1]

The published sources on the life and death of Crazy Horse are almost exclusively the accounts of the white men who fought against him. The exceptions to this statement are a twenty-page sketch by Charles A. Eastman and a few scattered reminiscences in a book by Luther Standing Bear.[2] Both these writings are very informal in matter and method. Believing that some Indians still living could throw light on an interesting personality and a debated episode in American history, the writer spent two weeks in July 1930 on the Pine Ridge Reservation interviewing witnesses of various events in the life of Crazy Horse. These interviews are presented as nearly as possible exactly as they were translated by the interpreter, being written up each evening from notes taken at the interview. In some places they have been condensed somewhat, and irrelevant matter is omitted.

Some notes upon the standing and personal connections of the persons interviewed are necessary to help in evaluating their evidence:

He Dog (Sunka Bloka) is the last surviving representative of the Oglala grand councillors. These were appointive chiefs of the highest rank, officially known as "owners of the tribe" or "supreme head men" (wicasa yatapika). As these titles proved too heavy for Oglala democracy, these functionaries were popularly nicknamed "shirt-wearers" because of a particular type of ceremonial shirt they wore as a robe of office. Red Cloud and Crazy Horse were among these "shirt-wearers," together with the other chiefs, less known to the white people, whom He Dog names in his narrative. Although a nephew of Red Cloud, He Dog sided with Crazy Horse in the fighting in 1876, and he and his brothers took a very active part in several of the battles of that year. Together with Crazy Horse, he surrendered at Fort Robinson on May 7, 1877. When the Court of Indian Offenses was established upon the Pine Ridge Reservation in the 1890s, He Dog was made a judge of it. He served in this capacity for many years until his advanced age and failing sight made further service impossible. At present he lives near the town of Oglala with his great-niece, upon whose family he is dependent.

In spite of his ninety-two years and his infirmities, He Dog is possessed of a remarkable memory. He is the living depository of Oglala tribal history and old-time customs. Anyone digging very deeply into these subjects with other old-timers is likely to be referred to him: "He Dog will remember about that." In interviewing He Dog one can hardly fail to be impressed with his strong historical sense and with the moderation and carefulness of his statements.

Two long interviews with He Dog are presented here. The third, dealing with the battles of the Sioux war of 1876, is not reproduced for the following reason. Shortly after the interview of July 7, 1930, He Dog was told by a young Indian that the interviewer was very likely a government spy hoping to lure the old-timers into admissions of depredations alleged to have been committed during the war of 1876. The claims of the Sioux nation against the United States government for compensation for the taking of the Black Hills are pending in the United States Court of Claims, and the Indians were expecting an early hearing upon them. It appears that a counter-claim has been filed charging damages against the Sioux for all soldiers and civilians killed and property damaged during the war. On this account the old chief was advised not to talk too freely with us for fear his words might be twisted into evidence in support of this counter-claim. Unfortunately the next interview, on July 10, dealt with the war of 1876, and He Dog's statements were so extremely guarded as to add practically nothing to what is already known of this fighting.[3] Accordingly, this interview is omitted. The misunderstanding was straightened out, thanks to the help of John Colhoff and to He Dog's own fair-mindedness. But the interviewer thereafter confined her questions to the personal biography of Crazy Horse. It was feared that the existing situation might color any accounts given of the war of 1876. Later He Dog's brother, Short Buffalo, volunteered a brief but comprehensive account of this war from the Oglala point of view, which is presented.

Short Buffalo (Tatanka Ptecila) is the youngest brother of He Dog and shares the remarkable memory which seems to be a family characteristic.[4] Anyone who will take the pains to compare his account of the John Bruguier incident or of the surrender of Crazy Horse with the accounts by white officers published thirty-five years or more ago will be struck by Short Buffalo's accuracy after so many years. None of the men interviewed had any means of access to the published accounts. In certain other instances Short Buffalo's version of events differs sharply from the published accounts but in such a way as to suggest that the Indian version deserves at least consideration. Short Buffalo was in his early twenties at the time of the events described here.[5]

Little Killer was connected with Crazy Horse by marriage, being the younger brother of Club Man, who married Crazy Horse's older sister. He was a member of Crazy Horse's band and a personal admirer, as his narrative testifies. He is approximately the same age as Short Buffalo.

Red Feather was the younger brother of Crazy Horse's first wife. He was a member of Crazy Horse's band during the fighting of 1876 and up to that chief's death. At this time he was one of the younger men. Later on he became a prominent figure upon the reservation and used his influence to support the government authorities during the unrest of 1888 to 1890. He became a Catholic and attends mass three times a week at the Holy Rosary Mission. His friendship with the fathers at this mission and his relations with the agency have brought him into frequent contact with white people. He receives a government pension. Red Feather has the reputation of being a skilful diplomat and a shrewd judge of character. The reader may perhaps find some indications of these qualities in his narrative. He lost a leg through blood poisoning a few years ago while in the agency hospital, and this experience may help to account for the poor opinion of physicians revealed in one of his observations.

Red Feather and He Dog had apparently had differences of a personal nature over a matter of historical fact, and each of them warned us to be skeptical of the other. In spite of these warnings, the actual disagreements between their narratives are not greater than one would expect to find between witnesses of events that took place more than fifty years ago.

White Calf was a government scout at Fort Robinson during the year 1876. He was a witness of the stabbing of Crazy Horse. He did not know the chief personally at all well. His family and political connections were with the Red Cloud band. He was twenty-three or twenty-four years old at the time of the events narrated.

All the persons interviewed here except Red Feather are either relatives of Red Cloud or close neighbors of relatives of Red Cloud. The Red Cloud connection appeared to take a certain interest in the movements of the interviewer, and members of it were present at the interviews with Short Buffalo and Little Killer. When this series was completed, the interviewer drove up to Manderson, South Dakota, where the few surviving blood relatives of Crazy Horse live. But their testimony could not be obtained. Luke Little Hawk, approached by John Colhoff on behalf of the interviewer, replied in effect that no questions had been asked about Crazy Horse at the time of his death, and he did not care to answer any now. Black Elk said he felt he ought to be paid for telling us the biography of Crazy Horse (He suggested a rate of two cents a word!) and that it would require about two weeks. This was taken to be another form of refusal. The interpreter, Emil Afraid-of-Hawk, told us that Crazy Horse's relatives had repeatedly refused to make any statement about him to white people or indeed to Indians of the opposite faction.

Some points not brought out in the interviews were added by our interpreters. It was one of them, Thomas White Cow Killer, who told us the character he had heard given the informer Woman Dress [This name usually appears in the literature as "Woman's Dress," but Hinman consistently uses "Woman"] when the Indians are talking among themselves: "He was like a two-edged sword against his own people." Killer was asked why our informants evaded the questions we asked them about Woman Dress: "That is the way with our people. We don't like to say anything against one of ourselves to someone from outside." Another interpreter, Samuel Stands, became so much interested that he went of his own initiative to "an old-timer" (whose name he would not tell us), and asked

184

some questions of his own. The old man's reply as quoted by Stands was, "I'm not telling anyone—white or Indian—what I know about the killing of Crazy Horse. That affair was a disgrace, and a dirty shame. We killed our own man." This remark is quoted to illustrate the difficulties of getting to the bottom of the problems involved and not to exculpate the white officers, who asked no questions at the time when questions were in order.

With the possible exception of Red Feather, the Indians seem to have been as unaware of what went on among the white men at the fort and the Spotted Tail Agency outside their immediate range of observation as the white men were unaware of the alarms and rivalries among the Indians.[6] For a well-balanced view of events, therefore, the Indian testimony must be studied in connection with the white sources already published.

He Dog
Oglala, South Dakota, July 7, 1930
Thomas White Cow Killer, Interpreter

I will be glad to tell you about Crazy Horse or any others of our old-time chiefs about whom you may wish to know because I am an old man now and shall not live many years longer, and it is time for me to tell these things. Whatever I tell you will be the exact truth because I was in a position to know what I talk about. There are a lot of old Indians hanging about the reservation who like to talk to the white people and would just as soon tell you anything, whether it is true or not. They are men whom we would not have had as servants, those of us who were chiefs in the old days.

I and Crazy Horse were both born in the same year and at the same season of the year. We grew up together in the same band, played together, courted the girls together, and fought together. I am now ninety-two years old, so you can figure out in what year he was born by your calendar. When we were seventeen or eighteen years old, we separated. Crazy Horse went to the Rosebud band of Indians and stayed with them for about a year.[7] Then he came home. After he had been back for a while, I made inquiries about why he had left the Rosebud band. I was told he had to come back because he had killed a Winnebago woman.[8]

Less than a year after Crazy Horse left camp, I joined in a trip against the Crow Indians. When I got home, the crier was announcing that Crazy Horse was back in camp. Only his name was not Crazy Horse at that time. He had three names at different times of his life. His name until he was about ten years old was Curly Hair. Later, from the time he was ten until the time he was about eighteen years of age, he was called His-Horse-on-Sight, but this name did not stick to him. When he was about eighteen years old, there was a fight with the Arapahos, who were up on a high hill covered with big rocks and near a river. Although he was just a boy, he charged them several times alone and came back wounded but with two Arapaho scalps. His father, whose name was Crazy Horse, made a feast and gave his son his own name. After that the father was no longer called by the name he had given away but was called by a nickname, Worm.

Crazy Horse, the son, was one of three children. The oldest was a sister, the next was Crazy Horse, and the third was a brother. All are dead now.

When we were young men, the Oglala band divided into two parts, one led by Red Cloud and one by Man-Afraid-of-His-Horse, the elder. I and Crazy Horse stayed with the part led by Man-Afraid-of-His-Horse. Later this half subdivided again into two parts. I stayed with the more northern half, of which I and Big Road, and later Holy Bald Eagle and Red Cloud, were appointed joint chiefs ("shirt-wearers," so called from a particular kind of ceremonial shirt worn by this class of chieftain as insignia of office). Crazy Horse remained with the southern quarter of the tribe. The council of this division awarded the chieftainship to Crazy Horse, American Horse, Young-Man-Afraid-of-His-Horse, and Sword. It was many years after our first battles before we were made chiefs. A man had to distinguish himself in many fights and in peace as well before he could be chosen as a chief.[9]

(Part of an interview held by John Colhoff with He Dog is inserted here because it bears on this subject. The material obtained through John Colhoff is in brackets.—E. H. H.)

[The name of Crazy Horse's band was the Hunkpatila ("End-of-Circle") band because, when the tribe was encamped together, it occupied one end of the tribal crescent.]

At about the time these appointments were made, Crazy Horse moved up toward the White Mountains (Indian name for the Big Horn Mountains). Crazy Horse and I went together on a war trip to the other side of the mountains. When we came back, the people came out of the camp to meet us and escorted us back and at a big ceremony presented us with two spears, the gift of the whole tribe, which was met together. These spears were each three or four hundred years old and were given by the older generation to those in the younger generation who had best lived the life of a warrior.

[Crazy Horse was still single when he was made a "shirt-wearer." A few years after this he began to pay attention to the wife of a man named No

Water. No Water did not want to let the woman go. In the battle "When They Chased the Crows Back to Camp," He Dog and Crazy Horse were the lance-bearers of the Kangi Yuha (Crow Owners' Society).[10] About ten days after that battle Crazy Horse started on a smaller war expedition, and No Water's wife went along with him.]

No Water followed them and came to the tipi of Bad Heart Bull and asked to borrow a certain good revolver which Bad Heart Bull owned.[11] He said he wanted to go hunting. Crazy Horse and the woman were sitting by the fire in a tipi belonging to some of their friends. No Water entered the tipi, walked up to Crazy Horse as near as I am to that stove (about four feet) and shot him through the face. The bullet entered just below the left nostril. That is how Crazy Horse got his scar. No Water took his wife back.

Because of all this, Crazy Horse could not be a "shirt-wearer" any longer. When we were made chiefs, we were bound by very strict rules as to what we should do and what not [to] do, which were very hard for us to follow. I have never spoken to any but a very few persons of what they made us promise then. I have always kept the oaths I made then, but Crazy Horse did not.

Later on the older, more responsible men of the tribe conferred another kind of chieftainship on Crazy Horse. He was made war chief of the whole Oglala tribe. A similar office was conferred on Sitting Bull by the Hunkpapa tribe. This was still early, a long, long time before the Custer fight. At this time the government did not know who we were.

Crazy Horse always led his men himself when they went into battle, and he kept well in front of them. He headed many charges and was many times wounded in battle, but never seriously. He never wore a war bonnet. A medicine man named Chips had given him power if he would wear in battle an eagle-bone whistle and one feather and a certain round stone with a hole in it. He wore the stone under his left arm, suspended by a leather thong that went over his shoulder. The one central feather that is in the middle of the war-eagle's tail, that was the feather he wore in his hair (He Dog denied, with a chuckle, various stories told about how Crazy Horse on certain occasions threw away his rifle and charged in with a war club or a riding quirt—a characteristic Indian mode of seeking death in battle—E. H. H.). Crazy Horse always stuck close to his rifle. He always tried to kill as many as possible of the enemy without losing his own men.

He never spoke in council and attended very few. There was no special reason for this; it was just his nature. He was a very quiet man except when there was fighting.

[Crazy Horse was married three times. The first time was to No Water's wife, but she only stayed with him a few days. Shortly after that he married Red Feather's sister. By her he had one child, a little girl who died when about two years old. A long while after, when he had surrendered at Fort Robinson, he married a young half-breed girl. He did not have any children by her.]

He Dog
Oglala, South Dakota, July 13, 1930
John Colhoff, Interpreter

Question: Dr. Charles Eastman, whose Indian name is "Ohiyesa," has written in a book that Crazy Horse, when he was a young man, was intimate friends with a famous Oglala war chief called Hump or High Back Bone.[12] We wonder if He Dog can tell us anything about this man and his friendship with Crazy Horse.

Answer: High Back Bone and Crazy Horse were sworn friends and went on nearly all their war expeditions together, and the one was as great a war leader as the other. The first and last time these two disagreed was the time when High Back Bone got killed. He and Crazy Horse were on a war expedition together against the Shoshones. They had stationed their men at the Wind River. It was in the fall, and there was a drizzly rain turning into snow. Crazy Horse said, "I wonder if we can make it back to Cone Creek. I doubt if our horses can stand a fight in this slush. They sink in over their ankles."

Messengers took this word to High Back Bone, who said, "This is the second fight he has called off in this same place! This time there is going to be a fight." He came to Crazy Horse and said, "The last time you called off a fight here, when we got back to camp, they laughed at us. You and I have our good name to think about. If you don't care about it, you can go back. But I'm going to stay here and fight."

Crazy Horse said, "All right, we fight, if you feel that way about it. But I think we're going to get a good licking. You have a good gun, and I have a good gun, but look at our men! None of them have good guns, and most of them have only bows and arrows. It's a bad place for a fight and a bad day for it, and the enemy are twelve to our one."

They fought all the same, but the Shoshones had the best of it. Pretty soon the Oglalas were on the run, with only three men left who were doing any fighting: Good Weasel, Crazy Horse, and High Back Bone. It was a running fight, with more running than fighting; only these three were fighting at all. Crazy Horse charged one side of the Shoshones and

High Back Bone the other. When they came back, High Back Bone's horse was stumbling. He said, "We're up against it now; my horse has a wound in the leg."

Crazy Horse said, "I know it. We were up against it from the start."

Both made charges. When Crazy Horse got back, he found only Good Weasel left. High Back Bone had fallen from his horse, and the Shoshones surged over him. That was the last seen of High Back Bone. Good Weasel and Crazy Horse got away.[13]

Q: About how old was High Back Bone? Was he about the same age as He Dog and Crazy Horse, or was he an older man?

A: Just about the same age as Crazy Horse and I.

Q: We have read that Crazy Horse had a younger brother, to whom he was very much attached, who died in battle. Can you tell us about this?

A: The younger brother went on a war expedition south of the Platte River and never came back. Crazy Horse wasn't along. This was during the time when No Water and Crazy Horse got into that scrape, and Crazy Horse was not yet well from his wounds.[14] When Red Cloud went to Washington (later in the same year [The year was 1870]), Crazy Horse went south and found his brother's body and buried it.

Q: What was this brother's name?

A: Crazy Horse's brother's name was Little Hawk. After the young man's death his father's brother took the same name. The old men claim the first Little Hawk would have been a greater man than his brother Crazy Horse if he had lived. But he was too rash.

All the time I was in fights with Crazy Horse in critical moments of the fight Crazy Horse would always jump off his horse to fire. He is the only Indian I ever knew who did that often. He wanted to be sure that he hit what he aimed at. That is the kind of a fighter he was. He didn't like to start a battle unless he had it all planned out in his head and knew he was going to win. He always used judgment and played safe. His brother and High Back Bone were reckless. That is why they got killed.

Q: When my friend and I got back to our camp after the other interview, we found there were several things in the story of the quarrel between Crazy Horse and No Water we did not understand the same way. We wonder if He Dog will tell that story again. In particular, we were not clear which No Water did the shooting, the No Water who is living now, the No Water who was the husband of the woman with whom Crazy Horse eloped, or the father of the woman's husband.

A: The old No Water did the shooting, the husband of the woman. The woman was the mother of this No Water who is living now. He was a little boy when it happened. The woman had three children; he was the oldest. She gave them to different people to take care of when she left with Crazy Horse. When her husband No Water got back, his wife and children were gone. He went around to the various tipis and found his children. Crazy Horse had been paying open attention to the woman for a long time, and it didn't take No Water very long to guess where she had gone. He gathered up a fairly strong war party and went after him.

Crazy Horse had taken the woman and a few followers and gone on a war expedition against the Crows. On the second night he came to a place on Powder River where several bands had joined together, and they stopped with friends.

Little Shield was with Crazy Horse at the time he was shot.[15] No Water overtook him on the second night after he had left camp with the woman. Crazy Horse and the woman were sitting by the fire in a friend's tipi when No Water rushed in saying, "My friend, I have come!" Crazy Horse jumped up and reached for his knife. No Water shot him just below the left nostril. The bullet followed the line of the teeth and fractured his upper jaw. He fell forward into the fire. No Water left the tent at once and told his friends he had killed Crazy Horse.

The woman went out the back of the tent, crawling under the tent covering, when No Water fired. She went to relatives and begged for protection. She did not go back to Crazy Horse.

It was Bad Heart Bull's revolver that No Water borrowed for the shooting. Yellow Bear brought back the revolver and the word that No Water had killed Crazy Horse. Later someone brought word that Crazy Horse was not dead.

No Water had a fast mule which he had ridden when he came to kill Crazy Horse. He left without it in a hurry. When Crazy Horse's men had convinced themselves that they could not find No Water to punish, they killed his mule instead. No Water's friends made a sweat lodge hot and purified him of the murder. Then he disappeared.

No Water was a brother of Holy Bald Eagle, nicknamed the Black Twin.[16] He really was a twin; the "White Twin," Holy Buffalo, was a little lighter in complexion. Holy Bald Eagle said to No Water, "Come and stay with me, and, if they want to fight us, we will fight."

Crazy Horse's men did not take him back to his people but to the camp of his uncle Spotted Crow to be nursed. They were very angry and thought they ought to have No Water turned over to them to be punished or else wage war on his people. For a while it looked as if a lot of blood would flow. But by good luck there were three parties to the quarrel instead of two. Bull Head, Ashes, and Spotted Crow, the uncles of Crazy Horse and the head men of that band, worked for peace. Also, Bad

Heart Bull and I thought we were involved in it since Bad Heart Bull's revolver had been used for the shooting. We did what we could. After a while the thing began to quiet down. No Water owned a very fine roan horse and a fine bay horse; he sent these and another good horse to atone for the injury he had done. Spotted Crow, Sitting Eagle, and Canoeing brought No Water's wife to Bad Heart Bull's tent and left her there on condition that she should not be punished for what she had done. This condition was demanded by Crazy Horse. Bad Heart Bull arranged for her to go back to her husband in peace. If it had not been settled this way, there might have been a bad fight.

But Crazy Horse could not be a "shirt-wearer" any more on account of his adultery.

The trouble flared up once more after it was supposed to have been quieted. There were several bands encamped near the mouth of the Big Horn River. They had been hunting buffalo across the Missouri (Yellowstone?). Some were through dressing their meat and others were not. Iron Horse and Crazy Horse had finished and were coming back with their ponies loaded with packs of meat. A man named Moccasin Top was still dressing his kill. Moccasin Top owned a fast buckskin horse and had it tethered near him while he worked. No Water came along that way and saw Crazy Horse coming. He untied the buckskin horse of Moccasin Top and jumped on it and started off across the prairie pretty fast.

Then Crazy Horse came along and saw Moccasin Top. He said, "Are you here? Then who was the man that just rode off on your buckskin horse?"

Moccasin Top said, "That was No Water."

Crazy Horse said, "I wish I had known it! I would certainly have given him a bullet in return for that one he gave me."

Then he stripped off his pack, jumped on his pony, and gave chase. He chased No Water to the Missouri (Yellowstone?) River. No Water made the horse plunge into the river and swim across. Crazy Horse did not follow him any further. No Water quit camp and went south among the Loafer Indians at the Red Cloud Agency and never went back. He stayed at the agency all through the war with the white people and had nothing more to do with the hostiles. We only saw him once after that until we came down to the agency. My father and No Water's father were related; that was how Bad Heart Bull and I came to be drawn into the quarrel.

Q: What was the name of No Water's wife?

A: This woman was named Black Buffalo Woman. She was a daughter of Red Cloud's brother.[17] They claim that a few months after she went back to No Water this woman gave birth to a light-haired little girl. Many people believe this child was Crazy Horse's daughter, but it was never known for certain. This daughter is living now.

No Water's friends accused Chips, the medicine man who gave Crazy Horse his war medicine, of giving him a love-charm to make this woman run away with him. They were going to kill Chips. The Black Twin (Holy Bald Eagle) tried to get Chips to acknowledge that he had given Crazy Horse a love-charm, but Chips stoutly denied it. He said he knew nothing whatever about the affair. So after a while they let him go. After that Chips stayed away from the Badger band.

Q: When a "shirt-wearer" broke his oath, how did they go about it to take his office away from him?

A: There is an outfit called the White Horse Riders or the Short Hairs.[18] They are the ones that decide who are to have the ceremonial shirts. When a shirt-wearer died or broke his oath, the shirt was returned to the White Horse Riders or the Short Hairs. These chose who was to have it next.

Q: Who was chosen to succeed Crazy Horse after he had to return his ceremonial shirt?

A: The shirt was never given to anybody else. Everything seemed to stop right there. Everything began to fall to pieces. After that it seemed as if anybody who wanted to could wear the shirt; it meant nothing. But in the days when Crazy Horse and I received our shirts, we had to accomplish many things to win them.

Q: How long was it from the time when Crazy Horse received his shirt until he lost it?

A: (He Dog) It was about five years that he was a chief, maybe longer.

A: (Little Shield) It was about the fourth year that the trouble started.

He Dog
Oglala, South Dakota, July 7, 1930
Thomas White Cow Killer, Interpreter

I was present at the killing of Crazy Horse. I can tell you just what happened, who was present, and the condition of the weather.

In the year we fought with the white people (1876), the band I led had joined the Crazy Horse band during the fighting. In the winter after the fighting, Spotted Tail went north and persuaded Crazy Horse to come down to the agency the following spring. When we started in, I thought we were coming to visit and to see whether we would receive an annuity, not to surrender. I thought we would be allowed to go back home afterwards. But when we got near Fort Robinson, I found we were coming to surrender.[19] Spotted Tail had laid a trap for us. Later on I found that

Spotted Tail was telling the military things about Crazy Horse which were not so.

Spotted Tail and others kept urging Crazy Horse to go to Washington and talk to the president, as they wanted him to do. After a while Crazy Horse became so he did not want to go anywhere or talk to anyone. One day I was called in to see White Hat [the name for 1st Lt. William Philo Clark] and asked to bring Crazy Horse in for a talk because I was such a friend of his. I asked Crazy Horse, but he would not come. This made me feel bad, so I moved my people from where Crazy Horse was camping (on Little Cottonwood Creek) and camped over near the Red Cloud band. There was no quarrel; we just separated.

Crazy Horse said to me that if they would have the agency moved over to Beaver Creek, then he would go to Washington as they asked him. The reason he gave for this condition was that Beaver Creek was in the middle of the Sioux territory, while the location at Fort Robinson was on the edge of it.[20]

After I had moved camp to the Red Cloud Agency close to Fort Robinson, I was given orders to go and camp a couple of miles east of Fort Robinson at the foot of the White Butte.[21] Word was brought that Three Stars (Gen. [George] Crook) was coming that evening and all the Indian leaders were to have a meeting there next day with Three Stars. But Crazy Horse did not come to that council, and neither did Three Stars. After a while we were summoned to Fort Robinson and told that it would be necessary to arrest Crazy Horse.

The next day when I went to Fort Robinson I was told that Crazy Horse had escaped with a part of his band. The Indian police were given orders to bring him back. Next day they brought him back. I was still encamped at the White Butte, and they brought him past my camp on their way to the fort. I saw them coming and sent orders for them to bring Crazy Horse into my tipi. I meant to give him a good talking-to. But the police didn't stop; they took him straight on to the fort. When I saw this, I could only put on my war bonnet and get on my horse bareback and follow.

When I came to the fort, I found Crazy Horse in the lead on his horse, wearing a red blanket. A military ambulance followed; a couple of army officers were in it, but no Indians. I rode up on the left side of Crazy Horse and shook hands with him. I saw that he did not look right. I said, "Look out—watch your step—you are going into a dangerous place."

I was standing just south of the entrance to the adjutant's office at the fort. Red Cloud with his men stood to the east of the building which had the adjutant's office in it, American Horse with his men to the west.

Crazy Horse was taken into the office and after a little while led out toward a building just north of it.[22] I knew this building was the jail because I had been sent out by White Hat once or twice to get some Indians who had done something bad, and they had been taken to this building. But Crazy Horse did not know it. Turning Bear walked ahead of Crazy Horse; on either side of him were Little Big Man and Wooden Sword; behind him was Leaper.

Soon after Crazy Horse had gone into the jail, a noise began in there. Crazy Horse had a revolver with him and tried to draw it, but it was taken away from him. Then he drew his knife. American Horse and Red Cloud shouted to their men, "Shoot to kill!" The white sentry who was on guard outside the jail ran in behind Crazy Horse as he was fighting with the Indian police and lunged—twice—with his bayonet. Crazy Horse cried, "They have stabbed me!" He staggered backward and fell on the campus (parade ground). I looked around and saw that soldiers and cavalry had formed all around the edge of the parade ground. I stood there, ready to drop.

Then White Hat appeared and said I might go up to Crazy Horse. I did so. There were soldiers standing all around him. The bayonet was laying on the ground beside him and also the knife he had used, and they were red. I tore in two the large red agency blanket which I was wearing and used half of it to cover him. He was gasping hard for breath. "See where I am hurt," he gasped. "I can feel the blood flowing."

I pulled back his shirt and looked at the wound. He was thrust nearly through twice. The first stroke went from between the ribs in the back, on the right side, and very nearly came through in front under the heart. A lump was rising under the skin where the thrust ended. The second wound was through the small of the back through the kidneys.

Most of Crazy Horse's people had disappeared. Standing Buffalo and another Indian came across the parade ground and gave him their blankets. Then Dr. V. T. McGillycuddy came up.[23] Crazy Horse died early in the next morning.

He Dog
Oglala, South Dakota, July 13, 1930
John Colhoff, Interpreter

Q: The first time we came to see you, you started to tell us something about one time when two white men came to visit Crazy Horse and gave him a present of two cigars and a knife and shook hands with him in a way that made him suspicious. Our interpreter did not tell us this that day, but a few days later he came around and told us. We would like to hear about that again because we thought it might throw some light on how some of the stories perhaps got started, those that were told about Crazy Horse.

A: This was at the time when Crazy Horse was camped a few miles from Fort Robinson and orders came for everybody to go over and camp beside the White (Crawford) Butte because they were going to hold a big council there.[24] Everybody did so except Crazy Horse. Those in his camp who wanted to go to the council were told to move across the creek. I got up in council, and I said, "All who love their wife and children, let them come across the creek with me. All who want their wife and children to be killed by the soldiers, let them stay where they are."

Afterwards Crazy Horse asked me and Iron Hawk to come to his tipi. We did. He was leaning back on a pile of blankets and cushions, and he reached under it and pulled out a knife and two cigars. He said this was a present brought him by two visiting white men who had come to see him that afternoon. He did not like the way they shook hands with him, and he did not like their talk, and he did not like their gift. He thought the gift of the knife meant trouble was coming. He thought they shook hands with him as if they did not mean him any good. He was afraid there would be trouble at that council. One of these white men was the soldier chief from Fort Laramie (Gen. [Lt. Col. Luther Prentice] Bradley); the other was D. H. Russell(?).[25]

I said, "Does this mean that you will be my enemy if I move across the creek?"

Crazy Horse laughed in my face. He said, "I am no white man! They are the only people that make rules for other people, that say, 'If you stay on one side of this line, it is peace, but if you go on the other side I will kill you all.' I don't hold with deadlines. There is plenty of room; camp where you please."

After that White Hat sent for me and told me about these white men and wanted me to get Crazy Horse to talk to them some more. They sent over presents of food, and I made a big feast and invited the white men and sent a messenger to Crazy Horse. But he wouldn't come. He sent back word, "Tell my friend that I thank him and I am grateful, but some people over there have said too much. I don't want to talk to them any more. No good would come of it." I did not think he was really angry, but he had taken offense. They did not approach him right. He did not say whether he would or would not go to Washington.

Q: Yugata (Frank Grouard) says in his book that he listened outside Crazy Horse's tent and heard Crazy Horse plot to bring his men to that council at the White Butte—or else to an earlier council—with weapons hidden under their blankets. When Crazy Horse shook hands with the white officer, his men were to draw their weapons and kill all the white people present, according to this story.[26] We wondered whether perhaps Yugata might have been watching from outside when Crazy Horse pulled out the knife the white officers had given him and explained about the queer way they shook hands with him and got his idea about the plot from that.

A: It was Long Chin, Lone Bear, and Woman Dress who spied around Crazy Horse's tent and told the white people those stories about him. I never heard until now that Yugata was in it. But I don't know. He may have planned the whole thing for all I know.

Stories like that are what caused ill feeling. But I don't believe they were true. If I heard Crazy Horse say it once, I heard him say it many times: "I came here for peace. No matter if my own relatives pointed a gun at my head and ordered me to change that word I would not change it."

When we first came down to the agency, Crazy Horse was willing to go to Washington. He said to me, "First, I want them to place my agency on Beaver Creek west of the Black Hills. Then I will go to Washington—for your benefit, for my benefit, and for the benefit of all of us. And that is the only reason why I will go there."

Spotted Crow and others told him, "That about going to Washington is only a decoy. They want to get you away from us, and then they will have you in their power." After a while Crazy Horse got so he thought it might be true. At last he told the officers, "I am not going there. I wanted to go, but you have changed my mind. Still deep in my heart I hold that place on Beaver Creek where I want my agency. You have my horses and my guns. I have only my tent and my will. You got me to come here, and you can keep me here by force if you choose, but you cannot make me go anywhere that I refuse to go."

Red Feather
Pine Ridge, South Dakota, July 8, 1930
Mrs. Annie Rowland, Interpreter

What is the date by your calendar? Write it down that I am telling you the story of Crazy Horse on July 8, 1930. I will tell you the true facts about Crazy Horse because I am a Catholic now and it is a part of my religion to tell the truth.

"Black Beard" made a treaty with the Indians.[27] In this treaty boundaries were set to the country of the Dakotas. The Indians all stayed together inside these boundaries. The white people kept sending to Crazy

Horse to leave his country and come in to the agency, but he wanted to keep his own land. The Indians always stayed inside these boundaries, and they are still inside them. So are a lot of white people.

Some Indians who were staying at the agency kept coming out to Crazy Horse to ask him to come in to the agency. One of these Indians was named Keeps-the-Sword, the other Spotted Tail.

Crazy Horse and another chief named He Dog were camping on the Powder River. Keeps-the-Sword and Spotted Tail took tobacco out to them and killed a lot of buffaloes. They told Crazy Horse that the agent wanted him. If he would go in to the agency, the agent would issue rations, blankets, and clothing, and then allow him to go back home. Crazy Horse didn't want to go. He didn't answer them for a long time. He told them to go over to the other Indians (He Dog's band), and he would do the same as the others did. These others were camping in the White Mountains (Big Horn Mountains). Crazy Horse did not take the tobacco; he sent it over to the others.

After they took it over, they had a big council of all the chiefs of both bands. The man that took the tobacco said the agent sent them; that is why they came. One old man named Iron Hawk spoke first and answered, "You see all the people here are in rags; they all need clothing; we might as well go in." Crazy Horse said whatever all the rest decided to do, he would do. So they all agreed to go in. They promised to go over, get the rations and the clothing, and return west of the Black Hills again.

I was right there when Crazy Horse was killed. Crazy Horse had never been to an agency since he was a young man. Neither had I. The Indians who were in the Big Horn Mountains started for the agency. They found Crazy Horse waiting on the Powder River, and all came on in together. When they were only about one day's journey from the fort, the people from the agency brought out rations to them. When they got to the fort, the agent gave them rations, clothing, and blankets. Everyone was very jolly. All the women made new clothes. Before that they all wore buckskin, but now their clothes were of bright-colored cloth. After the agent gave them clothes, he told Crazy Horse to become a scout. It was about April when they came in.[28]

When we came in, we were promised that we might go back, but, after we were there, we were not allowed to go back. All the white people came to see Crazy Horse and gave him presents and money. The other Indians at the agency got very jealous.

One day the soldiers called Crazy Horse over to the fort. He didn't want to go. I coaxed him to go. When they got him over to the fort, they made him promise to become a scout.

Then old Billy Garnett told me the Indians were telling lies about Crazy Horse. One Indian named No Water promised the scouts he would kill Crazy Horse. All the rest of the Indians made a council. Crazy Horse called White Hat to the council. He wanted to tell White Hat that he and his people were ready to go back where they came from. Garnett was coming out to this council with White Hat. Three Stars, the white man, was with them. A scout named Woman Dress stopped them, saying Crazy Horse was going to kill them at the council. This was not true. White Hat asked Woman Dress if Crazy Horse said that, and Woman Dress said he heard it.[29]

(When Red Feather started to tell this story, he misspoke himself and said it was No Water who met Crook and Clark and turned them back. At this the interviewer exclaimed and said she had always heard the man's name was Woman Dress. Red Feather then corrected himself. At this point the interviewer asked if Woman Dress and No Water were two names for the same man. Red Feather's answer follows.)

No, they were different men. No, I do not know of any reason why Woman Dress should have wanted to do Crazy Horse an injury.

After White Hat and Three Stars heard this story, they went back to the fort and called together all the scouts. White Hat offered $100 and a sorrel horse to any Indian who would kill Crazy Horse. I heard about this and went over to the fort. After I went over, Garnett told me the scouts and soldiers were going after Crazy Horse. I went with another man to Crazy Horse and told him the soldiers were coming. Crazy Horse had given his gun and gun case to me the night before and had only his knife. He was waiting like that for the soldiers. When the soldiers were coming, I went out to meet them. The soldiers told me to tell Crazy Horse they were coming, and he was to do as they said. When I came back with this message, Crazy Horse wasn't there. He had taken his wife over to the Spotted Tail Agency; she was sick with a swollen arm. He left his wife with her mother in Spotted Tail's camp on Beaver Creek.[30] Some of the Indians said he had run away. But he hadn't run away. When he had left her where she would be out of the trouble, he went on to see the agent down there. Yes, this wife was my sister.

Some scouts met Crazy Horse going from Spotted Tail's camp to Touch-the-Cloud's camp which was near by. They brought him back to Fort Robinson where the soldiers were. I heard about it and went along over to the fort.

Three of the scouts bringing Crazy Horse in were from the Spotted Tail Agency and two from the Red Cloud Agency. The men of Spotted Tail's band who came along were telling the Oglalas they didn't want Crazy Horse and his people on their reservation. The scouts took Crazy

Horse into a little house. They told Crazy Horse's Indians not to go around there. I and another Indian named White Calf sneaked around behind and looked in.

White Hat was sitting in a room in the little house. After they took Crazy Horse in, White Hat said Crazy Horse should go in the next house and stay there all day, and, after they got through supper, they would take him to Washington. One Indian called Little Big Man or Chasing (Charging) Bear followed Crazy Horse in; he had promised to stay by him all the time. Little Big Man said, "We'll do whatever White Hat says."

The house where they told Crazy Horse to go was about as far away as from here to that stake on the hill (about 200 or 300 feet). They said go in there. A soldier was walking back and forth with a bayonet over his shoulder. When the soldier saw them coming, he lowered the bayonet and let them go in.

Afterward I heard talking and excitement inside. Spotted Tail's scouts cried out, "It's the jail!" and left Crazy Horse and ran outside. Crazy Horse drew his knife and started to follow them. Little Big Man, who had promised the soldiers to stay with Crazy Horse, caught his hands and held them behind his back. Crazy Horse cut his wrists as they were fighting for the knife. The sentry came in behind them and ran Crazy Horse through once. The thrust went through the kidneys. This was done a little before sunset.

An Indian named Closed Cloud picked up Crazy Horse's blanket, which he had dropped inside the jail, and spread it over him. Crazy Horse seized him by the hair and jerked him this way and that: "You all coaxed me over here, and then you ran away and left me!" They carried Crazy Horse into the house. Everyone was ready to fight. But they all cooled down.

Everyone ran away from him; that was why it happened. The scouts were the cause of it. If they had held him and had not run away, he would not have been hurt.

After Crazy Horse was taken into the little house, the other Indians were not allowed in. His father, Spider,[31] White Bird, and another were with him all night. Crazy Horse died later in the evening.

I asked one of the Rosebud men, Turning Bear, why they left Crazy Horse and ran out. I told them they made it worse when they said, "Look out; this is the jail!" and ran out. Turning Bear knew nobody was going to put *him* in jail. I said, "Why didn't you stay and hold him?" All those Rosebudders were cowards, and they ran away. I started to cry. I had my gun with me, and they thought I was starting to fight. The Rosebud men held me.

When Crazy Horse was dead, they brought a soldier's wagon with mules hitched to it and put his body in it and took him back to camp. After they took him back, I helped undress him and put a buckskin shirt on him. It was then I saw where the wound was.

Crazy Horse was a nice-looking man, with brown, not black, hair, a sharp nose, and a narrow face. Nobody on the reservation nowadays looks like him. His nose was straight and thin. His hair was very long, straight, and fine in texture. I knew him well, knew everything about him, but not his age or where he was born or where he was buried. His own people buried him, and not even his wife, who was my sister, knew what they did with him.

Crazy Horse married my sister six years before he was killed. He had only one child, a little girl who looked like him. She died when about three years old. Black Shawl was my sister's name. She died near here only a few years ago in the year when so many Indians had influenza. She must have been about eighty-four years old. She never took another husband.

Crazy Horse was a big chief over all his land. His father hid his body so not even my sister knew where it was buried. Before he was buried a war eagle came to walk about on the coffin every night. It did nothing, only just walked about.

Question: Does Red Feather remember about when they asked Crazy Horse to go and help fight the Nez Perce Indians? That happened maybe seven days before Crazy Horse was killed. We heard that Crazy Horse didn't want to go and that this had something to do with the misunderstandings that arose.

Answer: We heard the Nez Perce Indians were having a fight with the white people. The soldiers wanted Crazy Horse to go along and help fight them. Crazy Horse didn't want to go. Finally he told the soldiers he wanted thirty-five dollars a day for himself and each of his men if he fought the Nez Perces. When he came in to the agency, the soldiers had made him promise not to go on the warpath any more. They told him not to fight and then to fight.

Q: We would like to have Red Feather tell us about the time when Crazy Horse was a young man, before he came onto the reservation and before the fighting with the white people started.

A: I knew Crazy Horse ever since I was a little boy. The enemy killed his saddle horse under him eight times, but they never hurt him badly. During war expeditions he wore a little white stone with a hole through it on a buckskin string slung over his shoulder. He wore it under his left arm. He was wounded twice when he first began to fight but never since— after he got the stone. A man named Chips, a great friend of his, gave it to him. My son, young Red Feather, has it now. He was the leader in many fights. He was the leader in the Custer fight. I was in that Custer battle. He came in a year after that and made a treaty, as I have told you. All that land where the fighting was is full of white people now.

Q: How did Crazy Horse get to be a chief?

A: He was a chief ever since he was grown up.

Q: I have heard that when he was a young man Crazy Horse was great friends with a man named Hump, or Big Breast, or High Back Bone. We would like to know more about that.

A: High Back Bone was about the same age as Crazy Horse and was related to him. They used to go on war expeditions together. One time they went on a war expedition against the Shoshones, and High Back Bone was killed in the fight. I was in that fight. Four days later Crazy Horse and I went back to find High Back Bone and bury him. We didn't find anything but the skull and a few bones. High Back Bone had been eaten by coyotes already. There weren't any Shoshones around. When the Shoshones found out whom they had killed, they beat it.

Interview with Red Feather
Pine Ridge, South Dakota, July 11, 1930
Mrs. Annie Rowland, Interpreter

Question: I have been told that when Crazy Horse first came down to the reservation the white officers liked him so well that they wanted to make him chief over all the Oglalas in place of Red Cloud if he would stay at the agency, but he didn't want to stay. The doctor who took care of Crazy Horse while he was dying said this to me, and also Luther Standing Bear said it in his book.[32] Does Red Feather know if the officers ever said anything to Crazy Horse about this?

Answer: White Hat [Lieutenant Clark] told Crazy Horse that they were going to take him to Washington and ask him two questions: (1) to quit fighting and (2) to pick out a land for himself and make a homestead. Crazy Horse answered, "Yes, when I get over my tiredness I will go with him and when I pick out a land I will pick one right near the Black Hills." But White Hat didn't come for him until they killed him.

Crazy Horse's father told me he thought that doctor gave Crazy Horse poison. The doctor gave him some medicine, and he died awful quick after that.[33]

Q: We wanted to ask about a secret council said to have been held in Crazy Horse's tipi about five or six nights before his death. There was to be a council with White Hat the next day to decide whether Crazy Horse and others would go as scouts to help fight the Nez Perces. The night before this council with White Hat, this secret council is said to have been held. The scout Yugata (Frank Grouard), who claims to have been listening outside the tent, told White Hat that Crazy Horse was planning to bring his warriors armed to the council next day and that at a sign from Crazy Horse they would pull their weapons from under their blankets and attack. We wondered if there really was a council held in Crazy Horse's tipi the night before the council with White Hat, and, if so, what happened at it.

A: I do not know of any such council. I had never heard that Yugata had anything to do with those stories, until now. I had always heard that it was Woman Dress and Lone Bear who listened outside Crazy Horse's tent with their blankets over their heads and told those stories. I think maybe Yugata heard what they said and claimed to have done the listening himself. Yugata was the interpreter.

Q: We have been told that Woman Dress was closely related to Red Cloud. Is this true?

A: Woman Dress was Red Cloud's first cousin and always stayed with him.[34]

Q: Was Crazy Horse related to Spotted Tail?

A: I don't know.

Q: What were the names of Crazy Horse's father and mother?

A: Crazy Horse's father was named Crazy Horse until he gave his name to his son. After that he was called Worm (Waglula). I do not remember the name of the mother.

Q: What was the name of Crazy Horse's little daughter that died?

A: She was called "They-Are-Afraid-of-Her" (Kokipapi).

Q: Does Red Feather remember anything about the marriage of Crazy Horse with his sister Black Shawl?

A: All I can say about that is that both Crazy Horse and my sister stayed single much longer than is usual among our people.

Short Buffalo
[No location given,] July 13, 1930
John Colhoff, Interpreter

I will tell you about one of the war stunts that Crazy Horse pulled off that I thought was great. It was in a fight with the Shoshones in which the Shoshones outnumbered the Oglalas. Crazy Horse and his younger brother were guarding the rear of their war party. After a lot of fighting,

Crazy Horse's pony gave out. Crazy Horse turned it loose, and the younger brother, who did not want to leave him, turned his own pony loose. Two of the enemy, mounted, appeared before them for single combat. Crazy Horse said to his brother, "Take care of yourself. I'll do the fancy stunt." Crazy Horse got the best of the first Shoshone; the other one got away. He got the horses of the two Shoshones, and they caught up with their party. They had saved themselves and their party and got the two horses and the scalp of the Shoshone who was killed. This happened near the present agency.

Another time when the Crows pretty nearly got Crazy Horse was the fight on Arrow Creek, the same fight where Runs Fearless performed his great deed. Crazy Horse charged the Crows, his horse was shot under him, and he was surrounded by the enemy. The Oglalas tried to help him but could not get near him. A man named Spotted Deer made a last effort to reach him. He broke through the enemy, and Crazy Horse got onto his pony behind him, and they made a charge for the open. They both made it back to the Sioux lines, riding double and closely pursued. This battle is known to the Indians as "The Time Yellow Shirt was Killed by the Crows." Pictures of it are shown in the Bad Heart Bull manuscript.[35] Yellow Shirt was a member of the White Horse Owners' society; that is, he was one of the "shirt-wearers" of the northern Montana Sioux. At the time of this battle Crazy Horse and He Dog were the two lance-bearers of the Has-the-Crow-Skin (Crow Owners') Society.

(Short Buffalo was asked to tell about what happened from the time the hostiles decided to come in to the agency until Crazy Horse was killed. His narrative follows.)

About one hundred men went out from the agency to coax the hostiles to come in under pretense that the trouble about the Black Hills was to be settled. The bands of Crazy Horse, He Dog, Holy Bald Eagle, and Big Road gathered to hear these men and to hold a council at the forks of the Tongue River, where a big city of the white people is now (Sheridan, Wyoming). All the hostiles agreed that since it was late and they had to shoot for tipis (i.e., shoot buffalo) they would come in to the agency the following spring.

The next spring He Dog and the Cheyennes were camped on Powder River, working in slowly toward the agency. Early one morning a lot of soldiers sent by General Crook jumped them and took away everything they had—tipis, clothing, food, everything. Crazy Horse was camped a little further down the same river. He Dog and the Cheyennes were going toward him but had not yet reached him when they were jumped by the soldiers. The chiefs of the Cheyennes with He Dog were Little Wolf and Ice. A man by the name of Crawler had come out from the reservation and brought a message from Red Cloud saying, "It is spring; we are waiting for you." Crawler was fired on, too, although he came out there on behalf of the white people.[36]

This attack was the turning point of the situation. The following summer Crook attacked us, and then Custer got into it. If it had not been for that attack by Crook on Powder River, we would have come in to the agency that spring, and there would have been no Sioux war.

The first message we got that Custer was coming to fight us was early in the summer. A small band of Indians coming from North Dakota came in and told about an encounter with Custer. One of this band cited for great bravery in that encounter was named Long Elk.[37] After they joined us, we left that place and moved over onto the next river, the Rosebud. Here the Cheyennes joined us. They came north past Fort Laramie. What they reported was that a lot of soldiers were massing at Fort Laramie and that Crook had enlisted a lot of Crows and Shoshones and was coming north to capture all the Sioux.

So it wasn't long until we had a fight with Crook on the Rosebud and pushed him back. The Crows, Shoshones, and Crook together made up a strong force. In the Rosebud fight the soldiers first got the Sioux and the Cheyennes on the run. Crazy Horse, Bad Heart Bull, Black Deer, Kicking Bear, and Good Weasel rallied the Sioux, turned the charge, and got the soldiers on the run. Good Weasel was a kind of lieutenant for Crazy Horse; he was always with him. When these five commenced to rally their men, that was as far as the soldiers got.

Crook moved back to Goose Creek after the fight. If he had got word to Custer, he could have told him that there were a lot of us Sioux. But he didn't get word to him.

Crazy Horse used good judgment in this Rosebud fight.

Six days after the Rosebud fight Custer ran into us. In this Custer fight I was helping fight Reno and never noticed Custer coming. We had Reno's men on the run across the creek when Crazy Horse rode up with his men.

"Too late! You've missed the fight!" we called out to him.

"Sorry to miss this fight!" he laughed. "But there's a good fight coming over the hill."

I looked where he pointed and saw Custer and his blue coats pouring over the hill. I thought there were a million of them.

"That's where the big fight is going to be," said Crazy Horse. "We'll not miss that one."

He was not a bit excited; he made a joke of it. He wheeled and rode down the river, and a little while later I saw him on his pinto pony leading his men across the ford. He was the first man to cross the river. I saw he had the business well in hand. They rode up the draw, and then there was too much dust. I could not see any more.

The next day we saw Bear Coat coming from below along the river.[38] These soldiers are the ones that dug in the ground and didn't do much fighting. In the morning they joined forces with Reno on his hill. The Indians quit and went away.

There had been three armies after us—Crook, Custer, and Bear Coat (Terry). If all three forces had struck together, it might have been a different story. But each struck separately.

The day we saw Bear Coat, Crazy Horse was in charge. He placed scouts to see Bear Coat did not follow us. But he did not. His soldiers made racks (litters) and hauled the wounded to the mouth of the Big Horn. I was one of the scouts who saw this and reported to Crazy Horse.

Our next fight was the Slim Buttes fight. In that, five leaders were prominent: Crazy Horse, Kicking Bear, Wears-the-Deer-Bonnet, He Dog, and Brave Wolf. There was no one commander. No leader did anything extraordinary.

This was the last battle I myself saw Crazy Horse take part in. The Indians call it "The Fight Where We Lost the Black Hills." Six Indians were taken prisoner in this battle; we call them the Black Hills Captives. Charging Bear (Little Big Man) was one of the captives.

(Here the interpreter, John Colhoff, put in a word, saying that he had read in a book that the Chief American Horse was mortally wounded and taken prisoner in this battle; but that was a mistake. American Horse was not taken prisoner in this battle; neither did he die of wounds received there. Short Buffalo confirmed the younger man in this. Asked who the man was who was shot through the intestines while concealed in the sand-pit, and who died that night and was left for the Indians to bury, Short Buffalo replied:)

Iron Plume was the man shot in the sand pit. There were women in that pit, too. Iron Plume didn't give up until he was too badly wounded to live. It was Iron Plume, not American Horse. One woman was wounded; they let the injured woman and the dead man's wife go. Three women and one child were found dead after the battle. The story might have been different here, too, but most of the men were out trading for ammunition when the attack came, and they had not got back.[39]

After this we went north to the Tongue River and sent eight men to make a treaty. Our peace envoys ran into the Crow camp and lost five men. The other three came home. Then we had the fight where Big Crow got killed. Crazy Horse was in this fight, although I did not see him. His horse was killed under him. He was one of four men who served as a rear guard to cover the retreat of the others and then made their getaway. The Big Crow who gave his name to this fight was a Cheyenne. The Cheyennes spent that winter with Crazy Horse and He Dog.

(Short Buffalo was asked if there was anything to the story that Crazy Horse had refused to share his scanty supplies with the Cheyenne refugees from the Battle of Hole-in-the-Wall, led by Dull Knife, and that they were at odds with him on this account. This story is told by Major Bourke in *On the Border with Crook,* page 394, and denied by George Bird Grinnell on the strength of Cheyenne testimony in *The Fighting Cheyenne,* page 368. Short Buffalo said:)

There is nothing to that story. We helped the Cheyennes the best we could. We hadn't much ourselves.

After that we started toward the Rocky Mountains to hunt. An Indian (half-breed) named Big Leggings [John Bruguier] brought back three women captives taken by General Miles and asked the hostiles to consider peace. Big Leggings, interpreter for General Miles, was a Hunkpapa. His coming to us that way was a brave deed. He would have been killed, but He Dog protected him until the ill feeling was over. There was always a pretty good bunch of men hanging around He Dog in those days. As soon as people knew what Big Leggings came for, and that the women had not been hurt, then it was all right.[40]

While we were up there, Crow Hawk, Running Fire, and Sword came out to us with a message. They wanted us to come back to the Red Cloud Agency and quit fighting. When the messengers came to He Dog we learned that Crazy Horse had already come down to Lodgepole Creek near the Powder River; he was already moving toward the agency. So at this Powder River we all met and had a big council and decided to go in together. The Cheyenne chiefs, Two Moon, Ice, and Little Wolf, took another course in.

When we got to the head of the Powder River, we found Red Cloud with one hundred other chiefs to bring us a welcome message: "All is well; have no fear; come on in." Some squaw-men came with him, the two Genise (Janis) boys and others. From there we all went in to the agency in good spirits. There was no bad feeling among the chiefs or anybody. When we had all come together as far as Hat Creek, we sent messengers ahead and followed slowly.

On a big flat near Fort Robinson, Red Cloud and White Hat with two troops of cavalry met Crazy Horse. They shook hands and said they were glad to see him; everybody had come in peace. Crazy Horse spread out his blanket for Red Cloud to sit on and gave his shirt to Red Cloud; He Dog did the same for White Hat. This meant that they gave up to these two. He Dog gave his war horse and saddle to White Hat. You can see by this that there was no ill feeling toward the whites.[41]

In all the talk they had on this day, Crazy Horse said, "There is a creek over there they call Beaver Creek; there is a great big flat west of the headwaters of Beaver Creek; I want my agency put right in the middle of that flat." He said the grass was good there for horses and game. This flat is near where the town of Gillette, Wyoming, is today. After the agency was placed there, he would go to Washington and talk to the Great Father. There was another site he had picked for an agency over near the White (Big Horn) Mountains. This was near where the town of Sheridan, Wyoming, is today. But if he couldn't go there, this place near Beaver Creek would be all right. This was the only cause of misunderstanding at that time. Crazy Horse wanted to have the agency established first, and then he would go to Washington. The officers wanted him to go to Washington first. The difference of whether Crazy Horse should go to Washington before or after the site of the agency was settled upon brought on all the trouble little by little. When Iron White Man (a relative of Crazy Horse) made his trip to Washington, he tried to make that clear.[42]

He Dog, I, and all our family are related to Red Cloud. So after a while we naturally moved over and camped near Red Cloud. Right away after that I joined the scouts and went out with a bunch of them to try to persuade the Lame Deer band to come in. I was away on this errand when Crazy Horse was killed. So this is as far as I know about Crazy Horse.

Crazy Horse was a man not very tall and not very short, neither broad nor thin. His hair was very light, about the color of yours.[43] He was a trifle under six feet tall. Bad Heart Bull was the same general type. But Crazy Horse had a very light complexion, much lighter than the other Indians. He usually wore an Iroquois shell necklace; this was the only ornament he wore. His features were not like those of the rest of us. His face was not broad, and he had a sharp, high nose. He had black eyes that hardly ever looked straight at a man, but they didn't miss much that was going on all the same.

I have seen two photographs of Crazy Horse that I think were really he, both showing him on horseback. One showed him on a buckskin horse he owned, one on a roan. I have seen a third photograph that I am sure was he because it showed him on the pinto horse he rode in the Custer fight. I could not possibly make a mistake about that horse, and nobody rode it but Crazy Horse. The man who owns these pictures got them from soldiers who used to be at Fort Robinson. He has quite a collection of pictures of chiefs. I think he lives out in California now, near the national park there. I do not remember his name.

Interview with Carrie Slow Bear
Oglala, South Dakota, July 12, 1930
Samuel Stands, Interpreter

Before Crazy Horse came down to the agency, all I knew about him was that I had heard he was brave. A big part of the tribe was away off beyond the Black Hills. Crazy Horse was off there with them. He was one of the bravest. He said he wanted to stay out back there in the desert with his people. Red Cloud had come in to the agency. He wanted to make friends with the white people. Crazy Horse did not.

The white people wanted Crazy Horse to come in to the agency and quit fighting. Slow Bear went out with Red Cloud to get Crazy Horse to come in. Finally they got him to come in.

Then the white people wanted Crazy Horse to go to Washington, but he didn't want to go. So after a while they arrested him and brought him to the fort. They were going to take his fighting materials away from him—his gun and his knife—but he wouldn't let them do it. So then they stabbed him with a sword. That is all I know.

Question: I have read in a book that Crazy Horse was related by marriage to Red Cloud. Is that true?

Answer: Crazy Horse was no relation to Red Cloud.

Q: Red Cloud acted like a good friend to Crazy Horse when he got him to come in to the agency, because if he had not, the soldiers were going to set out with a bigger expedition than ever and the hostiles would have had a hard time. But how did they get along together after Crazy Horse came in? I have been told that some people wanted to have Crazy Horse made chief of all the Oglalas instead of Red Cloud and that they got to be envious of one another on this account.

A: Crazy Horse was killed when he had only been at the agency a little while. I do not think there was time for them to have quarrelled, or to have got jealous of each other.[44]

Q: Did you know a man named Woman Dress?

A: Yes, I knew him.

Q: He told some queer stories about Crazy Horse, which was the reason why the officers decided to arrest him. Do you know anything about the character of this Woman Dress, whether he could be believed or not?

A: Woman Dress was a scout for twenty years at Fort Robinson. I don't really know what sort of a person he was, whether he was a good man, or whether he was a bad man. The white people at the fort liked him.

Q: Do you have any idea why Crazy Horse was unwilling to go to Washington?

A: Crazy Horse was willing to go there in the first place, but so much was said about it that he got afraid something would be done to him there. Red Cloud and Slow Bear told him the truth when they went out and got him to come in. They told him that he ought to go to Washington and that it would be all right. But another Indian told him they would kill him either at Fort Robinson or in Washington.

Q: Who was it told him that?

A: (slowly) Little Big Man told him that.

White Calf
Pine Ridge, South Dakota, July 11, 1930
Philip White Calf, Interpreter

The first I knew of Crazy Horse he was out on the Cheyenne River. I was in Red Cloud's band at the old agency near the fort. I was a scout at the fort. Red Cloud received word that Crazy Horse was coming in to meet us. So then he came in and made a treaty with the soldiers.

I was right there at the time when Crazy Horse was killed. A bunch of Rosebud Indians brought Crazy Horse to Fort Robinson. The soldier chiefs had called him to the fort four times. They called him three times, and he would not come, so the fourth time they were going to arrest him. The fourth time the crowd brought him back and took him to jail.

When they got to the jail, all the Indians cried out, "It's the jail!" and they would not go in with him. Only one went in with him. It was Little Big Man—Chasing (Charging) Bear—who went in with him. The others who came with him were Iron Hawk, Turning Bear, Big Road, and Long Bear. Crazy Horse and Little Big Man went in.

When Crazy Horse found it was the jail, he turned back and took out his butcher knife. He wanted to hurt somebody. Little Big Man caught his hands behind his back. Crazy Horse dragged him through the door out onto the parade ground. He cut Little Big Man in the wrists. The soldier who was walking up and down outside the jail stabbed Crazy Horse from behind with his bayonet. Crazy Horse fell, crouching. I was about twenty-three or twenty-four years old at the time these things happened.

Then someone said they were going to take Crazy Horse to the hospital. He died there, and they brought him back to camp the next morning. Do you want to know how Crazy Horse was dressed at the time he was killed? He wore beaded moccasins, buckskin leggings, and a white cotton shirt. He had a red blanket.

Little Killer
Oglala, South Dakota, July 12, 1930
Samuel Stands, Interpreter

I was with Crazy Horse all the time, like that (both forefingers pressed close together). But I was not with him when he was killed. If I had been, maybe I would have been killed too.

I was with Crazy Horse's people when they came out to him from Fort Robinson with tobacco and asked him to come in. Crazy Horse said, all right, he would come to Fort Robinson in the spring.

Crazy Horse moved in a little ahead of me. I trailed him when he was coming in and joined him. When we were a little distance from Fort Robinson, people came out bringing us meat. This meat was not buffalo meat but beef and other food. Crazy Horse told me that he was "captured" (i.e., had surrendered) and was going to Fort Robinson and from there on to Washington. The white people at Fort Robinson wanted our guns and horses—the things we fought with. Crazy Horse said, "All right, let them have them."

When he let the horses and fighting materials go, he wanted to go to Washington. He wanted to tell the president he had picked out a place where he wanted to stay. The place where he wanted to go was back over near the White (Big Horn) Mountains near the Tongue River. Crazy Horse had a white man carve a stone marker and gave it to my brother to take over and set up in that country where he wanted to go. This brother was named Club Man. He is dead now. If he were living, he would be chief of the whole tribe. He had married Crazy Horse's older sister. He had eight children, but none of them lived long enough to get allotments from the government.

When Crazy Horse first came to Fort Robinson, he wanted to go to Washington. But other Indians were jealous of him and afraid that if he went to Washington they would make him chief of all the Indians on the reservation. These Indians came to him and told him a lot of stories. After that he would not go there. So then he was arrested and killed.

I was not with Crazy Horse when he was killed. I had been sent to the Spotted Tail Agency with a message. When I got back, I heard about it.

Question: Were you at the Spotted Tail Agency at the time when Crazy Horse came there to see the agent, Capt. Jesse M. Lee?

Answer: No, I was not there then. I heard about that afterward.

Q: Can you tell us what Crazy Horse looked like?

A: Crazy Horse was a short, little man. He did not have black hair; he had brown hair like a white man's and a long straight nose. His eyes were black like a Lakota's.

Q: Can you tell us about Crazy Horse's family, to whom he was married and if he had any children?

A: All the time I knew Crazy Horse before he was "captured" he was married to one woman. Afterwards he was married to two, one a white woman (mixed breed). His first wife was Red Feather's sister. She was the only one by whom he had children, a little girl who died young. Crazy Horse's sister and her children all died before 1901.

Portions of Letter from Dr. V. T. McGillycuddy to Eleanor H. Hinman
May 6, 1930
Interviewer's Questions, Dr. McGillycuddy's Answers

Question: When and how did you first meet Crazy Horse and what were your first impressions of him?

Answer: I first met or became *distantly* acquainted with Crazy Horse at the battle of the Rosebud, June 17, 1876, eight days before the Custer fight, when he attacked General Crook's command of 1,100 with his 3,000 warriors (in which command I was surgeon of the 2nd U.S. Cavalry) and in September following when he again attacked Crook's command at the Battle of Slim Buttes on our starvation march to the Black Hills, after the Custer battle.

From my observation of his leadership and tactics employed in these two battles, and from the close association and friendship established between us after his surrender at Fort Robinson early in May 1877, I could not but regard him as the greatest leader of his people in modern times. He was but thirty-six.[45] In him everything was made secondary to patriotism and love of his people. Modest, fearless, a mystic, a believer in destiny, and much of a recluse, he was held in veneration and admiration by the younger warriors, who would follow him anywhere.

These qualities made him a danger to the government, and he became *persona non grata* to evolution and to the progress of the white man's civilization. Hence his early death was preordained.

At about eleven P.M. that night in the gloomy old adjutant's office, as his life was fast ebbing, the bugler on the parade ground wailed out the lonesome call for Taps, "Lights out, go to sleep!" It brought back to him the old battles; he struggled to arise, and there came from his lips his old rallying cry, "A good day to fight, a good day to die! Brave hearts . . ." and his voice ceased, the lights went out, and the last sleep came. It was a scene never to be forgotten, an Indian epic.

Q: You speak in your article in the *Nebraska History Magazine* of last December and also in your official report of 1879 of the jealousy and resentment felt toward Crazy Horse by Red Cloud and possibly (although he is not named) by Spotted Tail. Have you any idea at what date this hostility began to take active shape? Spotted Tail and Red Cloud had both seemed to play a friendly role in helping to negotiate Crazy Horse's peaceful surrender the preceding spring and in allaying the suspicions felt by the officers when he was so slow about coming in to the fort. If at that time they had wanted to do him an injury they had an excellent opportunity, but did not take it. What had happened between May and September to make them change their minds?

A: While the Custer battle, or massacre as it is termed, was a great victory for the Sioux, preceded as it was by the Battle of the Rosebud, it was a victory but temporary, ending in the scattering of the Sitting Bull and Crazy Horse forces, and the retreat of the bulk of the hostiles under Sitting Bull into British America for food and shelter, for the United States troops were increasing in numbers and in extent of country. The leaders of the Sioux, including Red Cloud and Spotted Tail, were forced to a realization that they had made their "last stand," and that the time had come for a final and lasting peace. Hence these two chiefs turned in honestly and assisted in every way to bring about the peace.

Spotted Tail and Red Cloud, however, did not realize or anticipate the "hero worship" that always follows the return to his people of a success-ful great military leader, which Crazy Horse had developed into. Hence the jealousy. Spotted Tail, more of a diplomat, did not show it so much.

In the fall of 1876 there was held in Washington a peace conference between the president and the leading agency chiefs of the several Sioux agencies. Present were Spotted Tail, Red Cloud, and General Crook. In this meeting Crook practically ignored Red Cloud as untrustworthy and threw his weight to Chief Spotted Tail.

The following spring, early in May, Crazy Horse after many months of solicitation from General Crook came in with his people and surrendered at Fort Robinson and entered into a solemn peace treaty with Crook to abstain from all war for the future. He intended to and did keep the prom-ises entered into, subsequent reports to the contrary notwithstanding.

Gen. George Crook, department commander, made a brilliant record in the Civil War and had become a past master in his dealings with the

Indians. He studied and became thoroughly acquainted with their nature, psychology, view points, and so forth, and enjoyed their confidence. From the British line south to the Mexican border, they trusted the "Gray Fox," and he never betrayed that confidence. In the south he had met marked success in overcoming Geronimo and his Apaches. . . . In Crazy Horse however he had a different problem to deal with, an Indian leader who had established his military leadership at the Battle of the Rosebud and eight days later at the Battle of the Little Big Horn.

Crazy Horse was the "Stormy Petrel" of the Great Plains, idolized by the young fighting element of the Sioux and Cheyennes, thousands in number. He asked not toleration, sufferance, or protection from the white man. He was willing to agree to a treaty of peace, and did so. But he retained a right to a free life on his hunting grounds, and to live on the game, instead of the beef of the white man. These things were his heritage from the Great Spirit, given to his people ages before the coming of the white man.

To solve the problem the general contemplated supplanting Red Cloud, who was an old confirmed reactionary and opposed to civilization, by having Crazy Horse made head chief of the Oglalas. But the inactivity of agency life palled on the young Indian leader. He was not intended to lead his young fighting men into the paths of civilization, but preferred the free hunting life which he claimed as his right. He did not however contemplate again going on the war path, unless attacked. He was a freeborn, aboriginal leader, neither a politician nor a diplomat.

Notes

[1] See P. E. Byrne, *Soldiers of the Plains* (New York: Minton, Balch and Co., 1926); John G. Neihardt, *The Song of the Indian Wars* (New York: Macmillan Company, 1925); Grace Raymond Hebard, *Washakie* (Cleveland: The Arthur H. Clark Co., 1930).

[2] Charles A. Eastman (Ohiyesa), *Indian Heroes and Great Chieftains* (Boston: Little, Brown, and Company, 1918), 83–106; Luther Standing Bear, *My People, the Sioux* (Boston and New York: Houghton Mifflin Company, 1928), 83–88, 100.

[3] For example, here is a specimen: Question—About how many fighting men were there with you and Crazy Horse at the Battle of the Rosebud? Answer—In the old days we did not stop to count whether there were two of us or whether there were two thousand. We just went ahead and fought.

[4] The name is commonly translated Short Bull, but it is rendered Short Buffalo here to escape confusion with the Brulé medicine man of Ghost Dance fame.

[5] The question of the attitude of He Dog and Short Buffalo toward their uncle Red Cloud may be of some interest in evaluating their testimony in view of the accusations

made by Dr. Valentine T. McGillycuddy and others that the rumors of treachery on the part of Crazy Horse originated with the Red Cloud party. Both the men quoted here maintained a policy independent from that of their celebrated uncle. Short Buffalo's personal attitude is reflected in a statement made to Helen H. Blish about a year before this in an interview on the subject of Oglala chiefs' societies: "Red Cloud was never a Short Hair (i.e., a member of the Pekin Pte Pte Cela or Han Skaska, a certain Oglala society of chiefs). Those whose prowess and battle accomplishments and characters were *undisputed* were feasted and honored. He Dog and Short Buffalo were so honored many times, while Red Cloud was not, although he was a chief." Notes of an interview with Short Buffalo by Helen H. Blish, July 23, 1929.

[6] For example, all the Indians interviewed say that Crazy Horse was brought back under arrest from the Spotted Tail Agency, while Gen. (then Capt. [2d Lt.]) Jesse R. Lee, who brought him back, says that he came back voluntarily upon the pledge that he would be heard.

[7] That is, to the Brulés, of whom Spotted Tail was afterward chief.

[8] According to ancient Lakota custom, coup could be counted on an enemy woman if she was killed in the sight of the fighting men of her tribe. The theory was that the enemy would fight even harder to protect or avenge one of their women than one of their men. But the Brulés were already agency Indians, and the authorities took a different attitude. Apparently Crazy Horse himself changed his mind about the ethics of this custom, if the speech of his reported by Fred M. Hans in *The Great Sioux Nation* (Chicago: M. A. Donohue and Company, 1907), 532–34, is correct.

[9] After consultation together He Dog and the interpreter dated these appointments as having been made about 1865 by the white man's calendar. On the duties and qualifications of a "shirt-wearer," see Clark Wissler, "Societies and Ceremonial Associations of the Oglala Division of the Teton–Dakota," *Anthropological Papers of the American Museum of National History* 11 (1912):7,36,39–40.

[10] The battle "When They Chased the Crows Back Into Camp," a Sioux–Crow fight which is celebrated in tribal annals, took place in 1870. On the Crow Owners' Society and the somewhat exciting duties of its officers, see Wissler, "Societies and Ceremonial Associations," 23–25.

[11] Bad Heart Bull was a brother of He Dog. He is now dead.

[12] Eastman, *Indian Heroes and Great Chieftains*, 90.

[13] This fight has been dated as 1870.

[14] Spring or summer of 1870.

[15] Little Shield is a brother of He Dog. He was wandering around outside the cottage when this was said, so the interpreter went out and invited him in. He was present during the remainder of the interview and contributed to it.

[16] A "shirt-wearer" of one division of the Oglala tribe, a colleague of He Dog, Red Cloud, and Big Road.

[17] This makes her a first cousin of He Dog, Bad Heart Bull, and their brothers.

[18] The chief's society in the northern division of the Oglala tribe was called the Short Hairs, that in the southern or "Red Cloud" division, the White Horse Owners. See Wissler, "Societies and Ceremonial Associations," 7, 36, 39–40.

[19] This statement illustrates one of the misunderstandings that were the curse of negotia-

tions with the Indians. The officers thought they were promising the Indians that they might leave the agency temporarily for a buffalo hunt the following summer when things had quieted down. He Dog thought he was being promised that he could go back west to stay. As it turned out, things had not quieted down much by the following summer, and the officers withdrew even the permission for the promised buffalo hunt. See Gen. Jesse V. Lee's account of this trouble in *Nebraska History* 12 (Jan.–Mar. 1929):7–12.

[20] Beaver Creek in eastern Wyoming is meant. The interpreter, T[he]. W[hite]. C[ow]. Killer, added that he believed Crazy Horse wanted to get his people farther away from the military.

[21] Apparently the Crawford Buttes, near where the town of Crawford is now.

[22] The directions given in this paragraph are wrong. He Dog was speaking under the impression that the guardhouse was north of the adjutant's office; judging from the blueprints of the old fort, it was west-northwest. This error throws his other directions off a little. Fort Robinson is not oriented according to the points of the compass, and it is easy to become confused about directions even when one is there in person.

[23] Assistant post surgeon and Crazy Horse's white friend.

[24] September 1 or 2, 1877.

[25] He Dog gave this man's Indian name. The interpreter gave the identification with the same hesitation.

[26] Joe De Barthe, *The Life and Adventures of Frank Grouard, Chief of Scouts, U.S.A.* (St. Joseph, Mo.: Combe Printing Co., 1894), 337–41. Considerable doubt has lately been thrown on Grouard's reliability as a witness. See the narratives of Lee and McGillycuddy in *Nebraska History* 12 (Jan.–Mar., 1929):12–17,36–38.

[27] This was the Treaty of 1868–69.

[28] It was May 7, 1877, when they reached Fort Robinson. They started in April.

[29] For a full account of the Woman Dress incident, see William Garnett's narrative in Byrne, *Soldiers of the Plains*, 235–43.

[30] Beaver Creek in southern South Dakota is meant. This is a different stream from the Beaver Creek in Wyoming, where Crazy Horse wanted his agency.

[31] A nickname of American Horse.

[32] Standing Bear, *My People, the Sioux*, 88. McGillycuddy's statement is given later in this article.

[33] Doubtless an opiate. Dr. McGillycuddy was a warm admirer of Crazy Horse.

[34] Lone Bear was a brother of Woman Dress. In later years, however, Lone Bear earnestly denied both that he had ever heard Crazy Horse plot such treachery as was charged to him and that he had ever said he had heard of such a plot. See the Garnett narrative referred to earlier. The story reached the officers from Woman Dress and Grouard.

[35] The Bad Heart Bull manuscript is a pictographic chronicle of Oglala tribal history and customs. It was drawn by Amos Bad Heart Bull, a nephew of Short Buffalo and He Dog, now dead. It is being prepared by Miss Helen Blish for publication.

[36] This is the Powder River fight of March 17, 1876. The whites thought they had hit Crazy Horse. For a white account, see John G. Bourke, *On the Border with Crook* (New York: Charles Scribner's Sons, 1891), chap. 16.

[37] These were apparently the Yanktons under Inkpaduta.

[38] Bear Coat is the Indian name of Gen. Nelson A. Miles, but Short Buffalo obviously means Gen. Alfred H. Terry, more commonly called The Limping Soldier or The-One-with-No-Hip.

[39] For a white account of the battle, see John F. Finerty, *War-Path and Bivouac, or The Conquest of the Sioux* (Chicago: M. A. Donohue & Co., 1890), 249–66.

[40] For a further account of this incident, see Nelson A. Miles, *Personal Recollections and Observations of General Nelson A. Miles* (Chicago and New York: The Werner Company, 1896), 239–40.

[41] For an account of this same scene from the white officers' point of view, see Bourke, *On the Border with Crook*, 412–15.

[42] Apparently Crazy Horse was afraid that, if he went to Washington before the site of his agency was settled upon, the authorities might try to intimidate him into signing a transfer of his people to the Indian Territory, where, in fact, his Cheyenne allies were sent in June of the same year with disastrous consequences both to the Cheyenne and to neighboring Kansas settlers. Either this, or he feared that he was to be punished for the Custer affair. The Indians interviewed seem to have been reluctant to state these suspicions in so many words to the white interviewer.

[43] The interviewer could be described as "medium blonde."

[44] Crazy Horse surrendered on May 7 and was killed on September 5, 1877.

[45] He Dog's narrative makes him thirty-nine at the time of his death, and Eastman, *Indian Heroes and Great Chieftains*, 83, makes him thirty-three.

Epilogue

The Pageant Revisited:
Indian Wars Medals of Honor
in Nebraska, 1865–1879

James E. Potter

Sergeant Patrick Leonard and the four privates were caught by surprise when Indians came boiling out of the ravines near Spring Creek. Their horses shot down by the warriors' first volley, the men fought for their lives from behind the makeshift breastworks the animals' bodies provided. Recognition for bravery was far from their minds that May morning in 1870; saving their lives was all that mattered. Nevertheless, for successfully defending themselves during this obscure skirmish in Nuckolls County, Nebraska, all five soldiers from Company C, Second Cavalry, would receive the Medal of Honor.

The Medal of Honor, created by Congress in 1862, has been presented many times to soldiers with Nebraska connections. In a group by themselves are the fifteen men who garnered the nation's highest award for gallantry while performing military service *within* Nebraska's borders. These Medals of Honor, earned between 1865 and 1879, resulted from the U.S. Army's efforts to subdue the embattled Sioux and Cheyenne during the Indian wars on the Plains.

The decades-long conflict with the western tribes was hardly war in the conventional sense. The foe was elusive and mobile, fought in small groups, and lived off the land. Large-scale, pitched battles were rare. The nation's attention was easily drawn to a Little Bighorn or a Sand Creek, while hundreds of minor encounters escaped notice, except in official dispatches or in the editorial columns of western newspapers always ready to raise the specter of settlements laid waste by "savages." Despite their obscurity, the small-scale actions typical of Indian fighting often were brutal affairs that took the lives of combatants and noncombatants on both sides.

Nebraska saw its share of bloodshed during the 1860s and 1870s. During most of this period Nebraska was defended by soldiers from the

Epilogue

Department of the Platte, commanded from Omaha. They garrisoned military posts large and small, carried out hundreds of scouts and reconnaissances, and occasionally battled elusive warriors. Although many examples of bravery doubtless went unrecognized, fourteen soldiers and one civilian scout who saw action in Nebraska, were singled out for award of the Medal of Honor.

The names of Indian wars Medal of Honor recipients are recorded in government publications, accompanied by brief, dry summaries devoid of detail and sometimes in error about what really happened and where.[1] Fortunately military records, pension records, and contemporary newspaper accounts more fully illuminate the personalities and events involved in each award of the Medal of Honor.

The first Medal of Honor earned in Nebraska, and the only one received by a soldier from a Nebraska regiment, went to Francis W. Lohnes in 1865. Lohnes was a private in Company H, First Nebraska Veteran Volunteer Cavalry. He joined the regiment when the Civil War began, fought with it at Fort Donelson and Shiloh, and reenlisted in 1864. In August 1864 the First Nebraska was dispatched to garrison stage stations and road ranches along the Platte Valley in the wake of raids by Sioux and Cheyennes. In February 1865 the company constructed a military camp at Midway Station near present Gothenburg, Nebraska.

On May 12, 1865, Lohnes left Midway in charge of a wood-gathering detail. Near Dan Smith's Ranche, ten miles to the west, his detachment blundered into a skirmish in progress between Indians and elements of Company A of the First Battalion, Nebraska Cavalry. Though wounded, Lohnes held his ground when ten Indians surrounded him. His stand enabled the men of both commands to escape to Smith's Ranche without loss of life or government property.

Brig. Gen. Patrick E. Connor, commander of the District of the Plains, recommended Lohnes for a Medal of Honor. Lohnes received the Medal on August 15 in an impressive ceremony at Fort Kearny attended by Maj. Gen. Grenville M. Dodge, Brig. Gen. Herman H. Heath, and Nebraska Governor Alvin Saunders. It was the only Medal of Honor ever awarded to a member of a military unit bearing Nebraska's name.[2]

Lt. John Breckinridge Babcock, commanding Company M, Fifth U.S. Cavalry, earned his Medal of Honor in a skirmish with Indians at Spring Creek in present Phelps County, Nebraska, May 16, 1869. Babcock, the lieutenant colonel of the 162nd New York Volunteers during the Civil War, received an appointment to the regular army in 1867 and was assigned to Maj. (Bvt. Maj. Gen.) Eugene A. Carr's Fifth Cavalry.

The Fifth Cavalry, soon to defeat the Cheyenne Dog Soldiers at Summit Springs in July 1869, was enroute from Fort Lyon, Colorado, to Fort McPherson, Nebraska, when on May 14, the command struck an Indian trail on Medicine Creek. Veering east, seven companies of the regiment pursued the Indians for two days. About noon on Sunday, May 16, a small party under 2d Lt. William J. Volkmar and scout William F. Cody advanced to reconnoiter, while the main command watered its horses at the crossing of Spring Creek. Fearing trouble, Carr ordered Babcock and M Company to support Volkmar's reconnaissance.

About two miles from the creek, some two hundred Indians sprang from ravines and completely surrounded Babcock's and Volkmar's contingent. For half an hour the isolated soldiers held on until Carr sent reinforcements.[3]

The skirmish itself was unremarkable; three enlisted men were wounded, and the Indians vanished when the reinforcements arrived. It was Babcock's behavior that distinguished the fighting and earned him the Medal of Honor.

As Carr explained later, Babcock's company "was somewhat demoralized, being like the rest, unused to Indian fighting." But Babcock encouraged and steadied his men, "remaining on his horse altho urged to dismount." Cody, who knew capable leadership when he saw it (and who was grazed by a bullet during the skirmish), testified that Babcock "displayed remarkable coolness and courage, handling his men with excellent prudence and military judgment."[4]

The circumstances surrounding the 1870 award of the Medal of Honor to Sgt. Patrick Leonard and Privates Heath Canfield, Michael Himmelsbach, Thomas Hubbard, and George W. Thompson were remarkably similar to Babcock's experience. The five soldiers belonged to Company C, Second U.S. Cavalry, stationed during the summer of 1870 at temporary Camp Bingham on the Little Blue River west of Hebron, Nebraska. The company had been sent from Omaha Barracks to protect the settlements springing up along the Little Blue, Spring Creek, and the Republican River.[5]

Several scouting expeditions from Camp Bingham had found no trace of Indians. Leonard's detachment was not expecting trouble when it was sent to search for some lost horses near the settlements on Spring Creek.[6] About seven miles southwest of Camp Bingham on the morning of May 17, 1870, fifty Indians fell upon Leonard's little party without warning. After a two-hour skirmish in which Private Hubbard was wounded, the Indians withdrew when they mistook a party of surveyors for a military column. Despite losing their horses to Indian fire, the soldiers managed to make it back to Camp Bingham.

Epilogue

While Leonard and his men were fighting for their lives, other Indians killed a settler on the Little Blue and made off with a few horses. The rest of Company C pursued, but failed to catch any of the warriors, who escaped south of the Republican.[7] Despite the turmoil this raid created among the settlements in the region, it was the last Indian foray into southern Nebraska, and Camp Bingham was abandoned in the fall of 1870. For their conduct in the skirmish of May 17 the soldiers of Leonard's command received Medals of Honor by order of Secretary of War William W. Belknap.[8] More Medals of Honor were awarded for this fleeting engagement than for any other episode in the annals of the Indian wars in Nebraska.

Sergeants John H. Foley and Leroy Vokes, Pvt. William H. Strayer, and scout William F. "Buffalo Bill" Cody received the Medal of Honor in 1872. On April 25 Capt. Charles Meinhold's Company B, Third Cavalry, left Fort McPherson on the trail of some Minneconjou Sioux, who had stolen horses from a nearby station on the Union Pacific. The next day Meinhold's command reached the South Loup River (in the vicinity of present Stapleton, Nebraska), where the captain detached Cody, Sergeant Foley, and ten enlisted men to scour the south bank of the river. The main command crossed to the north side.

Under Cody's skillful guidance, Foley's party managed to approach within fifty yards of the Indian camp before it was discovered. In the ensuing exchange of gunfire Cody killed one Indian, while two others were shot down by the main command as they fled. Six Indians, who were hunting away from the camp, made their escape.

In his report Meinhold commended Cody and three of the soldiers. Sgt. John H. Foley "charged into the Indian camp without knowing how many enemies he might encounter. First Sergeant Leroy Vokes, who by his prompt, intelligent, and cheerful obedience to my orders, aided me essentially." Pvt. William H. Strayer "bravely closed in upon an Indian while he was fired at several times, and wounded him." Of Cody, Meinhold remarked: "Mr. Cody's reputation for bravery and skill as a guide is so well established that I need not say anything else but that he acted in his usual manner." Meinhold's superior, Col. Joseph J. Reynolds, commander of the Third Cavalry, recommended the four men for Medals of Honor, soon issued on May 22.[9]

Cody's situation was unusual; he received the Medal of Honor as a civilian. Four other civilian scouts also received the Medal for Civil War or Indian wars service. In 1917 a military review board stripped the scouts of their medals, along with several hundred other recipients whose deeds the board found inadequate to justify Medals of Honor. Cody's medal was revoked on a technicality: a 1917 regulation limiting the Medal to officers or enlisted men was applied retroactively. There was no suggestion that Cody's conduct was not deserving.[10] Military records provide ample evidence that he was brave, resourceful, and highly respected by the commanders under whom he served. In 1989 the army reinstated Cody's Medal of Honor and those of the other scouts.[11]

Cody seems to have paid scant attention to his medal. It was just one more honor in a life filled with accolades and public acclaim, and his recollection of the incident for which he earned the Medal grew hazy. In *An Autobiography of Buffalo Bill* (published posthumously in 1920, one of his several autobiographies), Cody embellished his exploits on that April day in 1872. He, not Sgt. Foley, was in charge of the party of soldiers that crept up on the Indians (only six soldiers instead of eleven). The nine Indians reported in the military dispatches had become thirteen. Cody shot three Indians himself, while the rest, instead of fleeing, "came rushing to the rescue of their friends." Altogether, says Cody, six Indians and one soldier were killed, though no soldier casualties are mentioned in Meinhold's report. Cody claimed to have suffered a scalp wound from an Indian bullet.[12]

Ironically, while Cody enhanced his own role in the fight, even claiming the wound he actually received at Babcock's Spring Creek fight in 1869, he omitted to mention his well documented Medal of Honor in his retelling of the 1872 skirmish on the Loup.

Cody's medal surfaces, however, in his account of an 1870 brush with Indian horse thieves that took place on Red Willow Creek. The incident turns up in at least two Cody autobiographies, as well as in *Deeds of Valor*, a 1905 publication detailing the exploits of Medal of Honor recipients.

In June 1870 Cody guided a company of the Fifth Cavalry out of Fort McPherson to recapture stolen horses, including his own favorite, Powder Face. In Cody's 1879 account, the Indians make off with the horse.[13] In *Buffalo Bill's Own Story* (1917), Powder Face is recaptured.[14] In *Deeds of Valor* Cody not only recovers his horse, but he has himself receiving the Medal of Honor after this fight, instead of for the skirmish on the South Loup in 1872![15]

Fort Hartsuff (1874–81) was a military post mired in the backwaters of the Indian wars. Established to protect settlements in Nebraska's North Loup Valley, the fort's most significant contribution lay in the employment its construction availed to settlers impoverished by the "hard times" of the mid-1870s. Never garrisoned by more than a company, Fort Hartsuff promised a quiet, even monotonous existence for the infantrymen stationed there. Yet the single instance in which troops from the fort fought

Epilogue

Indians garnered Medals of Honor for three members of Company A, Twenty-third Infantry.

On April 28, 1876, settlers sighted a small party of Sioux in the vicinity. Acting Post Commander 1st Lt. William C. Manning dispatched 2nd Lt. Charles H. Heyl and eight enlisted men to pursue the Indians who, under the army's policy at the time, were presumed to be a war party because they were roaming away from the reservation. After a chase extending twenty miles northwest of the fort, the soldiers, along with a group of civilians, found the six Indians entrenched in a blowout on top of a sand hill.

The sun was about to set, and Lieutenant Heyl realized the Indians were likely to escape after nightfall. Because the warriors were so well protected, Heyl asked the civilians to join his men in a charge to overwhelm the Indians by sheer force of numbers. When the civilians demurred, Heyl left four men to block the Indian's escape route, while he led three soldiers in a charge to the rim of the blowout. There was a simultaneous volley of gunfire, and Sgt. William H. Dougherty was shot dead. Heyl, Cpl. Patrick Leonard, and Pvt. Jeptha Lytton retreated; it seemed obvious that they had little chance to dislodge the dug-in foe.

As Heyl feared, the Indians escaped after dark. There was nothing to do but return to Fort Hartsuff with Dougherty's body, which was buried April 30 with military honors. Though the unfortunate Dougherty achieved only the notoriety of losing his life, Heyl, Leonard, and Lytton were given Medals of Honor for gallantry in their charge upon the Sioux. After the "Battle of the Blowout," life at Fort Hartsuff returned to normal. By 1881 the need for military posts to watch the Sioux reservations in Dakota Territory led to the closing of Fort Hartsuff and the establishment of Fort Niobrara near Valentine, Nebraska.[16]

The last Medal of Honor earned in Nebraska went to Sgt. William B. Lewis of Company B, Third Cavalry, in 1879. Company B was stationed at Fort Laramie when Dull Knife's Cheyennes broke out of their barracks prison at Fort Robinson on the bitterly cold night of January 9, 1879.

From Fort Robinson Companies C and H of the Third Cavalry pursued the fleeing Cheyennes through the pine-studded buttes northwest of the fort, gradually decimating the ranks of the starving and poorly clad Indians. Periodically the Cheyennes would hole up in the rugged terrain, later resuming their flight under cover of darkness. As the chase dragged on into mid-January, Companies B and D of the Third Cavalry were dispatched from Fort Laramie to block the Indians' escape to the west.[17]

On January 20 a band of Cheyennes entrenched themselves on a rocky eminence, and, as night fell, the Fort Laramie soldiers were posted to prevent their escape. At dawn the guards saw troops moving in the valley below, as if in pursuit of Indians. There was a call for volunteers to reconnoiter the Indian position, and Sergeant Lewis and two others stepped forward. Approaching the Cheyenne rifle pit, they were fired on by a wounded warrior, who had been left behind, and Lewis killed him.[18] The other Cheyennes had escaped, only to be killed or captured at Antelope Creek on January 22 in the final fighting of the Cheyenne Outbreak.

Lewis's commander, Capt. John B. Johnson, recommended Lewis for the Medal of Honor in a February 7 dispatch to the adjutant general of the United States. The Medal was presented at a ceremony in front of the garrison at Fort Laramie on April 17, 1879.[19]

Lewis's Medal of Honor is recorded in government publications as having been earned in Wyoming, and official dispatches place his deed "near Bluffs Station, Wyoming Ter." Bluffs Station, on the Cheyenne to Deadwood stage route, was headquarters for some of the troops pursuing the Indians, who by then had gained the westernmost reaches of Nebraska's Pine Ridge, miles from Fort Robinson. In the waning days of the Outbreak, military dispatches often used Bluffs Station as the nearest reference point by which to fix the location of troops, including Lewis's company. Nevertheless his medal, the only one earned during the Cheyenne Outbreak, was for action in Nebraska.[20]

During the nineteenth century, considerable discretion colored decisions to award Medals of Honor. The 1862 act creating the Medal specified only that it be awarded for gallantry in action and other soldierlike qualities.[21] These vague guidelines were of little help in evaluating conduct worthy of a Medal of Honor. Many brave acts went unrecognized, while performance seemingly "in the line of duty," sometimes earned the Medal. Only one medal was awarded posthumously for Indian war service, when evidence would indicate that many soldiers died performing deeds that should have qualified them for a Medal of Honor.

Many of the acts for which Medals of Honor were received during the Indian wars would not deserve the award by today's standards. Current regulations require medal recipients to have risked their lives above and beyond the call of duty, performing deeds that would not subject them to censure had they not performed them.[22] In the 1890s the army began to recognize shortcomings in the Medal of Honor regulations when it was deluged with requests for medals to reward actions that had taken place thirty years earlier. In 1897 the secretary of war ruled that medal claims had to be supported by affidavits of officers or testimony of two eyewitnesses, and further attested by official reports. A 1904 act of Congress required that medal recommendations be verified by copies of official records.[23]

The 1917 review board revoked more than 900 Medals of Honor on the grounds that their recipients had "not performed acts of sufficient merit."[24] The board confirmed the majority of the medals previously issued, including all of those from Nebraska except Cody's, noting that in some cases, the Medal had been a reward "greater than would now be given for the same acts."[25] After World War I, various secondary awards were created so that degrees of valor might be recognized. The Medal of Honor was reserved for bravery truly distinguished by gallantry above and beyond the call of duty at the risk of one's life. Award of the medal was to be made within three years of the action for which it was recommended, and no claims relating to deeds of greater antiquity would be considered.[26]

Under the present guidelines most, if not all, of the Medals of Honor awarded for military service in Nebraska would not have been justified. Records of the various skirmishes lead to the conclusion that the Medal's recipients were performing acts routinely expected of soldiers, albeit bravely and sometimes at the risk of their lives. Only Sergeant Lewis seems to have risked his life voluntarily; had he not volunteered, his decision would have been free from censure. In the judgment of the Medal of Honor review board, however, the men who received the Medal of Honor in Nebraska met the standards for gallantry in vogue at the time.

What became of these fifteen men? The career of William F. Cody has been well documented and need not be reviewed here. The two officers remained in the army, and their careers are outlined in Francis Heitman's *Historical Register and Dictionary of the United States Army*. The later lives of most other recipients are obscure; sometimes even their gravesites are unknown. Fittingly, Francis Lohnes, the only Nebraskan to win the Medal *in* Nebraska, is buried in the state.

Francis Lohnes left the army under a cloud; he deserted from his company at Midway Station in September 1865, a few weeks after receiving the Medal of Honor. Many volunteers on duty in the West when the Civil War ended had been in the service for four long years. Their enlistments had expired. As weeks stretched into months with no discharge in sight, men began leaving their units to go home. Among them was Lohnes.

He simply returned to his farm in Richardson County, Nebraska. The army lacked manpower or a compelling reason to track down deserters from the volunteer forces, and there is no evidence that it made the attempt in Lohnes's case. Between 1882 and 1889 Congress enacted procedures by which the charge of desertion could be lifted from soldiers who had served faithfully until their enlistments expired, or until May 1, 1865.

Lohnes probably never knew that he could apply to have his desertion forgiven. On September 18, 1889, he was scalded to death in a steam engine accident near his home. His widow, Mary Lohnes, succeeded in expunging the charge of desertion against her husband's name in order to qualify for a widow's pension. Francis Lohnes is buried in Maple Grove Cemetery near Verdon, Nebraska, his Medal of Honor recognized by a government marker erected in 1987.[27]

Lt. John B. Babcock went with the Fifth Cavalry to Arizona in 1871 and fought Apaches. By 1901 he had been promoted to colonel and had served as assistant adjutant general of the Department of California. He died April 26, 1909, and is buried in Evergreen Cemetery, Stonington, Connecticut.

Were it not for their Medals of Honor, the four privates with Patrick Leonard at Spring Creek in 1870 would hardly have been mentioned in military records. Heath Canfield was discharged at Camp Bingham barely six months after enlisting in the Second Cavalry. He died December 16, 1913, and is buried at St. Augustine, Florida.

Michael Himmelsbach stayed in the service and died of kidney disease at Fort Ellis, Montana, January 5, 1881. He was buried in the post cemetery, which was abandoned in 1883, and there is no record of where his grave was relocated.

Civil War veteran Thomas Hubbard joined the regular army in 1870, just two months before the fight at Spring Creek. He was discharged at Fort Laramie in March 1875. He died in his hometown of Philadelphia and was buried there in Monument Cemetery. The cemetery later was closed and the bodies, including Hubbard's, were moved to an unknown location.

George Washington Thompson, despite his patriotic-sounding name and Medal of Honor, was not an exemplary soldier. He deserted from the Second Cavalry on May 16, 1872, was apprehended the next day, and deserted for good on July 2. He got away clean, and left no further record for history.

Sgt. John H. Foley, who fought with Cody, Vokes, and Strayer on the South Loup in 1872, was a career soldier. A native of Ireland, Foley enlisted in 1865 and served until his death from a laudanum overdose at Benicia Barracks, California, November 18, 1874. Although he was buried at the post, his specific gravesite has not been identified.

Foley's fellow sergeant, Leroy Vokes, retired from the service at Fort Snelling, Minnesota, in 1880. He is reported to have lived at Rochester and later in the Minnesota Soldiers' Home. Lack of a pension file has kept his death date and burial site a mystery.

William H. Strayer, like so many of his fellow Medal of Honor recipients, dropped out of sight after his discharge December 18, 1874, at Camp Sheridan, Nebraska. No pension or medical files have been found.

Charles Heath Heyl, the lieutenant who led the charge at the Battle of the Blowout, attained the rank of colonel in the inspector general's office by July 1902. He died October 12, 1926, the only one of the fifteen Nebraska Medal recipients known to be buried at Arlington National Cemetery.

Cpl. Jeptha Lytton was discharged as a sergeant at Fort Reno, Indian Territory, on June 19, 1877. The years until his death on December 27, 1932, are a blank. He is buried in the Soldiers' Home National Cemetery in Washington, D.C.[28]

Sgt. William B. Lewis had enlisted in the cavalry in January 1874. He probably would have made the army a career had it not been for a freak accident. While serving as quartermaster sergeant of the Third Cavalry at Fort Leavenworth, Kansas, in March 1884, Lewis was bitten severely on the forearm by a horse he was doctoring. The wound led to paralysis of the limb and his eventual discharge on a surgeon's certificate of disability April 2, 1885.

While Lewis was living at the Soldiers' Home in Washington, D.C., he met recently widowed Mary Ann Williams. On December 26, 1887, less than a week after her first husband's death, Mrs. Williams and Lewis were married in New York City.

There is reason to believe that Lewis's remaining years were not happy ones. His health continued to decline, which doctors attributed to the injury from the horse bite. By the spring of 1900 he was a helpless invalid, unable even to feed himself. On November 1, 1900, the fifty-three-year-old Lewis died at Mamaroneck, New York. According to his widow, he had no children, no known relatives, and no close friends. He is buried in Beechwoods Cemetery, New Rochelle, New York.[29]

The name Patrick Leonard appears twice in the government's official list of Medal of Honor recipients. Both medals were awarded for service in Nebraska, the first in 1870 at Spring Creek and the second in 1876 for the "Battle of the Blowout" near Fort Hartsuff. Although the recipient of one medal was in the Second Cavalry and the other in the Twenty-third Infantry, the two were assumed to be one and the same. Supporting the assumption was the Irish nativity given in both medal citations.

Research by Ray Collins for The Medal of Honor Historical Society revealed that there were two Patrick Leonards and their awards of the

Medal of Honor were unrelated. The coincidence of their names, their nativity, and their receipt of the Medal for Nebraska service explain how the two became one in the government records.

Patrick *James* Leonard, who earned the Medal at Spring Creek, served in the Second Cavalry until discharged in 1880 and later lived near Bloomington, Nebraska, before moving to Norton County, Kansas. He died January 24, 1899, and is buried at New Almelo, Kansas. Patrick *Thomas* Leonard was discharged from the Twenty-third Infantry in 1881 after four terms of enlistment. He died in Leavenworth, Kansas, on March 1, 1905, and is buried there in Mount Calvary Cemetery.[30]

So little is known about most of these men that conclusions are hard to reach. They ranged in age from nineteen to forty-eight. Several were immigrants. Some were excellent soldiers, and others were almost worthless. None seems to have sought fame during or after their military service and none, save Cody, achieved it. They were fairly typical of the men and boys who served in the frontier army, with one notable exception: Chance singled them out for the Medal of Honor.

Notes

[1] See *Medal of Honor, 1863–1968*, Ninetieth Congress, Second Session, Subcommittee on Veterans' Affairs, Committee on Labor and Public Welfare (Washington: Government Printing Office, 1968).

[2] The circumstances relating to Lohnes's Medal of Honor are more fully described in the author's article, "A Congressional Medal of Honor for a Nebraska Soldier: The Case of Private Francis W. Lohnes," *Nebraska History* 65 (Summer 1984):245–56.

[3] James T. King, *War Eagle: A Life of General Eugene A. Carr* (Lincoln: University of Nebraska Press, 1963), 95–98.

[4] Award of the Medal of Honor file, John B. Babcock, Records of the Adjutant General's Office, Record Group (RG) 94, National Archives, Washington, D.C. Copies of MOH recipient files are at the Nebraska State Historical Society, Lincoln.

[5] Special Order 52, Department of the Platte, Mar. 24, 1870, in Omaha Barracks Post Returns, Mar. 1870, *National Archives Microfilm Publication No. 617: Returns from U.S. Military Posts* (Washington: National Archives, 1965), roll 879; Company C Letterbook, Second U.S. Cavalry, 1870–74, MS202, Kansas State Historical Society, Topeka (also on microfilm).

[6] This was not the same Spring Creek near which John Babcock won the Medal of Honor. The site of the Leonard skirmish is in Nuckolls County, west of Ruskin.

[7] The account of the skirmish and related events is in Capt. Edward J. Spaulding's report to Maj. (Bvt. Brig. Gen.) George D. Ruggles, assistant adjutant general, Department of the Platte, May 23, 1870, in Company C Letterbook.

[8] Brig. Gen. Edward D. Townsend, adjutant general, to John Potts, chief clerk of the

War Department, June 22, 1870, Letters Received, RG 94.

⁹ Reports and related documents relating to Meinhold's expedition are found in Award of the Medal of Honor file, RG 94.

¹⁰ Unpublished paper by Paul Fees, Buffalo Bill Historical Center, Cody, Wyoming, delivered to the Order of the Indian Wars, Sept. 9, 1988 (copy in possession of the author).

¹¹ Department of the Army, Proceedings in the case of William F. Cody, Docket Number AC88–10374, Jan. 12, 1989 (copy in possession of the author).

¹² William F. Cody, *An Autobiography of Buffalo Bill (Colonel W. F. Cody)* (New York, 1920), 250–53.

¹³ William F. Cody, *The Life of Hon. William F. Cody Known as Buffalo Bill, The Famous Hunter, Scout, and Guide: An Autobiography* (Hartford, Conn.: Frank E. Bliss, 1879), 269–71.

¹⁴ William F. Cody, *Buffalo Bill's Own Story of His Life and Deeds* (Chicago, 1917), 198–203.

¹⁵ William F. Beyer and O. F. Keydel, eds., *Deeds of Valor: How America's Heroes Won the Medal of Honor* 2 (Detroit: The Perren–Keydel Co., 1905):154–58.

¹⁶ Fort Hartsuff Post Returns, April 1876, and Fort Hartsuff Medical History, RG 94 (both on microfilm at NSHS), provide the military version of the fight. A recollection by civilian C. H. Jones appears in *Garfield County Roundup: A History of the People, For the People, By the People of Garfield County, Nebraska* (Ord: Garfield County Centennial Committee, 1967). In the post medical history Surgeon George Towar implies that the civilians were cowardly in refusing to assist the troops. According to Jones, Lieutenant Heyl lacked experience fighting Indians and acted rashly. Heitman indicates that Heyl had previously fought Indians in Arizona in May 1874. Francis B. Heitman, *Historical Register and Dictionary of the United States Army* 1 (Washington: Government Printing Office, 1903):527.

¹⁷ Fort Laramie Post Returns, Jan. 1879, RG 94.

¹⁸ Theodore F. Rodenbough, ed., *Fighting for Honor: A Record of Heroism Written by Brave Men Who Have Been Decorated For Valor on the Field of Battle* (New York: G. W. Dillingham, 1893), 392–400. Rodenbough, himself a Medal of Honor winner, published three other variant editions of his Medal of Honor volume: *Uncle Sam's Medal of Honor Men* (1886), *The Bravest Five Hundred of '61* (1891), and *Sabre and Bayonet* (1897).

¹⁹ Rodenbough, *Fighting for Honor*, 399; Award of the Medal of Honor file, William B. Lewis, RG 94.

²⁰ *Medal of Honor, 1863–1968* gives the date of Lewis's Medal-winning deed as January 20–22, 1877. The Award of the Medal of Honor file leaves no doubt that the correct date is 1879, during the Cheyenne Outbreak. Agnes Wright Spring, *The Cheyenne and Black Hills Stage and Express Route* (Glendale, Calif.: The Arthur H. Clark Co., 1949), 296, places Bluffs Station "about thirty miles northwest of Red Cloud Agency." She quotes an error-filled statement by William Scanlon, Company C, Third Cavalry, about a skirmish with the Cheyennes near Bluffs Station on January 9, impossible because the Cheyennes did not escape from Fort Robinson until that night.

²¹ *Medal of Honor, 1863–1968*, 10.

[22] These criteria were identified as early as 1876 by a military board appointed to review Medal of Honor requests for the Battle of the Little Bighorn. See *The Medal of Honor of the United States Army* (Washington: Government Printing Office, 1948), 14.

[23] *Medal of Honor of the United States Army*, 15, 17.

[24] Ibid., 20.

[25] Ibid., 21.

[26] Ibid.

[27] See Potter, "A Congressional Medal of Honor, " 250–53.

[28] The author wishes to thank Harold "Sonny" Wells of the Medal of Honor Historical Society for furnishing much of the foregoing information on the Nebraska medal recipients.

[29] William B. Lewis Pension File, National Archives, Washington, D.C. A copy is in possession of the author. Charles E. Chambers, Medal of Honor Historical Society, to author, Sept. 30, 1993.

[30] Ray Collins, "Double Recipient Identified as Two Men," *The Annals* (Medal of Honor Historical Society, June 1984):80–83.

Suggested Reading

Since these articles originally appeared in *Nebraska History*, the following related readings have been published:

Part 1.
Seizing Control of the Platte and Republican Rivers

Jean Afton, David Fridtjof Halaas, and Andrew E. Masich, *Cheyenne
Dog Soldiers: A Ledgerbook History of Coups and Combat* (Denver and
Niwot, Colo.: Colorado Historical Society and University Press of Colorado, 1997); Thomas R. Buecker, "Fort Sidney: Its Role on the Upper
Plains," *Periodical: The Journal of the Council on Abandoned Military
Posts* 11 (Mar. 1981):22–36; Buecker, "Letters of Caroline Frey Winne
from Sidney Barracks and Fort McPherson, Nebraska, 1874–1878," *NH*
62 (Spring 1981):1–46; John R. Fisher, "The Royall and Duncan Pur-
suits: Aftermath of the Battle of Summit Springs, 1969," *NH* 50 (Fall
1969):293–308; Richard Guentzel, "The Department of the Platte and
Western Settlement, 1866–1877," *NH* 56 (Fall 1975):389–418; James T.
King, *War Eagle: A Life of General Eugene A. Carr* (Lincoln: University
of Nebraska Press, 1963); King, "Fort McPherson in 1870: A Note by an
Army Wife," *NH* 45 (Mar. 1964):99–108; Maury Klein, *Union Pacific:
Birth of a Railroad, 1862–1893* (Garden City, N.Y.: Doubleday & Company, Inc., 1987); Merrill J. Mattes, *The Great Platte River Road* (Lincoln: Nebraska State Historical Society, 1969), chaps. 6,7, on Fort Kearny;
and Gary D. Olson, ed., "Relief for Nebraska Grasshopper Victims: The
Official Journal of Lieutenant Theodore E. True," *NH* 48 (Summer
1967):119–40.

Part 2.
Pawnee Triumph, Pawnee Tragedy

Garland James Blaine and Martha Royce Blaine, "Pa-Re-Su A-Ri-Ra-Ke:
The Hunters That Were Massacred," *NH* 58 (Fall 1977):342–58; Martha
Royce Blaine, *Pawnee Passage, 1870–1875* (Norman: University of Okla-
homa Press, 1990); Thomas R. Buecker and R. Eli Paul, eds., "Go South
and Be Free: John W. Williamson's Account of the Pawnee Removal,"
The Chronicles of Oklahoma 65 (Summer, Fall, 1987):132–57,294–318;
Donald F. Danker, ed., *Man of the Plains: Recollections of Luther North,
1856–1882* (Lincoln: University of Nebraska Press, 1961); Thomas W.
Dunlay, *Wolves for the Blue Soldiers: Indian Scouts and Auxiliaries with*

the United States Army, 1860–90 (Lincoln: University of Nebraska Press,1982); "Interview with Luther H. North, April 21, 1917, Regarding the Battle of Summit Springs," in Bruce R. Liddic and Paul Harbaugh, eds., *Camp on Custer: Transcribing the Custer Myth* (Spokane: The Arthur H. Clark Company, 1995); Clyde A. Milner II, *With Good Intentions: Quaker Work among the Pawnees, Otos, and Omahas in the 1870s* (Lincoln: University of Nebraska Press, 1982); and R. Eli Paul, ed., "Lester Beach Platt's Account of the Battle of Massacre Canyon," *NH* 67 (Winter 1986):381–407.

Part 3.
Red Cloud Agency in the Spotlight

These suggested readings relate to the areas of material culture and photography as well as to the history of Red Cloud Agency: Charles W. Allen, *From Fort Laramie to Wounded Knee: In the West That Was,* ed. Richard E. Jensen (Lincoln: University of Nebraska Press, 1997); Harry A. Anderson, "Indian Peace-Talkers and the Conclusion of the Sioux War of 1876," *NH* 44 (Dec. 1963):233–54; Thomas R. Buecker, "A History of Camp Robinson, Nebraska, 1874–1878," Master's thesis, Chadron State College, Chadron, Nebraska, 1992; James A. Hanson, *Famous Indians of Northwest Nebraska* (Chadron, Nebr.: Privately printed, 1983); Hanson, *Spirits in the Arts from the Plains and Southwest Indian Cultures* (Kansas City: The Lowell Press, Inc., 1994); Paul L. Hedren, *With Crook in the Black Hills: Stanley J. Morrow's 1876 Photographic Legacy* (Boulder: Pruett Publishing Company, 1985); Hedren, "The Crazy Horse Medal: An Enigma from the Great Sioux War," *NH* 75 (Summer 1994):195–99; Hedren, "Postscript," *NH* 77 (Summer 1996):114; Hedren, *Traveler's Guide to the Great Sioux War: The Battlefields, Forts, and Related Sites of America's Greatest Indian War* (Helena: Montana Historical Society Press, 1996); Robert H. Keller, Jr., "Episcopal Reformers and Affairs at Red Cloud Agency, 1870–1876," *NH* 68 (Fall 1987):116–26; Douglas C. McChristian, *The U.S. Army in the West, 1870–1880: Uniforms, Weapons, and Equipment* (Norman: University of Oklahoma Press, 1995); James C. Olson, *Red Cloud and the Sioux Problem* (Lincoln: University of Nebraska Press, 1965); Catherine Price, *The Oglala People, 1841–1879: A Political History* (Lincoln: University of Nebraska Press, 1996); Gail DeBuse Potter, "The Crazy Horse Scalp Shirt," *NH* 77 (Summer 1996): 96–98; and Phillip G. Twitchell, ed., "Camp Robinson Letters of Angeline Johnson, 1876–1879," *NH* 77 (Summer 1996):89–95.

Suggested Reading

Part 4.
Sioux War Saga

Thomas R. Buecker, "'Can You Send Us Immediate Relief'?: Army Expeditions to the Northern Black Hills, 1876–1878," *South Dakota History* 25 (Summer 1995):95–115; Thomas R. Buecker and R. Eli Paul, eds., *The Crazy Horse Surrender Ledger* (Lincoln: Nebraska State Historical Society, 1994), introduction by Harry A. Anderson; Richmond L. Clow, "General Philip Sheridan's Legacy: The Sioux Pony Campaign of 1876," *NH* 57 (Winter 1976):461–78; John S. Gray, *Centennial Campaign: The Sioux War of 1876* (Fort Collins: The Old Army Press, 1976); Jerome A. Greene, *Slim Buttes, 1876: An Episode of the Great Sioux War* (Norman: University of Oklahoma Press, 1982); Greene, *Yellowstone Command: Colonel Nelson A. Miles and the Great Sioux War, 1876–1877* (Lincoln: University of Nebraska Press, 1991); Paul L. Hedren, *First Scalp for Custer: The Skirmish at Warbonnet Creek, Nebraska, July 17, 1876* (Glendale, Calif.: The Arthur H. Clark Co., 1980); Hedren, *Fort Laramie in 1876: Chronicle of a Frontier Post at War* (Lincoln: University of Nebraska Press, 1988); Oliver Knight, *Life and Manners in the Frontier Army* (Norman: University of Oklahoma Press, 1978); R. Eli Paul, "An Early Reference to Crazy Horse," *NH* 75 (Summer 1994):189–90; Joseph C. Porter, "Crazy Horse, Lakota Leadership and the Fort Laramie Treaty," in *Legacy: New Perspectives on the Battle of the Little Bighorn*, ed. Charles E. Rankin (Helena: Montana Historical Society Press, 1996):41–62; Don Russell, *Campaigning with King: Charles King, Chronicler of the Old Army*, Paul L. Hedren, ed. (Lincoln: University of Nebraska Press, 1991); and Robert M. Utley, *Frontier Regulars: The United States Army and the Indian, 1866–1891* (New York: Macmillan Publishing Co., 1973).

Five relatively recent biographies on four military leaders, whose actions and decisions were felt in Nebraska, are: Paul Andrew Hutton, *Phil Sheridan and His Army* (Lincoln: University of Nebraska Press, 1985); Michael D. Pierce, *The Most Promising Young Officer: A Life of Ranald Slidell Mackenzie* (Norman: University of Oklahoma Press, 1993); Joseph C. Porter, *Paper Medicine Man: John Gregory Bourke and His American West* (Lincoln: University of Nebraska Press, 1986); Charles M. Robinson III, *Bad Hand: A Biography of General Ranald S. Mackenzie* (Austin: State House Press, 1993); and Robert Wooster, *Nelson A. Miles and the Twilight of the Frontier Army* (Lincoln: University of Nebraska Press, 1993). A new and much needed biography of Red Cloud by Robert W. Larson (1997) appears in the *Oklahoma Western Biographies* series of the University of Oklahoma Press.

Suggested Reading

Some of the Eli S. Ricker interviews appear in the following publications: Donald F. Danker, ed., "Big Bat Pourier's Version of the Sibley Scout," *NH* 66 (Summer 1985):129–43; Danker, ed., "The Violent Deaths of Yellow Bear and John Richard Jr.," *NH* 63 (Summer 1982):136–51; Danker, ed., "The Wounded Knee Interviews of Eli Ricker," *NH* 62 (Summer 1981):150–243; Jerome A. Greene, ed., *Battles and Skirmishes of the Great Sioux War, 1876–1877* (Norman: University of Oklahoma Press, 1993); Greene, ed., *Lakota and Cheyenne: Indian Views of the Great Sioux War, 1876–1877* (Norman: University of Oklahoma Press, 1994); and Richard G. Hardorff, *Lakota Recollections of the Custer Fight: New Sources of Indian–Military History* (Spokane: The Arthur H. Clark Co., 1991).

Index

Index

Index

Index

Index

Index

Index